TRANSITIONS

Leading Churches through Change

Edited by David N. Mosser

WESTMINSTER
JOHN KNOX PRESS
LOUISVILLE · KENTUCKY

© 2011 Westminster John Knox Press

First edition
Published by Westminster John Knox Press
Louisville, Kentucky

11 12 13 14 15 16 17 18 19 20—10 9 8 7 6 5 4 3 2 1

Book design by Sharon Adams
Cover design by Eric Walljasper, Minneapolis, MN

Library of Congress Cataloging-in-Publication Data

Transitions : leading churches through change / edited by David N. Mosser. — 1st ed.
  p. cm.
Includes bibliographical references.
ISBN 978-0-664-23543-7
  1. Change—Religious aspects—Christianity. 2. Church renewal. I. Mosser, David, 1952– II. Title: Leading churches through change.
BV4509.5.T693 2011
253—dc225

2010036892

To the sacred memory of our sister preacher, Ella Mitchell, and our brother preacher, Rodney Wilmoth—your words always offered us grace.

". . . After these things the word of the Lord came . . . in a vision,
'Do not be afraid, [for] I am your shield; your reward shall be very great'"
(Gen. 15:1).

Contents

Foreword

While my sons and I were rafting through whitewater rapids, the guide barked out commands to "paddle hard left" or "back paddle right" as we careened between boulders the size of houses. When we reached an area of open water, we still were instructed to keep paddling gently even though the water was pushing us along with unrelenting strength and power. One of my sons asked the guide why we still have to paddle when the water was driving us forward anyway. He explained that the only way for us to maintain any ability to steer the raft is to move across the surface of the water just a little faster than the rushing current below. If we stopped paddling, the current would turn us sideways, and then over and under. We'd become entirely subject to the powers of the swift current. If we wanted to navigate with purpose rather than becoming victims to forces beyond our control, we had to keep paddling.

We live in a whitewater world, driven by the powerful and unrelenting forces of change. The world my children have grown up in would be utterly unrecognizable to their great-grandparents. Technology, medicine, communication, transportation, entertainment—every institution and every element of our working and living completes a new revolution with every half-generation. Change is an inevitable and persistent element of our culture.

How can we live fruitfully and meaningfully in face of change? Fast-forward living makes it hard to listen for God. Speed and spirituality seldom go well together. How do we deepen the spiritual life and keep a focus on the upward calling of God during tumultuous times? Can we live deeply rather than thinly in a world where the surface tangibles churn and change without ceasing, and where temporal distractions draw us away from lasting truths? These are questions of the heart that require our attention more today than ever before. We underestimate the risk of living merely a surface existence, buffeted along by the recurring urgencies of making a living, fulfilling family obligations, maintaining our health, paying the bills. Sometimes there's hardly any opportunity to reflect on where all this is taking us. How do we find God and tap the eternal and unchanging resources of the spiritual life in a whitewater world?

Our churches also face unrelenting change. One hundred years ago, most of our congregations included three generations in worship together, and these generations all shared the same vocabulary for interpreting their world, the same experiences of growing up and learning, and the same tastes in music and entertainment. Now our congregations commonly include four or five generations, each of which has a distinctive way of understanding the world and expressing its faith. They each enjoy a different style of music and use a unique vocabulary for describing interior experience, and within each generation, there exist countless niche cultures and ethnic subcultures. Congregations trying to reach new generations find themselves in an unending pursuit of new innovations with alternative worship styles, multimedia technologies, experimental music, off-site settings, and attempts at social networking. Remaining faithful to the mission requires congregations to adapt, learn, grow, and change. How can leaders preach and teach and counsel in such contexts? Many face a trap. If they don't adapt more rapidly, they betray their mission of reaching the next generation, and they fail to be outwardly focused; but if they don't support the worship styles and faith expressions of generations already present, they lose the financial foundation and reservoirs of talent that are necessary to lead. How do we embrace change at a pace that fulfills our mission without dangerously unsettling those already present?

Ronald Heifetz suggests that people do not resist change per se. People resist loss.[1] Congregations authorize pastors and leaders to take them to new and necessary places, but they resist changing the habits, values, and attitudes that are part of their identity. Change feels somehow disloyal to their origins. Change asks people to suffer loss, experience uncertainty, and redefine aspects of their identity. Change stimulates disequilibrium, and no one absorbs more stress than the leader. Pastors may be asking people to leave behind values and behaviors that they have lived with for years. People will only make such sacrifices and suffer such losses when they see the reason why and when they know the stakes are worth it, and this requires deep discernment and profound interpretative skill from the pastor. The role of the leader during change, Heifetz suggests, is to create a relational holding space in which people can stay engaged with one another and do the learning together that helps them

---

1. *Leadership on the Line: Staying Alive through the Dangers of Leading* (Boston: Harvard Business School Press, 2002), 11.

address the adaptive challenges that are required for them to fulfill their mission. The leader keeps the conversation and learning going, holds people together, and applies just enough pressure to motivate people to learn without applying so much pressure that the whole project explodes. Pastoral leadership and preaching in a changing world is risky, stressful, complex, and costly.

The Hebrew Scriptures include a church relocation story that captures the immensely complicated emotions, callings, and temptations that come with extraordinary change. The third chapter of Ezra records the rebuilding of the temple, and the celebration and anguish that come with leaving behind what is old while celebrating what is new. As the builders lay the foundation of the new temple, they celebrate with trumpets and cymbals and vestments, singing, praising, and giving thanks to the Lord, for "he is good and his steadfast love endures forever. . . ." The Scripture says that all the people responded with praise because the foundation of the Lord was laid. "But many of the priests and Levites and heads of families, old people who had seen the first house on its foundations, wept with a loud voice when they saw the house, though many shouted for joy . . ." (Ezra 3:12). The intermingling of joy and sorrow, hope and memory, longing and losing was so powerful that the Scriptures tell us that "the people could not distinguish the sound of the joyful shout from the sound of the people's weeping . . ." (Ezra 3:13).

Learning to lead through change has become an absolutely essential quality of pastoral leadership if we are to fulfill the mission of our congregations. But how do we lead through change in such a way that our people understand that grieving the loss of the old ways does not betray the new vision, and that seeking to fulfill a new vision represents no betrayal to the traditions and people of the past?

David N. Mosser has provided a significant and helpful service to pastors and congregational leaders by gathering together a widely diverse collection of essays and sermons that help us preach and lead through change. *Transitions* serves to stimulate our own thinking and imagination. Key pastors and congregational leaders share vital skills, insights, and experiences that provide an interpretive context for understanding the meaning of change in our society, in our churches, and in ourselves. I'm delighted to commend to you this collection. May these sermons and conversations help us navigate the white-water world in order that we may more faithfully and fruitfully lead our people toward the great tasks given us by God.

Robert Schnase, Bishop
Missouri Conference of the United Methodist Church
Author of *Five Practices of Fruitful Congregations* and *Five Practices
of Fruitful Living*

Introduction

This book is for pastors who happen to preach and for preachers who happen to pastor. In other words it is a book for those who have been charged by God, their presbytery, their synod, their diocese, and their annual conference to care for the souls of the congregants in their care, or for those who happen to own their own church (in a terrestrial sense). These congregants are people who are wobbling from the whirlwind of change that washes over all people in an increasingly industrialized world. A mere four decades ago this target group might have simply been drawn over North America and Western Europe, but as able journalists such as Thomas Friedman help us understand, even the most far-flung areas of China and India have now begun to cash in on industrialized globalization. The concept of a global village is no longer simply a concept. When we suggest that our world's culture is now moving at "*warp* speed," there is biting irony in that supposition, for the speed of change has no doubt warped us in significant ways.

Thus it is hard to be alive in most places in the world without living in and through mind-numbing change. The whole planet is awash in change. Yet the phenomenon of change strikes even at the almost corpuscular level of individual persons. I remember the week that my mother ultimately realized that if she could not talk my brother or me into filling her car up with gasoline, then perhaps the automobile would never get filled again. The idea of someone, somewhere, compelling her to be a self-reliant "pump jockey" was an abomination. Yet change forced her to do what was necessary to keeping moving—or, in this case, to keep her 1968 Pontiac Tempest moving.

Paul writes to the church at Corinth, "When I was a child, I spoke like a child, I thought like a child, I reasoned like a child; when I became an adult,

I put an end to childish ways" (1 Cor. 13:11). However, if I might hazard a guess, I would suggest that someone "took away" Paul's childish ways; few of us relinquish our ways of being human without a struggle. We like to call our rut "a pathway," but in truth these ruts often are the beginning of a shallow grave of doing things "my way." Someone forced Paul, like they forced us no doubt, into the world of adults. I heard one of my colleagues once say with great insight and humorous wisdom that the only person who likes change is a wet baby. So here we are.

Even those hip "postmodern world–type people" would feel some dread as I did when my banker said to me recently, "David, I hate to break the news to you, but eventually if you cannot do online banking, then you will not be doing any banking at all." Did I believe him? I am not sure. Yet as we move though life, we all understand that it is a rare week when some tectonic shift or another does not confront our comfortable way of doing things the way we have always done them.

In his foreword to this book, Bishop Robert Schnase writes with great intuition, "Change asks people to suffer loss, experience uncertainty, and redefine aspects of their identity." Yet the issue may be even more visceral than this. Fear and the real possibility of failure if a change does not work are alive and well, just below the surface of human consciousness. In his *The New Organon* (*Novum Organum*), Francis Bacon writes about the reality that change is dangerous. Even in 1620, Bacon could see that new methods of finding knowledge always provided the discoverers a degree of power that others did not possess. Yet there is danger, too, in doing things a new way. As I write these words, British Petroleum is trying to figure out how to fix the technology that provided oil drilling one mile underneath the surface of the previously pristine Gulf of Mexico.

Risk taking is not a new enterprise. We could without difficulty imagine a scenario in which fifteenth-century farmers in a particular region dared to use a new method of agriculture in hopes of producing additional and enhanced crops. Yet if the farmers and their enterprise had failed, the price would have been starvation. This kind of change is more than an inconvenience—the change itself has the potential to put survival in peril. Trying important things a new way is like a heroine in a movie scene experimenting with an armed explosive device. She must decide which color wire (blue? green? red?) to cut to deactivate the bomb—one wrong snip and her life—and our movie—is over.

For people in our contemporary culture, especially those in institutions of faith or learning, change is threatening. For example, the "new math" methodology taught fifty years ago in public elementary schools has now, some experts suggest, created a generation of mathematical ignoramuses. Whether true or not, when wholesale change comes, we are often willing to jettison the "tried and true" methods of the past in favor of the "new and improved." Unfortunately, too often "new and improved" fails to deliver what it at one time had so hopefully promised.

As these writers reward the time you spend in reading these essays and sermons, you will see a recurrent theme emerge: change and grief have a lot in common. Of course at the intellectual level we already know this. But at an intuitive level we who are beginning to understand the mystery of pastoring people know that the more we address and face change, the more we address and face grief—both our own and that of those to whom we have been called by God to lead, shepherd, and pastor.

I have asked some of the best preachers, professors, pastors, and consultants I know to help church leaders think through how the church and our faith can help us in our times of high anxiety. Change and transitions in life are a given for human beings. What you will discover in the pages of this book are many perspectives and insights about how we can better understand and serve the people whom God has called us to lead as shepherds. If we are to do things a new way—in ways we have never done before—we need guides and leaders who infuse us with confidence and verve—and a double portion of the Holy Spirit.

David Neil Mosser
First United Methodist Church
Arlington, Texas
1 June 2010—Saint Justin Martyr Feast Day

PART ONE

The Clergy in Chaos

The essays and sermons in this section focus on pastors and how they cope with the diversity of demands the office brings. Some essays offer insight into mistakes made; others address inner turmoil and how pastors might manage it.

To begin, both E. Carver McGriff and M. Kent Millard write about their transition in an extremely large United Methodist church in the essay "For All That Has Been, Thanks; For All That Will Be, Yes!" In truth the gist of their sharing is pertinent to any church—and to upright and principled relationships. In a telling observation McGriff writes, "One selfish word, one snicker, one raised eyebrow could undo. . . ." This is so true. We pastors all know that a comment that on the surface sounds innocent, such as "I do not want to talk about it," can be heard as an indictment of another preacher—and some people who ought to know better specialize in the "vile innuendo." As the wise McGriff knows, the people who are hurt in the insinuation process are mostly the innocents. The outgoing pastor McGriff paved the way for good ministry to begin the day his successor walked in the door—and he and Millard became fast friends. To turn a successor/predecessor into a ministry resource is to be a person who takes the gospel wisdom to heart: "'Be wise as serpents and innocent as doves'" (Matt. 10:16).

The relationship between incoming and outgoing pastors is vital to seamless ministry and a credit to the egos held in check by both persons. As these pastors remind us, humility and gratitude look for signs of God's activity to celebrate and to validate. Carver McGriff and Kent Millard provide good models for pastoral transitions. Would that God bless any church with either of these two pastors.

In the essay "A Break in the Stained Glass Ceiling" Joanna M. Adams tells the story of how the largest church in her denomination with a female pastor selected her to this "honor." She then describes her subsequent struggles and victories, transparently sharing experiences that no pastor ever wants to go through. Many of the admirable suggestions that McGriff and Millard warmly make in the previous essay failed to develop for Adams. Surprisingly she shares the "on the one hand" admonition to "love the people" but "on the other hand" reveals a surprising "antifemale clergy view" held by some in her congregation. In one of the essay's most telling statements, Adams writes, "The congregation was surprised to learn that there was more than one way to do things." In this tricky situation Adams relates how she built relationships with the laity and tried to establish collegial staff interactions during retreats and weekly meetings.

Again illustrating the importance of pastoral transitions for churches, Adams learned that her true predicament was not so much that she was a woman as that she was not her predecessor. Adams shares what she learned in her role as a change agent and how she cared for her personal well-being. She reminds us all of some important things and spends the last few pages of the essay looking back at the things she learned in this experience some twenty years hence.

Frederick W. Schmidt's essay "Led by a Pillar of Fire: The Preacher in Transition," about how clergy can care for themselves in transition, merges agreeably with Joanna Adams's previous essay. Schmidt addresses five habits of clergy, among which are to avoid cynicism and to redirect that energy to passion instead. He also urges pastors to make it a habit always and continuously to ask where God is in the circumstance we find ourselves. This essay chiefly will be helpful to those pastors who are negotiating life in a new parish. It includes stories that illustrate concretely of what Schmidt writes.

In her fine essay "Poetry in Motion: A Case Study in Preaching in a New Pastoral Setting," Alyce M. McKenzie (with her former student, Mary Martin) opens a portal into the task of being a new preacher in a new place. The bishop appointed Martin, then one of McKenzie's students, as the new preacher at a small church in Poetry, Texas. Martin had worked until that time in McKenzie's congregation. In fact Martin had already enrolled in McKenzie's fall homiletics class. She approached McKenzie for help her in her new assignment because she had never preached before. Now she was to preach every Sunday. They discussed among many topics "exegeting the congregation" and its importance along with "exegeting the preaching texts." Martin and McKenzie identified preaching themes that connected to the congregation's self-identity. Near the conclusion of McKenzie's entertaining and winsome essay is what she calls "three principles for preaching in transition: continuity, identification, and commendation."

In addition, Martin and McKenzie share the results of sermon debriefing in the chapter's conclusion, material that is a boon to any preacher. They also include "Mary's Top Ten" (her lessons learned), and McKenzie's handout questions "Exegesis of a Congregation."

W. Craig Gilliam's "Leading through Anxious Times and Situations: More Than Meets the Eye" offers a practical guide through the bog of anxiety that presents itself to congregational leaders. He offers direction to help leaders know what to look for to discern high anxiety. Gilliam also provides courses of action when leaders/pastors find themselves stalled in anxious circumstances.

Gilliam writes that the essence of the mystery called "congregation" is relationship—a mystery to embrace rather than a problem to solve. A pastor leads through anxious times by lessening stress, increasing the possibility of positive movement for the community, and heightening awareness. Gilliam defines two types of anxiety (acute and chronic) and identifies both the indicators and triggers for anxiety. He also provides a helpful list of steps to move a congregation cooperatively through anxiety. One of Gilliam's continuous accents centers on the importance of the leader/pastor's knowing self and community. That relationships are vitally important to a community's structure is a mantra that Gilliam incessantly chants. Craig Gilliam's essay will be of great value to anyone who leads a congregation.

"Most Change Occurs in Ways We Would Not Choose," by psychologist Sharyn Pinney, addresses being a pastor and preacher in ways that offer relief from anxiety to congregations in the course of change. Pinney lists four parts of the mental health process in regaining equilibrium: self-reflection, self-observation, listening well, and sharing to mobilize hope and connections. She also catalogs what she calls "Relevant Mental Health Principles": trust, ambiguity, determining personality types, self-care, a life outside the congregation, and a sense of humor. Pinney encourages the sharing of warmth from the pulpit, which, as odd as it may sound, is a way to bring about one of Aristotle's approaches for speakers to establish the ethos so important in public speaking.

Pinney's essay is a fitting summary of many mental health guidelines, tailored so that preachers may become more self-aware of the anxiety-producing work that they do in congregations as pastor, teacher, counselor, and preacher.

Gary G. Kindley's essay "Leadership, Preaching, and Pastoral Care in Times of Anxiety or Conflict," like the essays of Craig Gilliam and Sharyn Pinney, shares insights about the inner life of pastors/preachers that help us recognize the private feelings behind the public persona. Kindley suggests that when a crisis occurs in the faith community, the pastor's role is to offer hope. Remarkably wise and alert pastors look for "anxious occasions" to offer Christ in the midst of change.

Kindley also shrewdly notes that human beings handle ambiguity better than they handle apathy. This is because people have an innate need for feeling that someone cares for them and that someone hears them. The most effective pastors in times of transition or change in parishioner's lives are pastors who can listen during a distressing time in the congregation or in individual lives. Kindley goes on to share the insight that often dialogue is more important than any outcome and recommends to those who lead in times of change to be aware of their own strengths and weaknesses. Effective pastors reflect the love of Christ to others, while at the same time maintaining their own self-care. Kindley's method to help pastors recall these themes is to offer lists and acronyms (for example, C.A.L.M.) as mnemonic devices.

In conflicted situations, if the adversaries or perceived opponents violate boundaries and acceptable behavior, then an astute pastor will find out why. It is often by listening and reflecting that pastors reduce anxiety, but also by offering the possibility for honest dialogue. Above all the effective pastor and preacher will maintain a non-anxious presence. Kindley, in addition, finally offers a series of Scripture texts that address anxiety, hope, and faith.

A charming feature of Jonathan Mellette's essay/short story "The Show Must Go On," the final piece in this section, brings to mind the cliché making the rounds a decade ago: "Been there—done that!" Anyone who has ever preached a sermon and had a family in tandem will relate to the Sunday morning circus about which Mellette writes. Those with similar experiences will find the story amusing—especially as it happens to someone else. Mellette in essence offers readers a day in the life of a self-conscious and mortified pastor—a day of crises. He points out that even in times of crises a faithful pastor must stay the course, persevere, and give his/her best—regardless of how grandly humiliated the pastor comes into view. Mellette brings an authenticity to his essay that will, no doubt, alarm his supervisors in ministry.

1

For All That Has Been, Thanks;
For All That Will Be, Yes!

E. CARVER MCGRIFF AND M. KENT MILLARD

THE PREDECESSOR: DR. CARVER MCGRIFF

A comedian from the past, Jimmy Durante, had a signature song line: "Did you ever get the feeling that you wanted to go, and yet you had the feeling that you wanted to stay?" That described my feelings as I prepared to retire from St. Luke's United Methodist Church in Indianapolis. There were a few situations I was happy to leave, responsibilities I was delighted to hand over to someone else. I was retiring at long last and had several plans for activities that seemed like fun. However, there was a sadness to it all. I loved the work of ministry. That relentless responsibility to create a sermon each week was, as most of us know, at once a demanding taskmaster and a source of a preacher's greatest joy. I would miss its energy. I had a staff of people whom I loved, and, dare I say it now, I was a bit jealous that they would go right on at the work I would now leave, off to begin that slow slide into the role of "old what's his name." It was like riding on a train with dear friends who are all leaving Chicago together for San Francisco, but you have to get off in Dubuque. As Shakespeare said, parting was, indeed, such sweet sorrow.

Some of this dilemma besets all pastors, at least good pastors, men and women who genuinely love their people, who sincerely intend to remain faithful to those early vows we made to be a Jesus Christ person through our ministry. We all know there are pastors who, as one of my superintendents used to say, "always have their bags packed." However, I find that most clergy I am privileged to number as friends are the real thing, men and women who try very hard to carry out the ministry of love to their congregations. It's to their kind that I address myself now.

5

Your congregation is, in an intimate way, your family. I served a small, two-point charge for two years. I was in every home at least once within a couple months, mostly for Sunday dinners. I knew them all. I later served a congregation of just under six hundred members, and I knew many of them, but there were also many whom I only recognized as people who attended on Sundays. At St. Luke's it grew from 900 to 4,000 members and by retirement time I could probably, at best, recognize a third of them on the street. I finally gave up being a shepherd and became a sheepherder. Kent Millard would later add another 2,000 members, and I can't imagine how he manages with over 6,000 parishioners.

Here's my point. All those people in those several congregations, regardless of the size of the congregation, knew me. They listened to me, trusted me, and took care of me, and they looked to me for a responsible and intelligent presentation of the biblical Christian faith. Though I sometimes failed, they continued to trust me. If I let them down, as I may have done more than once in all those years, they forgave me, encouraged me, and stayed with me. If I achieved a victory of some sort, they celebrated, commended, and urged me on. Regardless of the size of a church, whether you know all your people or not, they all know you, and you are an important part of their lives. Even the old soreheads—one bishop said every congregation has three of those— are part of the family. My people shared their lives and their love with me through my own tragedies and struggles. Not once was I ever forsaken by the saints who predominated in all my congregations. I knew I must not, I could not, I would not let them down now. As I prepared to leave, and as someone whom I did not know prepared to take my place, I knew I simply must demand of myself that what I said and did in the weeks before I left be in every way commensurate with the gospel I preached for so many years. One selfish word, one snicker, one raised eyebrow could undo twenty-six years of ministry at St. Luke's in someone's eyes. I vowed that must not happen.

Was I, therefore, to be a perfect person? Those who know me well would snort and howl at such a thought. Of course I'm not perfect. To do what I will propose here is to lay down your life for your successor, and that is a demanding request. We are not perfect, and we'll feel all those sinful emotions of resentment that someone who has never contributed to the progress of your congregation will now enjoy its benefits, that the new pastor will be paid more than you were ever paid, that the old parsonage is now being completely refurbished. It can be devastating to foresee that people who have loved you and been undyingly loyal to you for all those years will, in a few short weeks, if you do your work as you know you should, transfer that love and loyalty to someone else. Yet without that your successor may fail, and so you will have failed. One of my dearest professors in seminary said to us that the true measure of our ministry is what happens when we leave. I believed him. I knew that if whoever would follow me were to fail, then it was in part because of my failure. I knew that now, as much as at any time in my ministry, my integrity was at stake, the validity of all those sermons about obedience and faithfulness would be tested by what I said and did as my successor prepared to take my place.

Your people will quickly know how you feel when you open your mouth about your successor. When I arrived at St. Luke's for the first time many years ago, I was following the man probably most admired of all the men in our annual conference at the time. The congregation idolized him. For me to try to follow him was bound to be a demanding undertaking. But when I arrived, one of my new parishioners said to me, "You know, Dick told us last week that had he been the bishop, you were the man he would have chosen to pastor this congregation." Wow. Talk about a rousing send-off. Immediate acceptance, thanks to the man whose every word his people completely trusted. I would later learn he tried every way he could to get out of moving. I was the worst kind of interloper, or so he had a right to feel. But he did what Jesus would have had him do and that prepared the way for me.

You may already know your successor. It's conceivable you may harbor some reservations about the person, may disagree with the bishop about the appointment. You may have painful regrets at leaving people you dearly love in the hands of someone whose gifts and graces you aren't convinced are sufficient for the task. That's no excuse. To even hint at such a sentiment can only prejudice some people against that person, and if that successor should come with the most serious intention of being a good pastor, your negative comments can only defeat that intent, and the losers in the end will be those people you so piously claim to love. And you, my friend, will have unveiled your true colors, and they won't be pretty. I was a salesman for several years out of college, and we were repeatedly told the old axiom "Every knock is a boost." Every critical judgment rendered tells more about you than about the subject.

Many a pastor who has moved on returns all too often to perform a wedding or a funeral. That is an unforgivable no-no unless by invitation of the new pastor. When Kent Millard succeeded me, I had already committed to several weddings. Kent knew this and invited me to keep those commitments. Otherwise, I announced from my pulpit that from the day of my successor's arrival, I would not be able to perform any service—wedding, funeral, or baptism—for any member of that congregation. That felt like telling your children that I will never again attend your birthday party. I wanted to cry. But it had to be done. When you move away, stay away. Stay away unless and until the person who follows you invites you back. This situation should be made clear to the congregation, together with an explanation: How is the new arrival ever to be truly accepted as pastor if the old guy keeps showing up?

Point out the obvious to your congregation, that along with the new pastor will come a spouse, children, and any special situation they may face. They are moving to what for them is a new community. They will need some time to get organized, to adapt their emotions to the new situation. Remind them that the new pastor may have just departed from a congregation of people whom he or she loved and who loved him or her. They may be experiencing grief and loneliness, the same feeling you may be facing. Ask that the congregation give him or her time to reveal needs and personality. Don't overwhelm the new family with social demands, but don't ignore them either. Keep in mind school adjustments of parsonage children. Let your people know who these new people really are, and remind them that most of all they need to feel the love. And by all means find something positive to say about this new arriving pastor. When Kent Millard came to town, I made it a point to spend some time with him and Minnietta. Ten minutes into our conversation I knew he was the right man to follow me. I told that to my people.

There are also other ways to prepare for the transition. As every pastor knows or soon discovers, certain church members are your grapevine. Say something you shouldn't have said to one of them, and it isn't long until it comes back, often in revised form, from someone else. In comments made to individuals about the new pastor, extol that person's strengths. If you are a retiree who maintains friendships with people in what is now your former congregation, or if having moved to another congregation you still maintain some friendships with former parishioners, steel yourself, as my dad used to say to me on appropriate occasions, to "keep your big mouth shut." There will always be someone who doesn't like change, and if the new pastor has instituted some change, an unhappy parishioner may approach you for consolation and perhaps for a bit of reinforcement. Stop. Do not, on pain of betraying the Lord you claim to represent, entertain such criticism. Change the subject.

I vowed that I would never, ever, even by raised eyebrow or knowing smile, undercut my successor. It so happened my successor never did anything I thought wrong, and to this day as I see the continuing upward progress of my former congregation, I find nothing but good to say about its leadership. But I did, for a while, hear that one-in-a-thousand critic. I always took Kent's side. One of my dearest memories is of a retired minister in my first little church who, having served the congregation there, had chosen to retire and attend my church. I gulped when I heard such a person would be there. Bless his heart, he supported me in a thousand different ways. When I had a lousy sermon, he told people how kind I was; when I forgot a meeting, he commented on how smart I was; when I failed to show up for a town fish fry, he told them how busy I was. Always, as the kids say today, I knew he had my back. I wanted to be that kind of supporter.

In the years since Kent Millard succeeded me at St. Luke's that church has thrived and become a major force for the denomination. Because of Kent's kindness to me I have been able to follow that progress as an ardent advocate and appreciative friend. Because of Kent's unfailing encouragement I have derived rewards of a thousand kinds through my ongoing feeling that although I attend a nearby Methodist church I am really, deep in my heart, a part of St. Luke's. I believe God has blessed all of this, and I can now walk among them knowing in my heart that I kept the faith so that today the thousands who worship there can love their pastor with all their hearts. Yet for the many who were there before, they can love me too. And I them.

THE SUCCESSOR: DR. KENT MILLARD

Dag Hammarskjöld, the second secretary general of the United Nations, wrote these words in his book of personal meditations and reflections titled *Markings*: "For all that has been, thanks; for all that will be, yes!"

When I became senior pastor at St. Luke's, I used these words in preaching and leading my new congregation. I wanted to express my profound gratitude and appreciation for all of those leaders who came before me and to help the congregation say yes to what God might be doing among us in the future.

"For All That Has Been, Thanks"

Before I preached my first sermon at St. Luke's, I spent a lot of time reading about the founding and the life and the history of St. Luke's by visiting with key lay and clergy leaders. I had some long conversations with Dr. Carver McGriff about the history of St. Luke's and about some of the highlights of his twenty-six years of highly effective ministry there. I interviewed some of the founding members and asked them to share with me some of their most cherished memories from the past.

Out of these conversations I gained a deep and genuine appreciation and gratitude for all that God had done in and through this congregation during the past, and I could genuinely say, "For all that has been, thanks."

I thanked God for the vision, faith, and commitment of about a hundred and twenty laypeople who started a new worship service in the Methodist tradition in a rented American Legion Hall building forty years earlier. These lay leaders had no pastor, so they invited retired pastors or laypersons to preach and lead worship on Sunday mornings. The bishop and conference leaders were not convinced that a new congregation was needed on the far north side of Indianapolis in 1953, but when the district superintendent was invited to preach, and over a hundred and twenty men, women, and children came to the service, the bishop and cabinet finally decided to charter them and appoint them their first pastor, who came a few months later.

I realized that this event established the DNA of St. Luke's as a creative and innovative congregation that was willing to think outside the box in making disciples of Jesus Christ for the transformation of the world. Consequently, St. Luke's has always had strong, visionary lay leaders who are willing to explore new and creative ways of sharing God's love with all people.

I suspect that every congregation has some inspiring stories of the faith, commitment, and sacrifice of previous or founding members who gave freely of their time, talent, and treasure to launch and strengthen a community of faith. In times of transition it is important that the new leader discover these inspiring stories from the history of the congregation and express appreciation and thanksgiving for the faith and commitment of those who have gone before and who built the congregation which the new pastor is inheriting.

In a transition time the congregation needs to know if their new leader knows and appreciates their history and the vision, faith, and commitment that has brought them to this particular time in their life and ministry. The new pastor who cannot find something to affirm in the life and history of their new congregation may have a hard time being trusted and followed as the new pastoral leader.

When I first entered the narthex of St. Luke's, I saw a plaque on the wall with the identity statement of this congregation. It reads, "St. Luke's Is an Open Community of Christians Who Gather to Seek, Celebrate, Live, and Share the Love of God for All Creation." When I first read that plaque something within me said, "Thank you God for the opportunity of serving an open community of Christians who want to share your love with all creation." I have always believed that Jesus was a spiritual leader who was open to all sorts and conditions of people and who shared God's amazing grace and unconditional love with everyone and that the church should faithfully replicate the ministry of Jesus.

I also thanked God for the three outstanding senior pastors who had each led the congregation in growing spiritually and numerically over the past forty years before I came and for the outstanding visionary and committed associate pastors, staff, and lay leaders who had led the congregation to this point in its life and ministry.

I was especially thankful to Dr. Carver McGriff for his deep faithfulness to God in serving St. Luke's so effectively for twenty-six years, his outstanding preaching ability, and his gentle, kind, and affirming spirit. I am deeply grateful that I have a predecessor who has been more supportive than I deserve and has become a mentor, guide, and friend.

In Deuteronomy 6:10–11 God told Moses that he would come into a land where he would live in houses he did not build, drink out of wells he did not dig, and harvest vineyards he did not plant. When I came to St. Luke's I realized that I was worshiping in a house of God I did not help build, drinking out of wells of faith I did not dig, and harvesting growth from vineyards I did not plant. Whenever any new pastors come to any new congregation, they should come with deep humility and gratitude because they are inheriting the opportunity of leading a congregation they did not build, drinking from the wells of faith they did not dig, and harvesting growth from vineyards they did not plant.

Some pastors come into new congregations with the attitude that they are the "saviors" of the church and that they have to correct all of the mistakes of the previous pastor. This arrogant and self-righteous attitude undermines the ministry and leadership of a new pastor with a new congregation and may lead to a short and unhappy tenure as a pastoral leader in that congregation. Humility, not arrogance, is the chief underlying spiritual characteristic of great leaders, and during times of transitions great leaders will be humbly aware of the debt they owe to the leaders who served before them and will find ways to honor and respect those who have been leaders in the past.

When we come into a new congregation with humility and gratitude for this new opportunity of service, we will say from the depths of our hearts: "For all that has been, thanks."

"For All That Will Be, Yes"

When I preached my first sermon at St. Luke's, I invited the congregation not only to look back and thank God for the wonderful leaders and ministries of the past but also to look forward and say yes to what God will be doing among us in the future. I explained that God had just finished a wonderful twenty-six-year chapter in the life of St. Luke's under the leadership of Dr. McGriff and now God was starting a new chapter in the life of this congregation. Our task would be to discern where God is calling us and say yes to the future into which God is leading us.

When I arrived, people often asked me where I was going to lead the church. I suggested that was the wrong question. The question is not where does our new pastor want to lead the congregation but "what is God going to do next in and through this congregation."

Shortly after I arrived, we started a visioning committee to discern God's vision for the church going forward. I explained that discerning God's vision is like putting the pieces of a picture puzzle together. The puzzle provides an image of the vision God has in mind for this congregation. God has put a piece of this picture puzzle into each of our hearts, and while none of us has the whole puzzle, each of us can share the part of the puzzle we have, and together we will begin to see a picture of where God is leading us.

Our visioning committee began to discern that God was calling us to expand our facilities because we were severely overcrowded in worship and educational space and regularly turned people away for lack of space. We decided that if we are really an open community of Christians, we would provide a place for people to sit when they came to worship and a place for their children and youth in Sunday school.

Our first response to overcrowding was to open a satellite service at a dinner theater to accommodate more people in a nontraditional setting and to reach more unchurched people. Dr. Linda McCoy, an associate pastor on our staff, started "The Garden," which now reaches seven hundred people each week in worship services in two different off-site locations.

Yet growth at the central campus continued, and we knew we would need to expand the facilities. Immediately our visioning committee divided in two camps. Half of our leaders wanted to expand at the present location, and the other half wanted to relocate to a new and larger site for the expansion. I thought, "Great; I've been here two years, and I've divided the congregation in half!"

I went on a one-day silent spiritual retreat to seek God's guidance in this dilemma. At the end of the retreat three ideas came to me clearly:

1. Don't be afraid. I realized that often when an angel appears in Scripture the angel usually says to human beings, "Fear not!" I realized that our fear about this issue was the problem.
2. Listen. Listen for the still small voice of God, and listen to all those leaders around you.
3. Look for a sign. God would give us a clear sign of whether we should stay or relocate.

I shared these insights with our visioning committee and asked us all to put away fear and just trust that God would lead us. I asked them to listen to one another, and put them in pairs with someone who disagreed with their position. I asked them to listen to their partner until they could articulate their partner's position to their partner's satisfaction. Finally, I asked them to look for a sign from God about which direction we should take.

At the end of the evening, after everyone had put away fear and listened deeply to someone who disagreed with them, someone suggested that those who wanted to relocate wanted to do so because they believed there was not enough space where we were to expand and those who wanted to stay felt there was enough space. It was suggested that it was fundamentally an architectural question, and someone moved that we hire an architect to help us answer the question. The group voted unanimously to hire an architect, and someone said, "Unanimous is a good sign from God."

The architect came back with drawings and costs for expansion at both the current site and the proposed site. The person who had led the charge to relocate had a change of heart after seeing the drawings and moved to expand at the current site. The motion passed unanimously, and again we saw unanimity as a good sign from God to move forward. Because we took time to seek God's guidance, God blessed us with the commitments to double our worship and educational capacity, and now hundreds of more people are able to worship God, grow in faith, and be used by God to transform the world into a compassionate, just, inclusive, and Christlike community.

When we say yes to God even when we don't know where it will lead, God is glorified and will lead us in ways we never could have anticipated.

I have also said yes when anyone asked if Carver McGriff could return to conduct a wedding, funeral, or baptism. When people need pastoral services, the question is not which pastor's ego we will stroke but which pastor can help us best through this transition time, and frequently it is the former pastor, who has had a long-term relationship with that family. Usually, Carver and I conduct the funeral or wedding together. It sometimes shocks people to see two pastors cooperating in providing pastoral services to a family, as if pastors are more known for their competition for people's affection than for cooperation in providing pastoral services.

In 1 Corinthians 3:6 Paul writes, "I planted, Apollos watered, but God gave the growth." Paul planted the faith in Corinth; Apollos came after him and watered the faith that was planted, but God gave the growth in faith.

When new pastors come to a new congregation, they need to realize that someone else labored and planted the faith in that garden. We are given the opportunity to water and tend the faith already planted, but we all realize that it is God who causes the plant of faith to grow. Our challenge is to say yes to God.

We have discovered that preaching and pastoring during times of transition between pastors is a time to offer this prayer: "O God, for all that has been, thanks; for all that will be, yes!"

2

A Break in the Stained Glass Ceiling

Joanna M. Adams

In 1991, twelve years after my ordination, with one associate pastorate and one solo pastorate under my clerical collar, I was called to serve a strong congregation in a thriving southern city. Although the South's traditionalism regarding women's roles certainly was a reality in those days, it is worth noting that for most of the eleven years I was there, this southern Protestant church was the largest in our national denomination to have a woman as senior pastor.

During those years, I was frequently asked how many members our church had, as if the number of names on the rolls indicated success or failure. I believe that the more important determinants of the health of a congregation are transformed lives and transformed communities, but our church did grow in every sense of the word. Along with significant expansion in number and in space for education and recreation, the church doubled its size, added five hundred children and youth to its rolls, established a community center in a nearby low-income neighborhood, built partnerships with faith communities in other parts of the world, and became a leader in interfaith dialogue and collaborative endeavors in the city.

When I arrived, the church was still recovering from the failure of a brief experiment of a copastor transition plan. Three interim pastors had done good work there, but the waters were still choppy. Prior to the copastor experiment, the church had been led by the same senior pastor for forty-two years. He was also the founding pastor. It was he who had built the first buildings, sustained the membership over the years, and guided the congregation during the difficult days of the civil rights struggle. He and his wife had raised their children in the manse on the church campus. Although he and I respected one another, my pastoral style naturally was quite different. The congregation was surprised to learn there was more than one way of doing things.

In the first months of my pastorate, I found myself offering up countless prayers for strength, patience, and wisdom. Those prayers were answered in part by a friend, an experienced head-of-staff pastor, who offered me an invaluable piece of advice: "Joanna, as you begin your new ministry, remember that your first and most important responsibility is to love the people as they are, without any conditions or expectations. Only when you and they have come to love and trust one another can you do what God has brought you together to do."

Actually, that advice was not always easy to follow, especially in those early, shaky months. Even before I preached my first sermon, I learned I had challenges to overcome. During the congregational meeting to vote on the report of the pulpit nominating committee, when the chairperson of the committee announced, "The best man for the job is a woman," the reaction was not universal joy. A few people stopped coming to church. An anonymous note or two or three found their way into my mail, complaining about various attributes I brought to the job, including, for instance, the sound of my voice. One elderly member, opposed to my coming, told me that since her sons had grown and her husband had died, her minister was the only man in her life, and now even that had been taken away. I tried not to be defensive and offered those who doubted my call an extra measure of respect, hoping that I might earn their respect over time. For the most part I did. An elder who was later interviewed for a book about churches and their women pastors commented, "[The choosing of] Joanna was about as likely as God appearing in the body of a Jewish boy in First-Century Palestine."[1]

From the beginning, I knew that preaching was paramount in this particular parish, and I worked hard on my sermons. I tried to speak both to the heart and to the mind, preaching sermons that spoke to the personal needs of the people and sermons that addressed many of the important issues of the time. I discovered that the congregation liked to be challenged, and so before the first year was done, I had completed a series of sermons dealing with such topics as "The Christian Faith and Sexual Ethics," "Life after Death," "The Earth at Risk," and "The Black and White Crisis in America."

Early on, I began to build relationships with the great laypeople who filled important leadership roles in the church. They told me the truth I needed to hear, reminded me to take care of myself, both spiritually and physically, and lifted me up when, like Peter, I had taken my eyes off my Savior and had begun to sink. I spent time building a collegial atmosphere with members of

1. Sally Purvis, *The Stained Glass Ceiling* (Louisville, KY: Westminster John Knox Press, 1995), 69.

the staff. We shared a lot of time together in retreat and in weekly meetings, making sure that what we devoted our energies to were endeavors that were congruent with the goals of the congregation.

I devoted many hours to visiting longtime members in their homes, going to the hospitals to visit the sick and welcome new babies, and stopping by the nursing and retirement homes where our elderly members lived. I discovered that frequently what was needed was simply my being there and listening. I became the repository of many secrets, the hearer of many confessions, and the comforter of many bearing heavy burdens.

One of my most vivid memories of those early months is of a hospital visit I made to a young woman in our congregation. The young-twenties daughter of one of the church's core families, she was moving into the last stages of a particularly virulent form of leukemia. Although I'd never met her, I went to see her at the nearby university hospital. I knocked on the door to her room, said my name, and asked if I could come in.

"No," she replied emphatically.

"Okay," I answered, "but listen. I drove all the way over here and parked in the parking lot. They won't let me park free if I haven't actually visited a parishioner."

She laughed and said, "Come on in."

Thus began perhaps the most precious pastoral relationship I have ever had. As the months passed, we became true sisters in Christ. I learned from her about faith and courage. She learned a few things from me too, I think. When she died, more than a thousand people, many of them young, came to the funeral. I spoke of the love that never ends. Through our tears, we were able to rejoice that what we still only knew in part on our side of the glass, she now knew in full. It wasn't enough, but it helped.

As time went by, it became apparent that the most daunting issues of the transition had much less to do with my being a woman than with my not being my predecessor. Forty-two years is a long time, and people had become accustomed to having things done a certain way. Whatever I suggested felt revolutionary to some, even if it was nothing more major than moving the church mailbox, which, for the record, evoked a great deal of consternation. When I suggested to the session's executive committee that we consider keeping worship at 11:00 a.m. throughout the year rather than changing it to 10:00 a.m. in the summer, the tectonic plates underneath the earth groaned in resistance. I made my case. I listened to the rebuttal. I realized that this was not a battle I needed to fight.

Getting Bibles into the sanctuary pew racks was, however, a struggle that I would not abandon. It wasn't that members of the worship committee objected to the Bible. I was assured that the Bible was fine with them. Nonetheless, the majority thought that putting Bibles in the pew racks might make the church seem too much like other churches. I was told, "We like the Bible, but we are not 'Bible thumpers.'"

"I see," I said.

A few months later, pew Bibles were donated by an anonymous couple in the church, and that was that. I remember thinking at the time that the Bibles in the pews marked what Winston Churchill would have called "the end of the beginning."

All of this took place almost twenty years ago, but I still feel the deepest sense of privilege for the experience. Ever since, I have benefited from the invaluable things I learned about ministry on the other side of that "stained glass ceiling":

- Don't worry about yourself so much. God calls. God equips. God sustains. Even when you are doing something that seems daunting to you, never forget that God's grace will be sufficient for all your needs, especially when you are doing your best to minister in Christ's name.
- Be respectful of others, even as you hope and pray they will be respectful of you.
- Realize that you possess neither all the answers nor all the skills necessary for success. Surround yourself with capable people; thank them every day for their commitment; listen to their constructive criticism; rejoice in their good ideas; and work with them to build a faithful, vibrant church.
- Don't lose yourself when you lose an argument or a vote, or when you disappoint yourself and the best you know. I have learned more from my missteps and failures than I have learned from all my successes combined. Churches do not need or expect leaders who are perfect but rather leaders who join them in being imperfect members of the human race, saved by God's grace and redeemed by divine love.
- Do not get into knock-down-drag-out arguments with wedding photographers. My story is still too painful to tell.
- Claim your gifts and authority, and use them forthrightly. The church is crying out for authentic, quality leaders who have both character and moral conviction, pastors who are not afraid to speak the truth in love, pastors who bravely challenge conventional wisdom without self-righteousness.
- Be a Christian. No one of us does this completely or without the influence of sin in our souls, but believe the gospel with all your heart. Preach the gospel with all your heart. Live the gospel with all your heart. A pastor with ambivalence about the resurrection of Christ from the dead is as of much use to his or her congregation as an attorney who is iffy about the Constitution of the United States.
- Don't be afraid to claim your role as change agent. In Isaiah 43:19, the Lord says, "I am about to do a new thing. Do you not perceive it?" Your job is to keep your eyes open to the wonders large and small that God works in our midst.

- Identify what will be for you concrete signs of progress. Perhaps it is not politically correct, but in those first years, I set goals regarding worship attendance, mission expansion, Bible study opportunities, and participation in hands-on service opportunities. If we missed the mark, we tried harder and introduced new approaches.
- Maintain personal well-being and a healthy family life.
- Have a life that involves friends and interests beyond the congregation.
- Remember, as a great friend from my pulpit nominating committee frequently reminded me, "Everybody isn't going to like everything."
- Pay attention to people, and be intentionally inclusive about it. Don't give all your energies to that small circle who are over at the church all the time. Connect on a human level, remembering especially that those who are new need to be made to feel welcome.
- Don't mess with what is working well; rather, ensure that the most outstanding programs are properly resourced and frequently celebrated. The music ministry was outstanding when I arrived and outstanding when I left.

One of my favorite conversations in the Bible takes place between Moses and God: Moses offers the Lord a long list of his personal inadequacies, even as God is trying to persuade him to take up the mantle of spiritual leadership for the sake of the Hebrew people. In the beginning, God had to have a similar conversation with me. My own self-doubts simply had to be replaced with my confidence in God's call and promise to equip.

I think of how Sarah, well into the AARP chapter of her life, laughed at the thought that she and Abraham would be the parents of a great nation. Before I arrived at that strong church in the South, I never would have imagined that I would play such a meaningful role in the generative purposes of God in that particular place.

As I ready myself to retire from thirty years in parish ministry, I give thanks to God that the church goes on, generation to generation. I rejoice that I was privileged to help a significant congregation claim its distinctive mission and move forward toward God's new tomorrow.

I am more confident than ever that the Spirit of the living God continues to call "both women and men to *all* the ministries of the church," including sizable parish posts.[2]

---

2. A Brief Statement of Faith, Presbyterian Church (U.S.A.).

3

Led by a Pillar of Fire

The Preacher in Transition

FREDERICK W. SCHMIDT

> "Clergy stink at helping people with change," my friend observed.
> "In large part because you aren't any good at it either. You preach
> dependence upon God, but you don't depend upon God at all.
> You depend upon the church, its support, the titles it uses, places
> to worship, and pension plans. When something happens and you
> find yourselves out on the street, you are just as much up the creek
> as the rest of us."
>
> *Anonymous*

Transitions have two faces—death and life, loss and gain, endings and beginnings, grief and anticipation. Transitions possess the power to make or break
us, renew or destroy us. The most significant transitions can rob us of our sense
of identity and security, our sense of belonging and mattering, our sense of
control. Invariably, even the most promising of transitions leave us for a time in
a place where our fate remains unnamed and the verdict on our future is lost in
the deafening silence. Sometimes our transitions are filled with pure terror.

TRANSITION AS SPIRITUAL TRIAL

Transitions are, then, inherently, inescapably, spiritual trials. They are leave
taking and journey, purgation and the search for something promised—the
exodus story in miniature.

To ignore the truth about transitions and the truth about our own inability
to navigate them, to therapeutize the experience, or to manage the details in

19

life's transitions is to miss the demands that they make on us. These are occasions filled with temptation and spiritual opportunity.

Worse yet, to resist entering the crosscurrents and riptides of own experience of transition as though we can stand above them is to fail those to whom we minister. Although some are likely to label the observation quaint or even dangerous, any preaching that fails to help people recognize the spiritual trial imbedded in the experience of transition also fails to aid the congregation in the deepest way possible.

For that reason, the preparation to preach effectively to the transitions that people experience does not begin in the pastor's study or on a blank piece of paper—never mind in the pulpit. This kind of preaching begins by cultivating a capacity for companionship by entering into the spiritual challenges that are inherent in the changes that shape our own lives. If there is any truth to the maxim that the preacher's life is the sermon, it is evident here. The pastor or priest or rabbi is not the resident expert; she or he is a companion on much the same journey. If, as my friend observed, we stink at helping other people through transitions, it is because we are so hapless at navigating our own.

How is that capacity for companionship cultivated? It is fostered by naming the behaviors we use to hold the spiritual challenges at bay and by defining the nature of the spiritual challenges and opportunities inherent in the transitions that we all experience.

TEMPTED IN THE WILDERNESS

There is no fixed or exhaustive list of distancing behaviors to which we all resort in our effort to avoid the spiritual trials inherent in transitions. The temptation to avoid transition's crucible reconstellates, depending on time, circumstances, and place. So our ability to enter into the wisdom to be wrung from the experience of transition requires spiritual honesty in naming our own habits. There are at least five such habits that are more or less common among clergy: (1) refusing to live aware, (2) managing the details, (3) baptizing fatalism, (4) resorting to primitivism and radical reform, (5) fighting change with change.

Refusing to Live Aware

I once participated in a mentoring program in which the rector of a large, complex parish graciously took the time to discuss the challenges he faced where he was ministering. Looking back on the demands that the transition had brought his way, he observed, "You know, like my peers who now serve as bishops, going in I was convinced that I could remain a priest and do this job, but that isn't possible."

At the time I remember thinking I was not quite sure what shocked me most, the fact that he could say something like that in public, that he took obvious pride in having reached an impasse of that kind, or that he thought it was a helpful observation to make in front of younger priests. But, of course, the truly stunning dimension of his remarks was the absence of awareness. He was clearly out of touch with the peril that anyone is in when one trades one's vocation as a bearer of sacramental presence for the mantle of CEO. No matter how complex or threatening the transition might be, trading true vocation for a less God-called role is making a pact with the devil.

That lack of awareness is perennial among preachers. Years ago I sat between two pastors who were twenty years my senior, anxious to get some insight into the way in which they balanced the challenge of listening for God's guidance in pursuing their vocation while navigating the exigencies of church communities that had a seemingly tin ear for such considerations. Both pastors, who presented on the face of it as satisfied practitioners of their vocation, spilled over with anger over the ways in which they had felt thwarted, ignored, and abused by the church. Yet there they were, passing on their fatalism, anger, and cynicism about the church.

Transitions can teach us something about the extent to which we have successfully remained aware of and alive to the prompting of the Spirit. We preachers, like countless laypeople, fail to learn from such experiences because we take the institutional structures within which we work as givens and depend on their largesse.

Tempted by not only the church's support but also its norms, we can easily lose sight of our calling and vocation. The absence of mechanisms and values that would recognize those commitments and their importance is, of course, deplorable. Nevertheless, our individual failure to face those challenges squarely robs not only us but those to whom we preach of valuable insights into the crosscurrents in their own lives at times of transition.

Not all transitions should be embraced. Living into our vocation, as vocation, is indeed deepened and refined in transition. But the transitions that are forced on us, the ones we choose, and those we refuse to enter all define the way we live out our vocation. To name transitions we choose and those where there are no choices we can make is to live in full awareness of their significance. Whether the transitions are welcome or unwelcome, we live more fully in God's presence when we live aware of where we are.

Yet as clergy, we are easily seduced by the temptation to identify the church's needs, charms, and appetites with God's call on our lives. Clergy are perhaps even more easily seduced than some laypeople are by their own work worlds. So in order to be the kind of guides who can cultivate a capacity for awareness, we ourselves need to practice living aware and wringing all the wisdom from experiences of transition that we can find.

The results will be a challenge to articulate from the pulpit. It is not enough—or even a good thing—to elicit cynicism. Modeling cynicism as a way of handling the challenge of transitions is all too common in the American pulpit. Far from cultivating the kind of vulnerability and passion that deepen the work of God in the lives of our congregants, it tends to inure them to the work of God. Cynicism cannot provide an opening to the work of the Spirit. Cynicism cuts us off from the Spirit, announcing that nothing good can come from the changes we face.

Our sermons could, instead, elicit innocence and passion, the kind of innocence and passion that so easily mark the beginning of the pilgrimage and are so quickly lost in the desert. This is not, of course, a matter of preaching blind obedience or naïveté. To do that is to err in the opposite direction. No one who approaches each wave of change as if they have never navigated it before can say that they have wrung the wisdom out of those experiences. Sermons shaped by the effort to live aware will be marked by the commitment both to listen and live in deep devotion to the call of God.

Managing the Details

A second temptation in times of transition is the tendency to manage the day-to-day details of life rather than face the fundamental changes in the way life is lived. Some argue that this is the temptation that has bedeviled leaders of every kind in the tectonic shifts that have marked the first decade of the twenty-first century.

Many thinkers observe that a difficulty we currently face is traceable in part to the fact that we are being led into the twenty-first century by leaders with a twentieth-century mind-set. In the case of the church, it might argued that our leaders have mind-sets shaped not by the twentieth century but by the nineteenth.

Having traveled widely in the last year, I have seen this dynamic at work almost everywhere in my own denomination. Globalization and conflicting understandings of the church and its mission have led to fissures in relationships within the Anglican Communion both globally and nationally.

Church membership is shrinking. Parishes and dioceses are contracting and disappearing. Others are exiting the denomination to found splinter groups that lack the kind of core, constructive commitments on which something new could be built. In most cases, none of the alternatives offered are thriving. Church as we knew it in the high-tide denominationalism of the fifties and sixties is dead.

Meanwhile we are entering into what may be one of the most dramatic intergenerational transitions in recent history. Boomers cling to leadership positions and label their views progressive while ever-larger numbers of younger adults exit the church, signaling that the boomers' claims to being progressive could not be further from the truth.

In the middle of it all bishops, priests, and academic deans of seminaries continue to manage the bureaucracy they were trained to manage with little to offer in the way of fresh vision. In one conversation about the absence of any meaningful statements from the House of Bishops about what we need in the way of clergy, one bishop observed, "We aren't going to have that conversation. There is no will to have it." The church, it seems, has lost its nerve and its ability to think about a vision for the next generation.

In an era when jobs, companies, and even ways of working are constantly changing and some are disappearing, it is unrealistic for clergy to believe that the church as we know it cannot pass from existence. A friend who recently retired looked back on the changes he has witnessed just in the last five years and expressed understandable dismay at both the changes and the seeming inability of the church's hierarchy to do more than manage the bureaucracy they prepared to lead. They cannot imagine a future different from the past, so they try to manage the institution they remember, not the institution that is.

In preaching to the vagaries of change, clergy would be better served not to take refuge in managing the details. If clergy are unable to acknowledge our radical dependence on God in the midst of transition, if we are unable to acknowledge in our preaching that even the institutions we serve cannot and are not passing away, then clergy can hardly speak with understanding or conviction to people who every day have that reality forced on them in the wider world.

I often tell my students that church history is more fun to read than it is to live. It may well be that the unwelcome but great gift in the early decades of this century is that we have not been spared the transitions the members of our congregations have faced. Our ability to enter into them, rather than trying to remain above them by managing the details of institutional life, will be the measure of our ability to receive the gift.

Baptizing Fatalism

As may be clear from what has been said thus far, we find the ability to speak to transitions in our ability to enter into them in all their complexity. One of the ways that clergy and others avoid entering into that complexity is through a baptized fatalism.

By baptizing fatalism and declaring what is as what must be, the capacity for imagining a different future is cut off at the source. Clergy "retire in place." They repeat the old programs and resort to the old formulas. This failure of imagination is not always evident and can often be confused with simple laziness. But more often than not it is flight from change—what Friedman describes as "a failure of nerve."

At every level some clergy deal with change by resorting to such fatalism, and the loosely linked bureaucracies in which we serve lack the mechanisms for identifying the malaise or addressing the causes. At other times, the very leaders charged with tending to the needs of preachers are themselves afflicted with the same malaise. A colleague who has traveled widely observed that he has seen bishops go through the motions, attending to as few administrative responsibilities as possible, passing on much of their work to others.

In its more forthright forms, fatalism credits itself with acknowledging the changes we face and thus masquerades as an embrace of transition. But the unthinking canonization of change that equates it with God's will and fails to ask serious questions about the changes that are taking shape and how they may or may not reflect the movement of God is not the embrace of change at all. It is a sign of despair and hopelessness. By contrast, the prophets—who preached their way through countless transitions—were never without probing questions about how and where God was at work. *Homo sympathetikos*, they were people who longed to understand what the spirit of God was doing and took none of the changes they faced for granted.[1]

Resorting to Primitivism and Radical Reform

It is not enough to ask questions, of course. However tentative, when we grapple with change, we find ourselves compelled to suggest a direction in which we might move in response to God.

The temptation for clergy is to resort to obvious, simple answers. In a religious environment that prefers bipolar answers to difficult questions about the will of God, it is not surprising to find preachers resorting to either primitivism or radical reform. The first harkens to some primitive and pristine past, often an idealized world of the New Testament. The second embraces the relativism of a world that divorces itself from asking and answering the difficult questions required by awareness.

---

1. See Abraham Heschel, *The Prophets* (New York: Harper & Row, 1962), 308–9.

The net result? Preaching that is often facile and predictable. The tendency to navigate the transition in such facile ways is common enough when the focus of preaching is the biblical text. Factor in the social, scientific, political, and economic complexities of change. and, sadly, most of what one hears from the pulpit amounts to little more than uninformed political opinion that differs only in whether the preacher's starting point is politically left or right of center.

Preaching of this kind is of singularly little help to congregations. It promises more than it can deliver. It aggrandizes personal opinion by wrapping the mantle of preacher around what would be better shared over the breakfast table at a diner, and it runs the risk of alienating laypeople who know better than the man and woman in the pulpit how difficult the challenges are.

I once heard a preacher who did a brief stint as a hospital orderly treat his congregation—which included some notable and distinguished physicians—to a screed about the way in which physicians could learn a bit of humility. He then went on to make sweeping assertions about the solution to the health-care debate. Not unsurprisingly, the apparent theological and exegetical basis of his remarks did little to assuage the justifiable anger of his congregants. Little was said that morning that was likely to assist the church in navigating the issues and transitions in health care that face all of us. The sermon did, ultimately, facilitate the transition in clerical leadership in the parish.

Fighting Change with Change

One of the most helpful works of a general nature on the subject of transitions is the work of William Bridges—not a bad name for someone writing about transition. Bridges argues that those who navigate transition take one of two approaches to the challenges that they face. Some are disillusioned; others are disenchanted.[2]

Bridges is not a theologian and does not take a theological approach to his subject. He argues that in the transitions we experience we confront the difference between our expectations and the nature of reality. To one degree or another, he argues, we are all "enchanted." That is, we have magical or unrealistic notions of what our jobs and relationships—or the future in general—can hold for us.

The disillusioned, he notes, are people who never realistically examine the difference between their unrealistic notions and reality to determine the extent to which this enchantment has shaped their expectations. So when they confront a difference between their expectations and reality, they are "disillusioned" by

2. William Bridges, *Transitions: Making Sense of Life's Changes* (Reading, MA: Addison-Wesley Publishing Co., 1980), 98ff.

it. In their disillusion they immediately begin looking for a new experience that will match their expectations. Disillusioned people, Bridges argues, go through multiple relationships and jobs, looking for the optimal experience yet never quite have it. Others are always to blame; they are forever the victims.

By contrast those who are mature go through a process of "disenchantment." The disenchanted experience the same dissonance that the disillusioned experience, but they also have the courage and patience to confront the degree to which their expectations are shaped by magical and unrealistic assumptions. Having taken that difference into account, the disenchanted then weigh the wisdom of making further changes. As a result, they are able to make realistic changes, hold themselves and others accountable, and avoid the perils of a life dominated by unrealistic desires and the inevitable disappointment that shadows it.

One could argue that a moment's reflection would reveal that Bridges's analysis, as psychologically astute as it is, might benefit further still from theological reflection. What is at stake here, perhaps, is not just our ability to confront the distortions in our perceptions and expectations—or the ability to recognize the way in which our life experiences can plunge us into transitions that are calculated to mask the greater inward, psychological transition needed. What is at stake is, at a fundamental level, our ability to confront the deeper transition that is repentance.

Spiritually, the disillusioned are not simply dogged by the dissonance between their expectations and their experiences—they are dogged by the spiritual presumption that their views are the measure of the way in which the world around them should perform, and they pridefully resist the need to examine that idolatrous presumption.

This is not to suggest that the spiritually mature preacher blithely accepts the status quo as somehow ordained and appropriate. To do that is to lapse back into a baptized fatalism and to cut the engine of spiritual and moral critique. Rather it is to suggest that we take ourselves out of the equation in ways that are presumptuous. We must not privilege our own views with a preeminence that only God's perspective rightly deserves.

This temptation is one to which everyone who preaches is subject. I have, in fact, seen a great deal of it in recent years. In debates over sexual orientation, clergy on both the left and the right of those debates have resorted to the politics of leverage, preferring the logic of the disillusioned to the more difficult task of patiently listening to one another, to say nothing of listening to God. This behavior is evident in the attempt of Episcopal dioceses and parishes to negotiate the tensions that arise out of those debates in their relationship to judicatories and, worse yet, in the relationships between the various parts of the Anglican Communion.

Disillusionment is common as well among second-vocation preachers, who are subject to it for understandable reasons. They enter seminary thinking that, at long last, they are exchanging conversations about money for conversations about meaning and corporate life for communal experiences. Then they enter the ministry and discover that there are ample conversations about money, just less of it, and plenty of corporate behavior rather than communal abounds. It could be that their disappointment is justified. In some cases the institution is itself spiritually in need of repentance. Still, until we as clergy go through the process of disenchantment and repentance, we are likely to offer sermons marked less by spiritual insight than by personal disappointment. Not unlike our counterparts in lay vocations of one kind or another, we are also likely to fight change with change, looking for congregants, parishes, and denominations that bend to our will.

DEFINING THE SPIRITUAL CHALLENGES

What then are the spiritual challenges and opportunities inherent in the transitions that we all experience? Beginning with the last point made, one of the challenges is, of course, to let God be God. Transitions take us straight into our need for control and our fear of being out of control.

It is an understandable, commonplace, and universal failing. It is at the heart of our sinfulness. Transitions exacerbate that tendency and heighten the spiritual crisis by forcing us to choose whether we or God will be the defining force in our lives.

Our ability to release the need to be God for ourselves is one of the sermons we find it easier to preach to others than it is to hear applied to our own lives. Perhaps the reason we preach so often about the need to let God be God is because we ourselves know how little progress we have made in responding.

Armed with that fundamental realization, we are then able to confront the other challenges latent in every life transition. In transition good things can be lost. When they are, we grieve. And we grieve not just the things we have lost; we grieve the loss of deeper, more important things that they represent. Everything ends—including this life. And we grieve the losses in retrospect and in anticipation of them. If grief and regret are all that we bring to the experience of transitions, then the final, great transition of death will color our experience and preaching of all the others.

Fear, not courage, will then define our lives and our ministries. Unless, of course, we remember that in each transition—and the wilderness that follows—we are led by that pillar of fire that is the presence of God.

4

Poetry in Motion: A Case Study in Preaching in a New Pastoral Setting

ALYCE M. MCKENZIE (WITH MARY MARTIN)

Poetry, Texas, is at the intersection of Farm roads 986 and 1565, six miles north of Terrell in northern Kaufman County. On July 22, 1845, Elisha Turner was awarded a patent to a league and a labor of land in this area by President Anson Jones for service to the Republic of Texas. He settled on the old Shreveport-Dallas road at a site that eventually became known as Turner's Point. A post office and school were established in 1858. A general store, hotel, Masonic lodge, and cotton gin eventually opened in the vicinity. The development of Terrell on the Texas and Pacific Railway in 1873 prompted such Turner's Point merchants as Joe Rushing and John Stevenson to move there. Others gradually moved their businesses the short distance to the present community. In 1876 the postal service requested that the community change its name to avoid confusion with a similarly named post office. Maston Ussery, a local merchant, suggested the name Poetry because the area in springtime reminded him of a poem. The post office was moved from the Turner's Point site to the Poetry site in 1879. In 1880 the estimated population of Poetry was forty. By 1904 the population was estimated to be 234. The post office closed in 1905, when service was consolidated in Terrell. On October 27, 1924, the business district was destroyed by fire. The churches escaped the fire, however, and their presence helped preserve the community. In 1941 the population was fifty. In the 1970s new growth began after two decades of little progress. Land developers enticed many new residents to the area, which is within comfortable commuting distance from Dallas. In 1984 an attempt was made to incorporate the community. The incorporation measure

passed but was later ruled invalid by the Kaufman County Com-
missioners Court due to technicalities. A new general store opened
in 1986. Sites of historical significance include the Poetry First
Baptist Church, the Poetry Methodist Church, the Cumberland
Presbyterian Church and adjacent Campground Cemetery, and
the Dry Creek Cemetery near the Turner's Point site. The latter cemetery contains graves of many pioneers who settled in this
area. In 1990 Poetry was listed as a community but without census
figures; "more than 600" people were said to live there.
                    —*Texas Online Handbook*, entry for Poetry, Texas

My name is Alyce McKenzie. I've been a United Methodist pastor since my
ordination in 1981. After seminary at Duke Divinity School in Durham,
North Carolina, I served several churches in central and eastern Pennsyl-
vania in the 1980s and 1990s. I got my PhD in homiletics from Princeton
Theological Seminary in 1994 and since 1999 have been teaching homiletics at Perkins School of Theology, Southern Methodist University, Dallas, Texas. David Mosser asked me if I would write an essay on transition
in ministry. I said yes because I like to be associated with anything David
does, and then I immediately asked myself, "What on earth will I focus on
in addressing this vast topic?" So it was that I sat at my desk in my home
office that May afternoon, contemplating various thematic approaches to
dealing with change and exercising pastoral care and leadership in times of
transition. I was about to get up and brew another pot of coffee when Mary
Martin called.

Mary Martin is a talented American actress who starred in many musicals,
most notably playing Peter Pan on Broadway. Since she passed away in 1990, I
knew it was not that Mary Martin calling. This Mary Martin is a bright, ener-
getic woman in her early forties with two teenagers who lives three minutes
from me in my neighborhood in Allen, Texas, a town of about 80,000 people
twenty-five miles north of Dallas. A couple of years ago Mary responded to
a call to ministry and started seminary at Perkins School of Theology. Soon
after that, she began working as the coordinator of adult ministries at First
United Methodist Church, Allen, where my husband and I sing in the chancel
choir, teach a Sunday school class, and are otherwise active in the life of the
congregation. Mary sounded a little nervous on the phone.

"Alyce, I'm registered to take your Introduction to Preaching class, in the
fall."

"That's good. I'll look forward to working with you," I said.

"And I've never preached before."

"Well, then a course in preaching will be a good thing." Saying obvious
things on the phone is one of my gifts.

"And I've just found out the bishop has appointed me to my own church in Poetry, Texas, pronounced 'Po (long o) tree.'"

I congratulated her, and we talked a bit about where Poetry is in relation to Allen, how many people are in the church, and what her job description would be. Then she cut to the chase of her call: "I will be preaching every week starting July 5. And your course doesn't start until the end of August. I don't have a clue what to do. Will you help me?"

Being an altruistic person, I would have said yes anyway. Being an altruistic person who was brainstorming ways to approach the topic of preaching in times of transition, I said yes enthusiastically. Why? Because a title had just popped into my head: "Poetry in Motion."

I hope you like double entendres as much as I do. "Poetry in Motion," at the literal level, describes Mary's new congregation, which is facing a pastoral change from a seasoned male pastor near retirement age to a forty-something newbie female pastor. "Poetry in Motion," at the metaphorical level, expresses the way we would hope that both people and pastor could respond to times of transition, with grace and energy. In this case study, the focus will be on preaching in a time of transition.

I agreed to meet with Mary a couple of times between May 15 and July 5, her first Sunday in Poetry. I asked her if she would mind if our reflections on preaching in a new setting, with intentional exegesis of congregation as well as text, formed the basis for the article I had been asked to write.

And that was how we came to be sitting in my living room one afternoon in early June 2009 with the Bible and a copy of the pamphlet *Poetic Beginnings: A History of Poetry Methodist Church* on the coffee table in front of us.

I suggested that we begin with talking about the congregation's needs, struggles, and strengths and allow themes and images to surface from our conversation. We would be working on the premise that exegesis of the congregation is the necessary complement to exegesis of the text in our preaching. I suggested she view preaching as local theology, a phrase used by Nora Tubbs Tisdale in her book on congregational exegesis, *Preaching as Local Theology and Folk Art*.[1]

Mary had been to a lengthy introductory meeting with the staff parish committee a few days before. I asked her to reflect on her impressions, on any clues throughout the conversation regarding what was important to them and what their personality and priorities were like. Ethnographers call this "thick description," looking not just at specific behaviors but at the context

---

1. Nora Tubbs Tisdale, *Preaching as Local Theology and Folk Art* (Minneapolis: Fortress Press, 1996), 48. Says Tisdale, "In preaching as local theology, exegesis of the congregation and its subcultures is not peripheral to proclamation but central to its concerns."

that shapes and gives them meaning.[2] The term has become commonplace in the fields of anthropology, literary criticism, and congregational studies. As a lover of mystery fiction, I see it as gathering clues. I gave Mary a copy of a handout I give to my Introduction to Preaching classes called "Exegesis of Your Congregation," which appears at the end of this chapter.

I started with a general question: "What are some things you've noticed about the people you've met so far?"

She thought for a moment, and then said, "Well, I thought it was significant that several of them asked me, 'Do you preach from the Bible?' They told me they didn't want to hear about my family stories, but they wanted me to bring the Bible alive. They were impressed that I have been to the Holy Land and seemed to take this as a very positive thing."

I got a little more specific with my questions. I asked Mary to reflect on the character of the congregation—their sources of pride, their personality—using any conversational cues she could recall. Among the features she mentioned were these:

- They are authentic people. They don't like pretense. They are not trying to be something they are not.
- They have a "can-do" attitude. They said when they see needs they like to do something about it. Somebody will quietly start an effort to take care of things. That's how the new pew covers came about. That's how the building fund got started.
- They open their church to a weekly quilting group that includes church members but is community wide. They make baby blankets and small "comfort quilts" for service people.
- Family is very important, and they like to see themselves as a family. They seem to be a forgiving and welcoming church.

From those observations we drew four qualities of the church, who they are and want to become: fearless (willing to be honest with each other), focused (on God as their center), forgiving (caring for one another), and welcoming. Though we tried to have them all start with the same letter, we didn't quite make it, but three out of four isn't too bad! We started brainstorming about themes or texts to take Mary through the summer. Since the first two weeks she would be there the lectionary texts were the rejection of Jesus at Nazareth and the death of John the Baptist, we decided not to give anybody any ideas! We began looking for themes and textual pairings beyond the lectionary. I told Mary about Nora Tisdale's advice to identify images and stories that express the congregation's identity as it is

2. Clifford Geertz first introduced this term to describe his methods in ethnographic study in *The Interpretation of Cultures* (New York: Basic Books, 1977), 5–6, 9–11.

and is becoming. I asked her if she thought the image of a quilt might spark a sermon series.

As we concluded this first session, I suggested to Mary that she meet with the former pastor and get his impressions, possibly by using the questions in the "Exegeting Your Congregation" handout I gave her. I suggested she use this instrument when talking with other church leaders. She asked if I would mind mulling over some ideas for texts to go with the quilt theme. I told her I'd do that and e-mail her some ideas in the next few days.

I gave her a copy of chapter 3 of the book *A Time for Change? Revisioning Your Call* by James E. Hightower Jr. and W. Craig Gilliam. Chapter 3 is titled "Managing Anxiety in Times of Change." I had read it a few weeks before and wished I had read it years ago. It is a family systems account of how we live in emotional systems, deeply connected to one another. W. Craig Gilliam, the author of this essay, says, "Because we are a part of a family system, we do not have the choice of whether to involve family. The family is already involved."[3] Change destabilizes the pastoral family. It answers the question "In times of transition, how we can maintain a non-anxious presence that will help the family equilibrium stabilize?"[4]

Reflecting on the topic of preaching in transition, it occurred to me that just about everybody I know is in transition, from my nuclear family, to my extended family, to my students and colleagues. I believe it was the obsessive-compulsive television detective Adrian Monk (played by actor Tony Shalhoub) who once said, "I don't mind change. I just don't want to be there when it happens."

Mary will be preaching out of her own transition to a people in transitions of their own. Mary is in transition—moving from serving on a staff in a large church to being the staff in a small church. Her new full-time appointment will cause her family to be in transition. The lives of her husband and two teenage children will be affected by her new role and duties. Her congregation is in transition between Pastor Bob and Pastor Mary, a male pastor in his sixties and a female pastor in her forties.

As promised, I mulled over the qualities Mary saw in her people and some biblical texts and e-mailed her the following:

> Mary:
>
> Here are some possible texts for your sermon series. As I recall there were four qualities you wanted to lift up as things you saw in them. You wanted to use the quilt metaphor:

---

3. James E. Hightower Jr. and W. Craig Gilliam, *A Time for Change? Revisioning Your Call* (Bethesda, MD: Alban Institute, 2000), 51.
4. Ibid., ch. 3, "Managing Anxiety in Times of Change."

Fearless (honesty with one another and about themselves; no
   pretensions)
Forgiving/Caring/Loving
Focused on God (have their priorities straight)
Welcoming

So I went to the concordance and found entries for "one another,"
remembering that I had once heard of a preacher doing a series on
"one another" from the New Testament, as models in how we are to
interact in Christ's new community. Here are some ideas.

Fearless (honesty with one another and about themselves; no pretensions)
James 5:16—"Confess your sins to one another."
Hebrews 3:13—"Exhort one another."
Hebrews 10:24—"Stir one another up to love and good works."
Colossians 3:9—"Don't lie to one another."
Galatians 5:26—"Don't envy one another."

Forgiving (loving, etc.)
1 Thessalonians 4:18—Comfort one another.
1 Thessalonians 5:11—Encourage one another.
1 Thessalonians 5:15—Do good to one another.
Romans 12:16; 15:5—Live in harmony with one another.
Ephesians 4:2—Forebear one another.
1 Peter 1:22—Love one another.
1 John 3:11; 3:23; 4:7—Love one another.
Romans 14:13—Don't judge one another.
Galatians 5:1—Be servants of one another.
Ephesians 4:32—Forgive one another.
Ephesians 4:32—Be kind to one another.
Ephesians 5:21—Be subject to one another.

Welcoming
Romans 15:7
Romans 16:16
1 Corinthians 16:20
2 Corinthians 13:12
1 Peter 5:14
1 Peter 4:9

Focused on God (In these texts readers are told to act a certain way to one another because it is how God acts or is toward us.)
Romans 15:7 (welcoming)
Ephesians 4:32 (forgiving)
2 John 1:3 (love)

1 Thessalonians 4:9 (love)
1 John 3:22 (love)
James 5:16 (pray for one another)

Of course, you can't preach all of these texts, but there's something to get started on anyway.

At the end of June Mary e-mailed me the following:

Alyce:

I went to Poetry yesterday for the afternoon to meet with the Staff Parish Relations Committee, as well as members of the finance and worship committees.

Do you remember when it hit you that you were the pastor, shepherd of a flock? Well it hit me yesterday. I was engaged, listening intently, made some decisions, and thought, "Wow, I am the pastor." We all acknowledged the fact that I will be somewhat nervous and they will be nervous on the first Sunday . . . and talked about what they will call me . . . we settled on "Pastor Mary" and in casual circles or one-on-one "Mary" will do. . . . I learned just be yourself, a sense of humor helps, and let them see that I am human too. Overall it was a good meeting.

Since my first Sunday is July 4 weekend, I'm thinking that not many people will be there, so I am going to save the theme we picked for after the first week.

After many soul-searching sessions I have chosen to use 1 Corinthians 12:12–27, Paul's metaphor of the church as the body of Christ, for my first few sermons. I'm going to use the lyrics of the hymn "I am the church; you are the church; we are the church together" to shape the sermon. Because I think that's what the text is saying.

What follows is the sermon that Mary wrote and delivered after our e-mail exchange.

I Am the Church; You Are the Church; We Are the Church Together

1 Corinthians 12:12–27

In 1 Corinthians 12:12–14, Paul sets out to establish that the body of Christ (the church) consists of diversity in unity. In 12:15–26 he extends this thought and applies the "body" illustration of the church. Finally in 12:27–31, he explains the diversity of spiritual gifts in the church. This passage makes the point that the church is identified by unity in Christ but with a diversity of members, personal abilities (gifts), and ministries (functions).

If I were to ask you to draw a picture of the church, what would you draw? Many of us would draw a building with a steeple, cross, and maybe stained glass. Some of you might draw people sitting, praying, or working together. A few might be more symbolic and draw a cross and flame or other images to represent the church. The most famous picture of the church does not hang in a cathedral or art gallery. It appears in the Bible. It is the image of the church drawn by Paul in his letter to the church at Corinth. He paints a picture with words of the church as the body of Christ. What better picture could there be? The body is a symphony of muscles, organs, nerves, tendons, bones, and other tissues functioning as a harmonious whole. This intricate, interrelated system is exactly what we the church have been called to become. We are the body of Christ in the world.

I learned this song in my church a long time ago. You may know how it goes: "I am the church; you are the church; we are the church together. All who follow Jesus, all around the world? Yes, we're the church together!" The lyrics describe the church as a community. Scripture encourages us to come together as we worship, care for each other, share our resources and tell our stories.

The following three affirmations help me understand how the church works:

First, *I am the church.* As pastor, I have been called by God and set aside by the church for the work of ordained ministry. It was in 2005 when I called Milton Guttierrez, the pastor at First United Methodist Church of Allen, and asked to meet with him regarding my call into the ministry. My faith journey has never been an overnight event. For me, being led by God continues to be a long and winding road with lots of curves, mountains, and flatlands.

At our first meeting, Pastor Milton reminded me of a verse in Luke 1:30–33 that says, "The angel said to her, 'Do not be afraid Mary, for you have found favor in God.'" This Mary became Jesus' mother and his first disciple. I, Pastor Mary, had been a practicing registered occupational therapist for over twenty years, and I was very content. I have helped many people learn to walk after having knee and hip replacements; I have taught patients to button their shirt and/or dress themselves after having a stroke; and I have taught others how to take a shower independently after being paralyzed from the waist down from a diving accident. God was asking me to "follow Him."

Does this remind you of the story in Mark 1:16 where Jesus was walking along the Sea of Galilee and saw Simon, Andrew, James, and John and asked them to drop their nets and to "follow Him"? I dropped my career and followed Him. But what I did not know was that God had been molding me over the years to become a disciple and to follow and serve Him so I may be able to serve others.

Serving God, while serving you, presents the ultimate challenge as I affirm as one of the pastors here, "I am the church."

It is for that reason I choose to wear this long robe. I remember when I put it on for the very first time in front of my family. As I zipped it up, I saw strange looks come across their faces. I asked what was wrong. My youngest daughter, Rebecca, the fashion expert in our house, said, "Mom, if you are going to wear that robe, you will need to find colorful accessories for it in order to look cool. I replied, "When I am ordained, I will wear a very colorful stole around my neck" that represents a lifetime of servanthood. She replied, "Hurry up, because black is just not the in color this year."

But the song goes on. It declares, "*You are the church.*" There is a ministry of all laity. All who are baptized are marked for ministry in the church. There is a phrase I don't like. The phrase is "I am *just* a." You've heard it used in such sentences as "I am just a layperson." "I am just a new member." "I am just a retired person." You are the church! You are not "I am just a." So if you come to me asking to visit or pray for someone who is in the hospital or home ill or who has some other need, I am likely to ask you how are you ministering to them. The most powerful witness in the church in this age does not come from the ordained or professional church staff. It comes from the rank-and-file members. More people join a church because a member invites them than they do from the urging of clergy or other professional staff. You are the church on the frontline at home, in Jack's Kountry Kitchen, in our quilting group, and in countless other relationships. You may be the only Bible someone reads or the only sermon someone hears. We gather as the church so that you may be equipped for the work of ministry.

The song finally declares, "*We are the church together.*" Just as the body needs all its parts to function, the church needs everyone working together to make an effective witness to the world. That first means to me that service is not measured by greatness but by faithfulness. Who is more important, preacher or community member? Sunday school teacher or piano player? Only as we serve together faithfully can the ministry of the church be realized. There are many gifts but only one Spirit. Second, it means that if there is a vacancy in an area of service in the church, someone is resisting the Holy Spirit. I am convinced that God provides all the necessary leadership for each church. If you are not presently serving in some area of ministry in the church, now is the time to start. When you accept your role, you will be filled with the Holy Spirit. It is never enough to have competent and committed pastors and staff. It is never enough to have loyal and dedicated laity.

It is only when all God's people move in the same direction with the same vision that the power of togetherness is achieved. When that happens the church becomes alive!

There is an old legend that tells about Jesus returning to the throne of God after his resurrection and ascension. The angels and heavenly host asked him about the experience. Jesus told them that his ministry was difficult and at times excruciatingly painful. He told how he banded together a few faithful women and men to be his disciples. He taught them all they needed to pass his word to others and so keep it alive in the world. One angel interrupted Jesus and asked, "But what if those people forget or ignore what you have taught and shown them? What other plan would you use?" Jesus looked at the heavenly host boldly and declared, "I have no other plan." I believe that Jesus has no other plan than us—the church together—for the salvation of the world! Do you? Amen.

Mary and I agreed to meet the week after she preached this first sermon and discuss its strengths and growing edges. In preparation for that meeting I got clear in my own mind about three principles for preaching in transition: continuity, identification, and commendation.

The first principle is *continuity*. A church in transition needs a sense that their tradition and contributions in the community are valuable and will continue under the new pastoral leadership. Affirming that tradition is crucial. I want to suggest to Mary that she needs to do more in this regard in the second and third segments of her sermon.

The second principle, *identification*, is a rhetorical principle for all preaching. The congregation needs to experience some identification with the preacher, to know that he or she has similar emotions and experiences, fears, and dreams. Mary does a good job sharing her experiences from her prior vocation. She needs to make sure she affirms the choices and ministries of those who, unlike her, have not chosen to leave their professions and jobs to pursue ordained ministry.

The third principle is *commendation*. When we ask people to change, we are asking them to build on something, no matter how slender a straw. Mary needs to commend the good service and faithful witness the congregation has been engaged in prior to her arrival on the scene.

SERMON DEBRIEFING SESSION

When Mary and I met a few days later, she began by asking me, "What did you think of my first sermon?"

"I thought it introduced you as a caring, practical, bold leader with a vision for the community as well as a sense of humor," I said. "When we break that down into several things the sermon did well, it looks like this: You introduced yourself and told a bit about your background, which is crucial for them. The detail you gave about the good work you did was very moving. Your sermon was clear. You used several examples that they could relate to and that related to the points you were making. Your ending did not drag on, and it made the point well. I appreciated the way you challenged the congregation in the 'you are the church' and 'we are the church' sections."

Here are some growing edges as I discussed them with Mary, section by section:

> In the section "I am the Church" I'd be careful to add that they all, in their various work, serve God just as you did when you were an occupational therapist. When you left that important work to enter the ordained ministry, God raised up someone else to do that work. You don't want to imply that ministry is the true calling and that everyone else's lifework is somehow second rate, that some people get "called up to the majors" and some have to stay in the minor league. Martin Luther had it right when he said that all baptized Christians have the same vocation—to be disciples. But that we have different offices. Yours is to ordained ministry. But there are police officers, office managers, people in retail sales, and elementary art teachers listening to you who are, like you, called to ministry.
>
> I would commend the congregation in the section on "You are the Church." Mention some of the positives about their ministries that you and I discussed—their welcoming, their community ministry (quilting), their "can do" attitude to meeting needs they see. This would be a place you could list the four qualities you noticed from your interactions so far: fearless, forgiving, focused on God, and welcoming. You could give them a heads up that these themes will appear in future sermons.
>
> In the section on "We are the Church" be careful you don't imply that, until they say yes to a responsibility at church they will not be filled with the Holy Spirit. The Holy Spirit is always at work in us. You don't want to veer into conditional salvation or works righteousness. In the sermon as a whole, I would underscore grace. It is God who sent Jesus Christ, who knits us into this body and energizes us to act together.

An e-mail from Mary on September 14 described some more of her eye-opening experiences:

> Two weeks ago, I found myself struggling to stay focused during the sermon. As I looked out into the congregation, I saw my daughter playing around and talking to another little girl. I wanted to put on

the Mom hat and tell her to straighten up. Then I saw one lady teary eyed, due to a death in her family that week. I wanted to put on the Pastor hat, and console her. Then I saw one of the men sleeping and just wanted to say "wake up."

Too much going on in my head and felt the sermon was just riding along on a train track with not any sparks flying. Also I did not center myself at the beginning of worship due to many last-minute changes to the bulletin with the piano player. I was very distracted and frustrated.

Lessons learned: 1) Pull back and center myself before the service starts, and let the piano player handle things. 2) Ask the Holy Spirit to help me center myself, gather my thoughts, and let the Spirit guide me. In time I am sure I will learn not to let the members of the congregation get to me as I preach. I can deal with them after church. Also I need to stop being so hard on myself. Preaching is a craft, not something that can be learned overnight. It is like when I started making hand splints for patients, I was terrible at it; the splint molds to the hand, not the hand to the mold. Preaching is a molding process; as time passed with assistance, many workshops, and my confidence as a therapist grew, the splints looked pretty good and functional. So, it is a marathon not a sprint.

Mary and I met for the final time the afternoon of August 25. My Introduction to Preaching Class, in which Mary was enrolled, met for the first time the next morning at 8:30 a.m. This would be our last conversation about our article. By this time she had preached her "I Am the Church; We Are the Church" sermon as well as several others. "How is it going?" I asked. "Pretty well," she answered. "They say things to me like 'Your sermons are clear and teach us the basics that we sometimes forget. You don't talk down to us. You are authentic. We like that you are getting us in touch with our roots as Methodists.'"[5]

"What can you tell me about your recent sermons?" I asked. She told me she'd been preaching from the lectionary, using the quilt metaphor as a kind of overarching metaphor for several sermons that lift up the qualities we talked about in our first session: 1) fearlessness (being honest with each other), 2) being focused on God (loving), 3) forgiveness, and 4) being welcoming. "So far I've touched on three of the four," she said. "I'm saving the topic of welcoming for our annual Homecoming service in October."

On July 26 she said she touched on the quality of honesty: telling the truth. "We can be honest with God and honest with ourselves so we can share

---

5. In focusing on the basics of their faith tradition, Mary has chosen an effective strategy for preaching in times of transition. Preaching Professor Craig A. Satterlee advises transition pastors (departing and arriving) to preach the gospel, showing the congregation "what is primary and constant" (*When God Speaks through Change: Preaching in Times of Congregational Transition* [Herndon, VA: Alban Institute, 2005], 118).

Christ's love with each other," she said. She preached on Ephesians 1:3–14 in a sermon called "The Seal of Truth," in which she talked about Jesus Christ as the one who promises the Spirit of Truth to lead us and about how that truth sets us free to love and serve one another in community.

On August 2 Mary preached on John 6:24–35, the discourse on the Bread of Life. In this sermon the theme was our need to focus on God, not on our needs. The sermon was called "Jesus, the Original Bread Machine," and it challenged people to replace self-serving motivations for religion with following Jesus to receive spiritual sustenance, the bread of life.

On August 9, she preached on Ephesians 5:25–32 with a focus on the quality of being forgiving. The sermon was called "Will the Real Jesus Christ Please Stand Up?" and was based on the old game show from the late 1950s. She focused on God's forgiveness through Christ and our need to forgive one another and ended it with the words of assurance "In the name of Jesus Christ, you are forgiven." She then asked each person to turn to someone else, look at that person, and say those words. "People responded to this positively," she said, "telling me that it meant a great deal to them, even though, at first, they were reluctant to look someone in the eye and say something so personal."

"I'm looking forward to learning more about the art of exegeting a text and putting a sermon together," she went on to say. "But I feel I've learned a lot about how to come into a new situation and size it up and craft messages that affirm the good qualities of the congregation and challenge their soft spots."

She thanked me, and I thanked her, but I think I need to thank her one more time, this time in print. Somebody, I forget who, probably George Burns or Mark Twain or some other witty wag, once said that "life is like learning to play the violin in public." I want to thank Mary for being gracious enough to let other people learn from her experience.

MARY'S TOP TEN

Here are the top ten lessons that Mary says she learned about preaching (for the first time) in a new appointment:

- Be yourself.
- Practice, practice, practice.
- Slow down in your delivery.
- Be open to the Holy Spirit and draw on God's energy for preaching.
- To be the pastor is not to be the parent or caregiver.
- You don't have to fulfill all their expectations or provide all the answers.
- Use images from everyday life.
- Respect their experiences, and connect with them through empathy.

- Don't try to do too much in one sermon.
- Don't use theological jargon.

EXEGESIS OF THE CONGREGATION

The Big Question

- What is my congregation's identity? That is, what are the persistent set of beliefs, values, patterns, symbols, stories, and style that make my congregation distinctively itself?

The Smaller Questions That Help Answer the Big Question

- Drawing Cards: What reason do new members give for joining your church? What reasons do those who visit once give for not returning?
- Skeletons in the Closet: What is something in the life or past of the congregation that no one wants to talk about?
- That Vision Thing: Is there a common dream or vision?
- Plot: What is the plot of your congregation's story over the past ten years?
- Imagery: Are there recurring images?
- What's New? What is new around the church lately?
- Change Is Good? What has changed, and has this been positive, negative, or both?
- Distinguishing Marks: What distinguishes this church from a nearby competitor?
- Dead Ends: What kinds of programs or projects are frustrating or seem unproductive here?
- First Impressions? What images and impressions would a newcomer walking in and through for the first time see?
- Rituals: What rituals are unique to this congregation?
- Attention Grabbers: Which events/activities/issues receive most attention, time, energy, and investment of resources (personal and financial)? Which types are more neglected?
- Controversies: Which events/activities/issues are most controversial?
- Sources of Pride: What is the greatest source of pride?
- Wise Ones: Who are the people others look to as having wisdom?
- Marginals: Who is on the margins, and why?
- Our Story: Summarize the congregational character in a meaningful narrative form.
- Our Mission: Does the congregation have a one-sentence statement of mission?
- Our History: What are the key events in the congregation's history? Is there a pamphlet on the history of the congregation? Does the congregation have an appointed historian?

5

Leading through Anxious Times and Situations

More Than Meets the Eye

W. CRAIG GILLIAM

All congregations are profound mysteries. The Colombian writer Gabriel Garcia Marquez said of his wife that he knew her so well that she was completely and utterly unknown to him. Those same words describe my encounters with congregations, these living organisms, these unpredictable communities with wonderful and frightening lives of their own. The more I know a congregation, the more it is completely and utterly unknown to me.

As we walk winding and wandering into the sacred mystery, deeper and deeper into its joys and pains, its challenges and opportunities, in and out, curving, stumbling, meandering on circular walkways, listening to the questions on the journey and hearing the emerging wisdom, we walk with awareness and sensitivity, always paying attention. The blade of each new crisis points the way and brings us closer to the larger question the community lives from its center. The essence of this mystery called congregation is relationship. Leading in this labyrinth of relationships involves our full attention, our words and our presence, our walking and our standing still, our way of doing and our way of being. It involves all of us: our minds, spirits, bodies, and emotions. All are part of what it means to be ourselves, the deep call of pastoral care, of preaching, of being a leader in religious communities. These components together make space for the deep, mysterious embrace.

While there are no simple checklists or "how-to" answers for leading through anxious times and situations in congregational life, this essay will strive to offer insights to help clergy pastor, preach, and lead in anxious times and settings, and do so in a way that lessens paralyzing stress, increases the possibility of positive movement for the community, and heightens awareness. I identify and give a working definition of anxiety, behaviors that are symptomatic of high anxiety, and common triggers of anxiety. Also, I offer insight for leaders to consider as they assist congregations and other organizations move forward through anxious times and situations. Finally, the essay moves into some new thinking about leading through anxious situations as we move toward a conclusion. Enjoy the journey. Like any body of relationships and life, *congregations are mysteries to be embraced, not problems to be solved.*

Whether the community is made up of 2 or 102 people, anxiety is always present. It is a deep-flowing powerful force. From a systems perspective, leadership involves learning to regulate and manage this hidden anxiety and its influence on oneself and the larger system. To do so, we must pay attention.

The word *anxiety* comes from a Latin root that means "to strangle, to have by the throat, to choke, to cause pain by squeezing." We all know the suffocating impact of anxiety when it becomes too intense. It is like a wet wool overcoat. It stifles, it restricts, it confines and blinds us from options for creative flow and adaptation.

There are two kinds of anxiety: acute and chronic. When gripped by acute anxiety, we know why we are anxious. It is a response to a real, immediate threat: "We are anxious because we have a church audit tomorrow, and we have none of our numbers together." The anxiety can be helpful, for it can motivate us not to delay any longer.

Systemic or chronic anxiety is different. It is a deeper, lingering anxiety. We can sense it; we might even feel its effect within, but we cannot clearly identify its source or reason. It is like a deep ocean current that we cannot see, but it is flowing, stirring the sands and making the vision murky and unclear. It is more imaginal and surfaces around the "What if . . . ?" question—not necessarily grounded in reality. It is the "cry wolf" that keeps whispering and sometimes shouting. Systemic anxiety can envelop us when we walk into it. When we get caught in it, and fear and panic become our modus operandi, the imagined reality we fear often constellates.

Chronic anxiety is contagious, bringing out the worst in human potential. If people are neither differentiated nor well-defined, it spreads like a highly infectious virus. The sign of its infection is the reactivity and resistance people display. When infected, we and they will often behave in ways we had never imagined.

Is it any wonder that Jesus said, "'Therefore I tell you, do not worry about your life'" (Matt. 6:25), and Saint Paul commented, "Do not worry about anything, but in everything, by prayer and supplication with thanksgiving let your requests be made known to God" (Phil. 4:6)?

The challenge and opportunity are how to regulate this chronic anxiety so that it does not choke, strangle, or stifle creativity. How do we assist in keeping it from becoming a force that drives us apart from our knowing? How can we regulate and manage it in a manner that creates mature Christian communities? How do we create environments where an "I-Thou" way of being is the accepted norm?

Anxiety is like the wind—you cannot see it, but you can feel it and observe its impact. To observe it, however, one must pay attention. For example, one cannot see the wind, but if you look at a flag on a flagpole, you can tell if there is wind, and if so, you can estimate its strength. You can also feel it against your skin.

The same is true for anxiety. When you are ministering in your congregation or working with a group, you cannot see the anxiety, but by observing the participants, you can tell if it is present, and if so, how strong. If you are sensitive and have developed the art of paying attention, and are intuitive or discerning toward self and community, you can feel the anxiety against and under your skin.

From working with congregations that are conflicted, stuck on that creative abyss looking to the next step, or trying to be intentional and reflective about the future they are being called to create, I have found there are clear, common indicators of chronic anxiety that can be observed and sensed:

- *Blaming.* Mature leadership and community foster responsibility, not blame. Blame and anxiety feed each other. As blame increases, so does anxiety. As anxiety increases, so does blame.
- *Horribilizing others.* When an individual or group is caught in anxiety, other people's faults seem larger.
- *Feeling victimized.* As a result of feeling like victims, those in the system do not claim, at least in a mature way, the power they have been given to use responsibly as creatures of God.
- *Exaggerating values.* Anxious groups inflate their values. Although the values may be positive, when they become exaggerated, they can become counterproductive.
- *Focusing on weaknesses and pathology.* When communities are highly anxious, they are unable to see or acknowledge strengths and celebrations of others or the community. Highly anxious communities do not see possibilities. They can only see challenges, problems, and cautions. As a leader, I have found that when I enter and focus on the pathology in the system, the people will go no further with me. But if I can help them discover what holds meaning and passion for them, what they really care about, then the organization's anxiety lowers and creativity rises, and they have greater possibilities to move forward.
- *Overemphasizing rules, regulations, and policies.*
- *Magnifying differences between and among people.*
- *Demanding certainty, while strongly resisting living with ambiguity.*
- *Focusing on self in an unhealthy, obsessive way.*
- *Not being open to creativity and diversity.* When groups are gripped by anxiety, they want everyone to see alike, act alike, be alike, believe alike.
- *Fomenting unhealthy triangles and secrets in the community.*

- *Focusing on "shoulds,"* the critical parent voice. I like the bumper sticker that said, "I will not 'Should' on anybody today."
- *Demanding quick fixes, saviors, and short-term relief.*
- *Overemphasizing who's right.*
- *Exhibiting reactivity, resistance, and lack of compassion.*

In addition to these universal indicators for high anxiety, we also have our personal indicators. I encourage you to spend time developing a list of indicators that tell you that you are getting caught in the anxiety of a group. For me, an indicator is when I can no longer think of questions to ask a group. One person told me that sarcasm was one of her indicators. Another person tells me that his indicator is that he withdraws and becomes quiet. He told the story of a time when he was with his family and his feelings were hurt. He began to withdraw as was his pattern when things did not go in the direction he desired. His daughter remarked, "Daddy is pouting." He said, "She caught me and named it. She helped me find my indicator when I am getting anxious." What are your personal indicators?

In congregational and organizational life, some common topics activate anxiety. I call these hot buttons or triggers of anxiety. When these topics emerge, anxiety appears and can easily escalate. Although the list is not exhaustive, it highlights the more common triggers:

- *Money*—In any church and in other organizations, follow the money trail, and you follow the anxiety trail.
- *Leadership style*—When this issue surfaces with groups, I am never immediately certain what that means. Thus, when I enter a congregation and leadership style is mentioned as an issue, I spend time unpacking its deeper, intended meaning.
- *Worship style*—Change the worship, and anxiety rises.
- *Conflict among the clergy and/or staff*—When conflict and anxiety exist in the leadership, it surfaces in the congregational body tenfold.
- *Growth and survival*—When a congregation moves into a survivalist mode, it becomes more difficult.
- *Old and new*—This can be applied to people, curriculum, or worship. When working with congregations and other organizations caught in this struggle, the conversation is to help them clarify what holds meaning, value, and identity. Also, the central question becomes how to preserve what holds meaning for them and is part of their identity while also staying relevant to the emerging culture around them.
- *Change of leadership*—Whenever leadership changes, anxiety rises. Think of the congregation as a giant mobile; you touch one part and the entire mobile quakes. When the leadership changes, the mobile shakes.
- *Governance/community decision-making process*—When the decision-making process breaks down or is unclear, anxiety is triggered.
- *Focus on internal or external*—A common button that triggers anxiety is whether to emphasize ministering to those within the church community

or reaching out into the larger community. Highly anxious groups often think in dichotomies—"either/or" not "both/and." The higher the anxiety, the more difficult it is to invite the parishioners to that "both/and" way of thinking and being.

- *Issues involving sex and sexuality*—Any issue around sex and sexuality is a hot button for anxiety in most congregations. In my opinion, sex and sexuality have been a shadow for the church throughout its history. Thus, whenever such an issue arises, whether heterosexual or homosexual, the anxiety skyrockets and reactivity heightens.

Am I suggesting that since these identified issues or buttons trigger anxiety that clergy should stay away from them? No, absolutely not! Around any issue that is important to us lies the potential for anxiety to heighten. It is our wish to escape from anxiety or a paralyzing fear of being swept away by it that steals our aliveness. What I am suggesting is to be aware that anxiety might surface around these issues, so when you deal with them, do your own inner and outer work. We do not have to be naïve or surprised if we encounter anxiety, sabotage, or resistance around these issues. When it occurs, be prepared, calm, and prayerful. See people as people to be cared for, not objects to be manipulated, defeated, discounted, or used.

To help clergy and other leaders move congregations through times of high anxiety, the following are several strategies that I have found helpful.

- *Work on your family of origin and extended family field.* One possibility is to do a genogram or at least revisit your family literally or metaphorically to understand the voices and persons who influenced you. The ways we lead and the manners in which we handle anxiety are strongly influenced by what we learned from our family of origin and our extended family field. We carry our ancestors with us. How did your family of origin and extended family deal with anxiety, and how do you deal with it? What is the same, what is different? The *communion of saints* still speaks to us from our past.
- *Remain calm, non-anxious, and responsive in the face of anxious situations and groups.* If I remain calm and responsive, the group has a greater chance of finding its way to a calmer and more creative way of responding. I tend my own hoop and focus on staying calm and non-anxious myself. One of the most important variables to remember in modifying communities is taking responsibility for yourself rather than trying to control others.
- *Remember to breathe.* When getting anxious, I take three deep breaths before speaking. Breathing helps us to relax, to focus, to maintain balance, and to be present.
- *Be present and listen with compassion and curiosity.* Listening is a sacred act. Listening means being fully present with the other. When we are present and listen to others, holy moments of insight can emerge, creative options

can surface, deeper connections happen, and possibilities for moving forward increase significantly.

- *Find sanctuaries where you can reflect on events and regain perspective.* Find an out-of-the-box place from which you see life, other people, and yourself differently. Sometimes sanctuary comes from being with an old friend or new acquaintance whose mere presence is a sanctuary or who allows you the space to get out of the box within.

- *Reach out to confidants with whom you can debrief decisions and actions and articulate your reasons for taking certain actions.* Ideally, a confidant is not a current ally within your congregation, your organization, your conference, or even possibly your religious denomination. An important criterion is that your confidant cares more about you than about the issue at stake. Also, she or he needs to be honest, compassionate, and insightful.

- *Use the spiritual practices from your tradition to nurture your soul and your spirit.* We are invited to engage our spiritual practices regularly in a disciplined manner. If we need support or guidance, getting a spiritual director can be a helpful resource.

- *Exercise, eat right, and nurture a positive attitude.* Healthy diets, good exercise habits, and positive attitudes fall under the broad umbrella of lifestyle and are indisputable contributions to one's health and excellence in ministry.

- *Don't lose yourself in your role/position.* Defining your life through a single endeavor, no matter how important your ministry is to you and to others, makes you vulnerable when the environment shifts. While your position or role is important and part of who you are, there is a whole host of mystery and personality to you that is beyond your role. Let the mystery live, not the role define.

- *Ask open, honest, high-level questions.* Good leadership for this century is less about having the answers and more about asking the difficult questions and not allowing the group to settle for easy answers. Open, honest questions can help groups move to a higher level of functioning and away from anxiety that paralyzes. In addition, asking questions gives the responsibility and anxiety back to the rightful owners and invites them to find their own solutions. What is an open, honest question? It is not "Have you ever thought of seeing a therapist?" That question is loaded. An open, honest question is something like "Help me to understand this situation more clearly. What do you think this circumstance is really about?"

- *Be transparent as a leader.* Congregations come through transitional times better when the leaders model openness and refuse to allow secrets to be part of the process. Secrets lock in the pain, impede progress, and breed mistrust. (Transparency does not mean leaders do not have boundaries or are not differentiated. Boundaries are important for leaders in anxious situations.)

- *Work to see the strengths, gifts, and graces of the community and its members.* In committee meetings and other gatherings, spend a few moments discussing what the congregation can celebrate about its community since the last time it met. It is not a way of ignoring the challenges; by affirming what it does well, a congregation can find the strength and energy to address the challenges.

- *Bring more of your emotional self to your ministry.* Appropriate displays of emotion can be an effective tool for change and regulating anxiety, especially when balanced with poise. Parishioners appreciate candor and honesty. Emotions/feelings are part of any decision and what it means to be human. When we deny rather than acknowledge them, they go "under the table," but still influence decisions.

- *Have a vision and articulate it regularly.* Both personally and for the organization, being able to articulate a clear vision is important for congregations.

- *Spend more time and energy on the motivated than the unmotivated; on the fruit-bearing, not the troublesome issues, people, and situations; on the emotionally and spiritually mature, not the immature.* Too often I have heard denominational leaders lament that they spend 80 percent of their time with the troublesome 20 percent. A district superintendent of a UMC commented that one of her convictions is "not to invest inordinate energy in helping people cross the street if they do not want to go." As leaders, what does it look like for you to focus more on the motivated, the mature, the fruit-bearing?

- *Love what you do, but not too much.* A poet is being interviewed. The interviewer asks, "With the demands of life, making a living, etc., how do you keep your attention on writing poetry?" She responds that she never takes a job that she loves too much. In other words, she stays clear on the difference between her job and her calling or vocation and on which is her deeper commitment. When we as leaders keep clarity between job and deeper calling, it affects us and the systems to which we are connected.

The word used in "systems vocabulary" to describe the strategies toward which the previous section is pointing is *self-differentiation*, a synonym for leadership. The concept involves defining oneself while staying in relationship with others. According to systems theory, the more self-differentiated the leader, the more mature the organization is or potentially can become.

While I appreciate the word "self-differentiation," my experience is that our common usage of the concept as a behavioral strategy overlooks a deeper component. Self-differentiation in its deepest meaning is about a deeper way of being—about the soul or heart. Religiously, we are talking about soulful transformation, not a new mask we wear. It is about a way of being in relationship with self, others, God, life, and community.

There is something deeper than behavior that people sense or intuit, as I learned from Martin Buber and my work with the Arbinger Institute (http://www.arbinger.com). When this deeper component that people sense or intuit is not right, it will sabotage even the most outwardly correct behavior. When the leader and community are in touch with this deep wellspring, the anxiety is more regulated and motivates positive change. When leaders and the community lose touch with this source, it escalates anxiety and creates unnecessary chaos and confusion.

Pastoral ministry is not about a particular set of "good" behaviors or "stronger" programs that ministers are supposed to employ, however important these might be. Behavioral strategies, although vital, will never be enough. Instead, pastoral ministry is about something deeper and more important than behavior.

Too often, I have watched ministers do ministry "right," practicing the recommended behaviors and launching great new programs and preaching excellent sermons, but somehow it all goes wrong. Other times, I have seen clergy do virtually everything "wrong," failing to use the specific techniques they've been told to use or using them poorly at best and preaching sermons that are not particularly strong, but their ministry goes right.

What accounts for the difference? One key variable may be the leader's *way of the heart, way of being,* or *way of the soul.* When ministers focus only on correcting what's wrong, on addressing the negative or pathological in the system, or when they work on looking "good," on working harder with more intensity, they can neglect their own way of being, inadvertently causing their ministries to lose the very depth of connection they had sought. If we focus first on our way of being or way of our heart, ministry can happen more naturally and easily at a deeper level. Whatever I do on the surface, people respond to who I am being when I am doing it. The way of the heart or the way of being determines influence.

So what is at the heart of pastoral ministry, this deeper way of being, this way of the heart? It goes back to Martin Buber's concept of "I-Thou," which fundamentally captures the two ways we have of being in relation to ourselves, the world, and others. When I stand in that place of "I-Thou," I see people as people. I respond to their reality because their reality is as real as is my own—their concerns, their hopes, their dreams, their needs, and their fears. When I am in an "I-Thou" relationship with others, they know it. They sense it. They intuit it. Trust is cultivated, and usually they will respond in kind. As a result, possibilities for soulful ministry happen. As Buber remarks, "All real living is meeting."[1]

---

1. Martin Buber, *I and Thou,* 2nd ed., trans. Ronald Smith (New York: Charles Scribner's Sons, 1958), 11.

But when my relationship to the world is an "I-It," I see others, if at all, more as objects than people. I see them as less than I am—less relevant, less important, less real. Their reality is of less importance than is my own. As a result, the possibility for ministry of any kind is slight. Ministry must first begin out of the soul, this *deeper way of being* with self and others.

While I am aware that this essay raises as many questions as it answers, I hope the reader has found some food for thought and a way of seeing into the mystery of this incredible body we call congregations and communities.

As a leader, your challenges might seem overwhelming at times. But within the challenges are also gifts and opportunities. Be open to God, whose middle name is Surprise! Trust yourself; trust God in the situation. We do not face it alone. God is with us as are others on the journey.

We are in the midst of unique times and a watershed moment in the life of our world. Never have the challenges been so great nor have the opportunities been so many. Congregations are microcosms of the larger macrocosm. What is happening "out there" gets brought into the community and often intensifies there. As leaders, we get invited to deal with what we and our parishioners carry, and the load and influence are deeper than meets the eye.

Because of the unique time and place in which we are living, the voice of a congregation, its role, and its collective wisdom has never been more needed. In some ways, I wonder, What would a church body look like serving as a functional model for our culture? Can we provide a space for people to think critically about the deeper issues we face as a world? Can we ask the difficult questions and make safe spaces for deep, grounded, soulful conversations with and for the larger culture?

To provide those spaces, our communities have to deal first with their own anxiety, learning to contain it, thus inviting ourselves and others into that sacred circle of questioning, connecting, listening, and speaking. What does it mean to become a place that models what it looks like to disagree but stay in relationship? How do we model moving into the deep, difficult conversations in a way that honors connection and differences? How do we live a life that makes the relationship with others and all of creation more important than the content of it?

> May the journey continue,
> and we find our way by walking.
> God's grace and peace be with you!

MANNA FOR THE JOURNEY

Workshop Conducted by W. Craig Gilliam for the Center for Pastoral Effectiveness

(From the Lewis Center for Church Leadership of Wesley Theological Seminary, Washington, DC, at www.churchleadership.com and adapted by Craig Gilliam. Used by permission.)

Best Practices for Beginning Ministry in a New Ministry Setting

1. Learn about the new church and community.

    Take 6–18 months to get to know the people and community.
    Demonstrate a willingness to learn the history of the congregation.
    Develop your skill in "reading" the congregation.
    Learn the mission and vision of the congregation.
    Consider using data-gathering methods to understand the church and community.
    Do careful assessment of strengths, weaknesses, challenges, and opportunities.

2. Spend time with people and build relationships.

    Visit members with key leadership roles.
    Visit people who have pastoral needs.
    Meet with the staff of the parish relations committee early and regularly.
    Pay particular attention to pastoral care and preaching.
    Make building relationships your highest priority.
    Meet community leaders, be visible in the community, and meet clergy colleagues.
    Develop a strategy to get to know the people. Communicate that plan, and stay with it.
    Ask everyone you visit to suggest others with whom you should be talking.

3. Don't change things at first, especially worship. (Keep your hands off the thermostat.)

4. Listen and observe with an open mind to discover strengths and needs. (Listen, listen, listen, . . .)

5. Build trust.

    Express joy in being there.
    Be authentic, honest, and genuine.
    Let people get to know you and allow the congregation time to learn to trust you.

> Focus on the congregation and their future, not your agenda.
> Earn the right to change things before initiating changes.

6. Honor your predecessor's ministry.

> Don't criticize a former pastor, even if criticism is warranted.
> Honor the progress and achievements accomplished before you
> arrived.
> Let people know it is OK to grieve the loss of their former
> pastor.
> Honor traditions long enough to understand the positive motiva-
> tion behind them.

7. Don't talk about your previous parish.

8. Don't complain, criticize, or make excessive demands.

9. Be patient. (It is a marathon, not a sprint.)

For Further Reading

Allen, O. Wesley, Jr. *The Homiletic of All Believers: A Conversational Approach* (Louisville, KY: Westminster John Knox Press, 2005).

Cameron, Julia. *Transitions: Prayers and Declarations for a Changing Life* (New York:
Penguin Putnam, 1999).

Friedman, Edwin H. *Generation to Generation: Family Process in Church and Synagogue*
(New York: Guilford Press, 1985).

Nieman, James R., and Thomas G. Rogers. *Preaching to Every Pew: Cross-Cultural
Strategies* (Minneapolis: Fortress Press, 2001).

Oswald, Roy M., James M. Heath, and Ann W. Heath. *Beginning Ministry Together: The
Alban Handbook for Clergy Transitions* (Bethesda, MD: Alban Institute, 2003)

Satterlee, Craig A. *When God Speaks through Change: Preaching in Times of Congregational Transition* (Herndon, VA: Alban Institute, 2005).

Tisdale, Nora Tubbs. *Preaching as Local Theology and Folk Art* (Minneapolis: Fortress
Press, 1996).

6

Most Change Occurs in Ways We Would Not Choose

Sharyn Pinney

Most change occurs in ways we would not choose. Change is constant, inevitable, and sometimes even sought. Most of us don't really like the arrival of change no matter what we might say in theory about its goodness or necessity. Often we behave badly in the face of change and protest the emerging new reality with further bad behavior. Change is hard.

These few sentences might elicit some memories or associations about yourself, your congregation, or people/communities you know. It might call you to reflect on how you or they faired through various changes. You might grimace, or laugh, or shrug.

As a clergyperson you have a unique opportunity to observe, share, and shepherd yourself and others through troubled times of overwhelming change—whether on a personal level, in a family, within a congregation or an entire community, or during periods of social upheaval. Is that good news or bad? It depends. For certain, what you can say from the pulpit could help a great deal.

Pastoring and preaching in a way that truly helps people through transitions and change is wonderful, worthy work. How it can look is as individual as every pastor and every congregation. I hope to share a way of thinking and feeling our way through a process that might be helpful to you in organizing yourself during times of change and stress. Also I want to share a few guiding principles from a mental health perspective that may also assist you in regaining and maintaining your own equilibrium during anxious times. The process has four parts: self-reflection, self-observation, listening well, and sharing to mobilize hope and connection.

SELF-REFLECTION

Self-reflection usually comes about with great difficulty because we are often too busy reacting to a source of stress or someone else's stress response. "Wait a minute, what's going on with me?" seems an obvious place to start but a place that pastors and other helpers often skip while running headlong into trying to be helpful to someone else. You see the folly in this, of course. So it's good to ask ourselves questions like, How do I feel? What am I thinking? Is this reminiscent of anything that's happened in the past? What are my tendencies and past patterns in similar situations? It is to be hoped that the answers will lead to insight that gives you some beginning boundaries for yourself and your role as a pastor. A simple question to get this process started is, Whose crisis is this? If it's yours, you have a beginning boundary to contain it. If it's someone else's, then you can calm down, manage your own feelings, and start to think.

There are some helpful tools and habits for ongoing and noncrisis self-reflection. Quiet time alone on a regular basis is the foundation. Your own spiritual formation and theological reflection habits spring from this disciplined quiet time. Journaling helps many; actual handwriting engages different parts of the brain than thinking or talking.

Writing one's own autobiography is a powerful tool, as is the continued refinement and rewriting of one's call story. Our own family dynamics (what we learned and experienced emotionally as members of our immediate family) and our fantasies about who we are and what needs can be met in our congregations are heavily at work—whether we are aware of them or not. The more you are willing to examine, alone and with others, your history and any familiar patterns you see in your present life at home and in your ministry, the more you will be able to perform well your job as clergy and live out your call to serve God's church. A helpful book is Dr. Robert L. Randall's *Pastor and Parish: The Psychological Core of Ecclesiastical Conflicts*.[1] In this slim book of fewer than two hundred pages, Dr. Randall, a self-described clergyman-psychologist, reviews basic elements of Heinz Kohut's self-psychology model as a preface to examining a model of common problematic pastor/congregation relationships.

Any of these activities can help you integrate your past with your present. As a therapist, I have a clear bias toward the advisability of psychotherapy for pastors. At a minimum I would suggest finding a mental health professional with whom you can consult on personal and pastoral issues.

---

1. Robert L. Randall, *Pastor and Parish: The Psychological Core of Ecclesiastical Conflicts* (Human Sciences Press, 1988).

SELF-OBSERVATION

Self-observation in this context is meant to describe a stance of self-awareness, genuine involvement in the present with the co-occurring ability to have a watchful attitude toward yourself. A mental health person might call this the observing ego. It is somewhat like instant replay or being able to watch a live video feed of yourself. This stance helps you remember your role as pastor and the obligations that come with it. It helps you be in the present and engage your ability to mobilize your thinking about the here and now. It helps you not lose yourself and your role or get overinvolved in an unhealthy manner with your congregation.

A small group of trusted colleagues meeting regularly can facilitate an enormous amount of growth for clergy willing to take this risk and make this commitment. Learning the skills of giving and receiving honest feedback, comparing your view of yourself with others' views of you, and having a confidential place to share congregational concerns make this kind of group a powerful method to have a healthy, effective ministry.

LISTENING WELL

Listening well will ultimately give you the information you need to formulate what is the primary problem or hierarchy of problems at hand. With your self out of the way (successful self-reflection) and the ability to observe your functioning as a pastor (self-observation), you are in a good position to truly listen to others. Listening is more difficult than you think, for helpers are usually eager to help. Talking, however earnest, well-intentioned, or brilliant, is not listening.

Much excellent material exists on active-listening techniques. I will not go into detail but will list these as the most important aspects: listen to understand and to learn, not judge; pay attention and maintain eye contact; affirm and connect with nonverbal acknowledgments; ask clarifying questions; and periodically summarize what you are hearing and ask for feedback to see if you are understanding what the person meant.

Typical initial reactions to stress or overwhelming change range from shock, fear, anxiety, anger, avoidance, protest, grief, helplessness, and depression. However, we often fail to remember that most people move through these disorganizing emotions to a new stabilization/acceptance of change. Most people cannot remain in a state of crisis very long; it is just too exhausting. Most will soon arrive as some sort of problem-solving approach and start on a path to acceptance of a new reality. Sharing with others, commiserating, and finding similar feelings/thoughts in others help most people to feel less alone. A sense of community as well as sharing resources move people into meaningful action. This is the normal, resilient adaptation to change that most people experience. The other side of the stress response is frequently excitement, curiosity, energy, enthusiasm, creativity, clarity, and motivation for a new purpose. Many people will get there naturally in their own time. Others will get stuck and can be helped by messages of perspective and hope from the pulpit. All can benefit from a sense of community that provides acceptance and understanding for all members of the congregation. It is a good practice to decide in advance how many individual pastoral counseling sessions you intend to have with a parishioner before referring that person to a mental health professional. Be clear in your own mind and in verbal agreement with your parishioner and stick with the plan. Unless you have had a good deal of formal clinical pastoral education (CPE) and related clinical field placements, you are likely to become entangled in a process best handled by someone other than the pastor. I find this area to be one of enormous stress to most new pastors.

SHARING TO MOBILIZE HOPE AND CONNECTION

Sermons provide many opportunities to share comfort and instill hope in others through the ancient stories which remind us all that not much is new, including the most recent personal crisis or shared community issues. Bringing perspective and meaning through faith is the task of the pastor from the pulpit. It is both natural and helpful to the congregation for the pastor to share some degree of his/her own experience, feelings, and thoughts. The exact nature and degree of self-disclosure is a very delicate aspect of preaching and pastoring. Going through a thoughtful process of self-reflection is the first step in deciding what exactly to share and what to keep to yourself. A good guideline is that you should be able to explain logically to a senior colleague and peer why the self-disclosure is a good and helpful idea and one that would move the congregation forward as group. If not, probably the self-disclosure is too self-serving. Sharing in general terms and themes what you have learned listening to others is generally very helpful. Usually this binds a group together by helping people realize how many share similar thoughts/feelings/fears. These universal, human concerns are more bearable in community. The pastor has an opportunity to remind the congregation that we are all learning, growing, and changing at different rates but that together we can comfort and inspire one another.

MENTAL HEALTH PRINCIPLES HELPFUL
TO CONSIDER

Trust is generally built over time and can be described as the ability to predict accurately an outcome or pattern. When we say we trust someone that usually means we have collected enough information over time to know that we are safe with that person. Establishing a basic sense of trust in others and the world in general is the psychological foundation of human development. Change often disrupts a person's sense of trust; it can be trust in an individual, a group, or an institution. Sometimes this change is when we will see a person "behave badly," meaning in a frightened or threatened manner. Sometimes a person behaves angrily or aggressively. Reacting angrily to anger seldom works well. Listening, empathy, and kindness usually work better. Conducting yourself as a constant, trustworthy person is best. Apologizing is another trust-building act because it demonstrates the ability to self-reflect, to arrive at a new assessment of one's previous behavior, and to care enough about others to say so.

Change is any variation from the norm. A perfect example is the arrival of a new baby in a family. The baby can be planned and greatly desired, and the parents can be as ready as possible. Nevertheless, the world of the couple is forever altered. New demands as parents often make the couple feel inadequate, and a former way of life is lost and replaced with a new way. Many couples quickly focus on the cuteness of the baby and the excitement of becoming a family while shoving down the sense of anxiety and loss. Those couples are likely to experience more stress as time goes by than those who acknowledge some sense of loss along with the gains of parenthood. It is helpful to recognize that most changes entail a loss of some size/significance and thus much of the reaction to change can be understood as a grief response—a reaction to a loss. Most pastors are familiar with the stages of grief described by Elisabeth Kübler-Ross: denial, anger, bargaining, depression, acceptance.

Grief does not progress orderly or neatly, nor does it have a typical time frame. However, this basic information is often helpful in an educational sense to individuals and groups. Mobilizing to connect to others (as in a grief-recovery group or career-transitions group) is usually a helpful first step in finding some purposeful action—something you can do something about—which combats that frozen inaction that often is the first response to a loss. Again, you as a clergyperson are vulnerable to having a previous loss of your own triggered by another's loss or a time of upheaval and change in the church at large. It is not always easy to know to what or whom you are reacting.

The ability to tolerate—if not embrace—ambiguity is a cognitive and psychological strength in a pastor. Many stressed persons will attempt to engage you along an either/or, black/white line. It is handy if you see this coming from a long way off so you can avoid the reactivity it usually generates. While listening helps, listening alone is usually not adequate when an individual or subgroup within the congregation is in an uproar. Setting limits with kindness, compassion, and an acceptance of the ambiguity of most dilemmas is usually a better course than allowing yourself to get caught up in an impassioned battle of extreme positions. Growing in skill in this area works against clergy burnout. Knowing as much as you can about your natural and preferred leadership style is a place to start. Many seminaries use the Myers-Briggs Type Indicator to examine both communication and leadership styles; it is often helpful in exploring problem areas in supervisor/supervisee relationships. Another tool to consider is the Enneagram, which describes nine types of personalities. Some like this model because it is said to speak more to a spiritual dimension of healthy personality types and give more information about individual motivational factors.

Your personal self-care is vital to both you and your family and also serves as a powerful model for members of your congregation. The usual advice of regular exercise, routine medical appointments and following medical advice, regular time off from clergy duties, date nights with your spouse, some protected family time, and active participation in your children's lives all stand as solid recommendations. Pastors I know can recite this list and mostly hit many of them much of the time. Sadly, other pastors recite the list with a sigh and attitude of fatalistic acceptance of sacrificing one's self to the endless hours and thankless work they have been called to do. This attitude is completely unnecessary and almost surely guarantees you will teach the congregation to engage in an abusive relationship with you.

At special risk are clergy who are single, divorced, or widowed. Family (also extended family and networks of friends who are our emotional families) serves as a natural balancing agent for the exciting and often demanding life of the church. Time alone is difficult to find if you are wanting to meet someone to date. I strongly advise against the great temptation to find these intimate relationships in the congregation you are serving. Unless you are an unusually enlightened and self-aware person, the boundary-related problems this poses are nearly impossible to navigate without undue misery. If at all possible, have interests/hobbies totally separate from and at a distance from your congregation. Try to think of these arenas as the best ones to meet a potential partner. Again, therapy is a good idea. It can help you be honest with your self and knowledgeable of boundaries that may be straining.

A healthy sense of humor is a critical life skill for a pastor. Our ability to laugh at ourselves and with others is vital. Laughter (like singing and whistling) reduces stress and brings perspective to difficult times. Laughter releases powerful, positive neurochemicals that immediately help you combat some of the stress hormones flowing through the brain and body. Singing and whistling regulate breathing and reduce anxiety in a natural way. A good sense of humor usually indicates a high IQ and the ability to abstract, to make novel connections, and to see the ironies of life.

Sadly, you will find many persons not able to laugh at themselves or with others—even in the best of times. Moments of high stress, whether a personal crisis, churchwide challenge, or a community disaster, reduce most folks' ability to find humor anywhere at first. Therefore, test the waters gently with your particular brand of humor to see how it fits your staff and congregation. Also remember to spend enough time with people outside of the congregation with whom you can really talk and laugh. Good, silly sit-coms, movies, and plays may be as necessary as good art and music to the mental health of the pastor.

The final and my favorite mental health principle to share is warmth despite differences. It is a philosophical position as well as a practical/behavioral one which acknowledges that differences (large and small) are natural and expected and that we can relate to one another at a minimum in a kind, respectful manner. It requires more than civility or good manners though both are very important and seem to be in quite short supply lately. On a higher level it sets the stage for relationship formation with an attitude of respectful curiosity. Greeting the world and all the people in it as potential friendly collaborators in navigating and understanding this life we share is an open, receptive, flexible stance that communicates a great deal of love. The openness to differences by definition makes conflicts, surprises, stress, trauma, change, and realignment much easier to bear than the typical adversarial, polarized stance. This message from the pulpit calms, builds bridges, and inspires the congregation to think/feel beyond their personal experience and expand into empathy with others. Especially in difficult times of transition and uncertainty, messages from the pulpit encouraging connection are vastly superior from a mental health perspective than a more typical stress response of anger and withdrawal.

In review, a clergyperson enjoys unique opportunities during difficult times for pastoring and preaching to his/her congregation if the pastor can maintain her/his own footing when stressed. I have offered a four-stage process for a practical way of maintaining or regaining your equilibrium from a mental health perspective. The process entails self-reflection, self-observation, listening well, and sharing for the purpose of instilling hope and connection. Relevant mental health principles that can aid this process include trust, change, the ability to embrace ambiguity, self-care, a sense of humor, and warmth despite differences.

7

Leadership, Preaching, and Pastoral Care in Times of Anxiety or Conflict

GARY G. KINDLEY

All of the great leaders have had one characteristic in common: it was the willingness to confront unequivocally the major anxiety of their people in their time. This, and not much else, is the essence of leadership.

—John Kenneth Galbraith

TIMES OF CHANGE, ANXIETY, OR CRISIS

It is the mark of an educated mind to be able to entertain a thought without accepting it.

—Aristotle

Most of us could name where we were and what we were doing on September 11, 2001. It is a day that is etched in the memory of Americans and of many others around the world.

Those with living memory of the assassination of President John F. Kennedy can likely recall what they were doing on November 22, 1963, almost four decades earlier. Even as a second grader, I remember the teachers at my elementary school inexplicably crying and our unexpected but eagerly received early recess from our usual classroom routine.

A significant crisis—and each person determines what is significant—can serve as a bookmark of a point in time along life's journey, recalling a memory of when life, as we knew it, changed. It is a time both of ending and beginning, a close of what was and the start of a new reality. The question of significance is so subjective that some would shrug off what others would find as watershed moments. In the life of a church, a seemingly minor change in the liturgy can be as momentous for some individuals as a change of pastor may be for the entire congregation.

A crisis in a community affects each congregation in a unique way. On May 12, 1982, Braniff International Airways ceased flight operations. The airline's pilots were told to land at their destination and park their aircraft, leaving flight crews around the world scrambling to find a way home. A number of those pilots and their families were members of a United Methodist church in Grapevine, Texas, where I was serving as an associate pastor, barely two miles from Dallas–Fort Worth International Airport. There were many numbed families that entered the sanctuary that following Sunday. Brows furrowed in worry and uncertainty. Tears shed in grief and fear. Very few members of this large congregation were unaffected by that event. Merchants knew their businesses could take a financial hit. The congregation was genuinely empathetic but felt powerless, uncertain what to do to help their friends and neighbors.

The senior pastor made a call to Dr. Charles Kemp, the professor emeritus of pastoral care and founder of the Pastoral Care and Counseling Center at Texas Christian University in Fort Worth. The pastor asked Dr. Kemp's advice on how best to address the issue from the pulpit and sought suggestions on approaches he might take for his sermons. Dr. Kemp's wise and seasoned answer was both simple and powerful: "Offer them massive doses of hope."

It is the role of the pastor to point the way to the transcendent, to help those fellow strugglers whom we serve and with whom we share the journey to be aware of the presence of God in their midst. The apostle Paul, in his celebration of love as written to the Corinthian church, was not discounting the importance of faith and hope by uplifting the power of love (1 Cor. 13). Faith, hope, and love are all essential if we are to face the constancy of life's unpredictability, which can overwhelm the best of us. Staying anchored in our faith in the God who was given form through Jesus Christ, claiming the hope that God's redeeming nature brings to our life, and offering to others the unconditional love that God has so graciously given and we have humbly received, is the way that Christ's followers face life's turmoil and uncertainty.

LEADING, CARING, AND COMMUNICATING IN ANXIOUS TIMES

Knowledge speaks; but wisdom listens.

—*Jimi Hendrix*

People's response to change or conflict is influenced by 1) the degree of the change or conflict, 2) the level of stress already present in their lives, 3) their coping skills and flexibility, and 4) their emotional/spiritual maturity. A wise and effective pastor or leader looks at the opportunities that change or conflict can hold, for such times can bring opportunities for personal, spiritual, and interpersonal growth for the entire congregation. Times of anxiety or conflict can become means of bringing about positive change for the faith community and can be compelling forces for renewed mission and vision.

Within the life of a congregation, changes in pastoral leadership, staff, or lay leadership; in traditions or customs; in ministry programs, salaries, or church budget; or in existing facilities or the construction of new facilities can increase anxiety. Although some people have anxiety about the smallest of changes, in general anxiety increases based on the level of change involved. When change occurs, individuals ask,

> What will the future hold?
> What about my needs and concerns?
> When will all of this take place?
> Is there anything good that can come of this?

On the other hand, anxiety decreases when people feel included in the process of change. There is diminished anxiety when people can say,

> My concerns were heard.
> I was taken seriously.
> I was kept informed.

Human beings can handle ambiguity better than apathy. We can tolerate uncertainty but we refuse to be ignored. Effective leaders understand this and know how vital it is to communicate, communicate, and communicate! An important reality of congregational care is that people feel cared for when they are heard and know that someone cares to listen. Conversations over coffee at the café on Main Street can be more essential and productive than a meeting of the board of deacons or the church council. Cultivating and nourishing relationships take time and care. Jesus changed the world with a handful of close followers. He spent three years with them before sending them out to fulfill their mission. Relationships take time, and people know that they are cared for when leaders take the time to listen and when those speaking know that they are actually heard.

A congregation once had three worship services. Judging by attendance and available resources, the church needed to offer only two services. They had added a third in order to start a contemporary service without having to choose which of the existing services would lose its traditional style. In other words, the pastor and leaders were trying to make everybody happy and avoid conflict. The additional service placed greater demands on the staff; was held during the Sunday-school hour, which affected class attendance; and was more popular with the youth, so parents desiring to attend Sunday school were unable to worship with their families. Most everyone agreed that two service times were best and that Sunday school should take place in-between the services, as it had in the past. It was also clear that one service should be a contemporary style while the other offered traditional liturgy. The anxiety of change was palpable, with the resolution having the potential for causing a rift in the congregation.

The pastor decided to hold eleven "listening meetings," small gatherings where people could express their opinions and concerns. The meetings were offered at different times and on different days so that all could attend. The pastor attended each meeting, usually held in people's homes over coffee and dessert, and personally took notes of each meeting's input. After all eleven were held, the minister shared a summary of people's opinions and ideas with the church's governing body. The executive leadership team brought forth a single recommendation that would be voted up or down by secret ballot so that no one would fear not voting their true conscience. The recommendation passed with one negative vote. Thankfully, the person who opposed the change identified herself to the pastor and said that she would abide by the decision and be present at her typical worship time—the service that was changed from traditional to a contemporary style!

Although smart leaders strive for a win-win outcome, it is not merely the outcome by which ultimately we measure success. It is in the development and fostering of meaningful relationships where true success lies. Wanda Holcombe, who has served as the Peace with Justice Coordinator for the Southwest Texas Conference of the United Methodist Church, said, "Don't have your success tied to the outcome. It is the dialogue that is vital and moves people closer to, or further from, agreement."

CARING FOR THE CAREGIVER IN ANXIOUS TIMES

Effective leaders also have self-awareness to know how their own particular personality, values, judgment, and biases contribute to the handling of a situation. It is thus essential to 1) claim your tendencies, 2) grow your strengths, 3) strengthen your weaknesses, 4) live in the Spirit, and 5) lead with a non-anxious presence (reflecting the love of Christ).

Self-awareness includes monitoring your own self-care so that you can remain as objectively empathetic as possible rather than becoming enmeshed in, and a victim to, the crisis at hand. No one can maintain perfect objectivity, for such is the nature of the human condition. Self-care and time away to distance yourself are essential. Taking time away for personal retreats, reflection, and sermon preparation needs to be a part of your routine and is best when it occurs at least quarterly. This is in addition to time for vacation or denominational meetings or conferences. In times of acute crisis, self-care is especially critical to keep the caregiver from becoming another victim of the crisis.

In the late afternoon of May 27, 1997, an F-5 tornado wiped out an entire subdivision of the community of Jarrell, Texas. Winds were so strong that one mile of pavement was removed from a roadway, heavy-gauge metal dumpsters were shredded, and only concrete slabs—not even debris—were all that remained of what was once a quiet neighborhood of brick homes. Twenty-seven people died. Another clergyperson and I were called to provide pastoral care to survivors and emergency responders the day following the disaster. It was a day of immeasurable grief and heartache as a community began to assess the magnitude of its loss. When I returned home that evening, the horror of the carnage I had witnessed finally hit me. The façade of "professional care-giver" melted into the reality of the human being who was also a spouse, father, son, and brother. As tears streamed down my face and sobs wrenched my body, I was compelled to release my own pent-up emotions. Exhausted, I slept for nine hours. My clergy colleague reported a similar response. Whatever the situation or the magnitude of emotion involved, make time to care for yourself.

THE C.A.L.M. APPROACH TO ANXIETY AND CONFLICT

> Conflict isn't so bad as long as things turn out the way I want them to be.
>
> —*Anonymous*

The C.A.L.M. approach to anxiety and conflict invites us to consider, assess, listen, and maintain. Let's examine each part of the acronym in more detail.

Consider the necessity of the anxiety or conflict

When an organization is overly anxious, consider if what is causing the anxiety, concern, or conflict is necessary. Is it an exaggerated response resulting from miscommunication or misperception? Is it the result of a plan that is ill-conceived or a goal that is unrealistic? Is a new pastor expecting too much too soon? Are demands being placed on a congregation whose resources of time, talent, and money are already stretched? Is a pastor trying to force "mega-church" ideas and programs on a congregation still needing guidance in how to grow in mission and ministry? How is the Spirit of God at work in what is happening? God leads, guides, encourages, and also uses others to point the way or to shut a door.

In such a context of congregational "militancy," when people are "riled up" at the pastor or church leaders, perhaps a military metaphor is apropos: It is better to lose a battle than lose a war (or an ultimate objective). Pastors and leaders should consider whether it is better to withdraw, regroup, and consider a diplomatic option, or to press forward, potentially fueling further conflict with possibly disastrous results. Better preparation with broader participation from the congregation can lay the groundwork for a more acceptable and accepted idea, plan, project, program, or mission that yields fruitful results for ministry.

Assess all of the factors involved

Are there other factors, dynamics, or agendas at work here that have not been recognized or, if denied, need to be brought into the light of day? Is there greater concern about personal power than faithful discipleship? Is the anxiety or conflict the result of a person or persons being reactive because of their own personal history or long-held belief (whether or not it is a rational belief) that has nothing to do with the present situation?

There was the woman who adamantly resisted the construction of a playground for children at her church. She recited every possible problem such a playground might bring, although church trustees had already assessed the risks and concerns and were wholeheartedly behind the project. She attempted to rally support for her objections from a variety of church members, appealing to their various interests. To the gardening enthusiasts she painted a verbal image of ruined landscaping and unsightly equipment. To those members more ensconced in "how things used to be" than what today and tomorrow might hold, she spoke of the playground attracting "trouble-makers," children from the poorer part of the community. Her objections were endless.

The pastor, sensing that something greater lay behind her persistent resistance, made a visit to her home. During their conversation over coffee in her living room, he noticed a collection of framed photos of a young girl. Upon inquiry he learned that it was her granddaughter. Through her tears, the woman's painful story poured out as if floodgates of emotion had finally been opened. Her granddaughter had been abducted from a public playground and killed. She could not bear the thought of coming to worship at her church and looking at a playground that reminded her of their family's tragedy.

When someone's reactivity or resistance seems disproportionate to the situation or change that is at hand, consider what other factors may be at work.

Listen and reflect on what people are saying

Observe what is going on around you. Listen beyond the words of any disagreement, complaint, worry, or resistance to the deeper feelings that lie beneath. Listen for the passion. What is held sacred by those who are anxious that they now perceive to be threatened? What core values are involved? What dreams, desires, or dreads are beneath their actions and anxious words? Where is the hurt? What causes their fear? How is faith involved?

Listening is a great teacher and an invaluable source of insight. Wise leaders listen before they speak and communicate that they have heard what has been said. Listening, even when parties involved disagree with or are uncomfortable with what the other party is saying, is the root of the possibility of positive change. Moses saw the bush and stopped to look and listen. Paul saw the light and couldn't help but hear. Jesus, in the midst of his suffering, listened to the confession of the one crucified beside him and offered him comfort and hope.

Listening is the Christlike thing to do.

Maintain a non-anxious presence

Effective leaders don't get so close to the issue at hand that they lose sight of the big picture. For Christian leaders, times of anxiety, turmoil, and conflict afford the opportunity to practice God's grace. Such times bring rich possibilities to offer the unyielding hope and assurance that come from being anchored in the Holy Spirit. Nourished by prayer and empowered by God's Spirit, effective leaders distance themselves just enough to have a healthy and less anxious perspective in the setting where they serve. As a result they learn to anticipate possible problems before they develop. They are more attuned to their own "triggers" that result in anxiety and reactivity.

A non-anxious presence helps to defuse conflict and engender peace before conflict occurs or anxiety develops. It puts things in perspective and brings greater likelihood of resolution or mediation for a solution.

A non-anxious presence is not passivity. An active leader knows when to sit and wait and when to take appropriate action, but even waiting is an action when it is intentional, and it is appropriate when it is purposeful and not the result of fear, denial, avoidance, or procrastination. An active leader challenges inappropriate behavior. When someone is verbally abusive or destructive, makes ultimatums, or sabotages the mission of the church, appropriate confrontation is necessary. It may be a teaching moment, a time to establish appropriate boundaries for behavior, or it could signal that a change of role or relationship is necessary. If a parishioner or clergy is unhappy in the congregation where he or she resides or serves, it may be a sign that the person needs to seek another congregation.

SOME SUGGESTED SCRIPTURES FOR PREACHING AND TEACHING IN ANXIOUS TIMES

The following Scripture passages are ones you might find helpful for preaching and teaching during times of congregational anxiety.

> And we know that in all things God works for the good of those who love him, who are called according to his purpose. (Rom. 8:28, NIV)

> "Love your neighbor as yourself." (Matt. 22:39b)

> Always be prepared to give an answer to everyone who asks you to give the reason for the hope that you have. (1 Pet. 3:15b, NIV)

> Draw near to God, and he will draw near to you. (Jas. 4:8a)

> There is a time for everything, / and a season for every activity under heaven. (Eccl. 3:1, NIV)

> Two are better than one, / because they have a good return for their work: / If one falls down, his friend can help him up. / But pity the man who falls / and has no one to help him up! (Eccl. 4:9–10, NIV)

> Who is wise and understanding among you? Show by your good life that your works are done with gentleness born of wisdom. (Jas. 3:13)

> And a harvest of righteousness is sown in peace for those who make peace. Those conflicts and disputes among you, where do they come from? (Jas. 3:18–4:1)

> They came to Capernaum. When [Jesus] was in the house he asked them, "What were you arguing about on the road?" But they kept quiet because on the way they had argued about who was the greatest.
> Sitting down, Jesus called the Twelve and said, "If anyone wants to be first, he must be the very last, and the servant of all.'" Mark 9:33–35, NIV)

> "But strive first for the kingdom of God and his righteousness, and all these things will be given to you as well." (Matt. 6:33)

> And I heard a loud voice from the throne saying, "Now the dwell-
> ing of God is with men, and he will live with them. They will be his
> people, and God himself will be with them and be their God. He
> will wipe every tear from their eyes. There will be no more death or
> mourning or crying or pain, for the old order of things has passed
> away."
>
> He who was seated on the throne said, "I am making everything
> new!" (Rev. 21:3–5a, NIV)

The previous text from the Revelation of John, along with several key
verses from Romans 8, is another way of approaching the redemptive nature
of God, who is both the beginning and the end and is always making new and
redeeming what is broken.

The Psalms are also rich with possibilities for teaching, preaching, and
praying in anxious times. Laments as well as psalms of thanksgiving and praise
all have great potential for homilies and messages of hope.

SOME CLOSING THOUGHTS ON PREACHING IN
TIMES OF ANXIETY OR CRISIS

We humans have two tendencies that work against us. First, we tend to think
dualistically: black or white, right or wrong, good or bad. The truth is, life is
often a mixture such that good people can do evil things. We blame and judge
others based on a literal interpretation of certain passages of Scripture, but
those same texts take on a different perspective when considered through the
life and teaching of Christ.

Second, we frequently seek a purpose or intention in almost everything
that happens. It is hard determinism to view all of life as happening for a
reason. The mother of a four-year-old boy who died of cancer explained his
suffering as "God doing something huge" through what happened to him.
God does bring redemption and hope from suffering, and that is a "huge"
truth that is bedrock to Christian teaching. Yet it does not necessarily mean
that God causes the suffering in order for there to be purpose and significance. We cannot understand all that is wrapped up in theodicy, any more
than we can explain childhood cancer, natural disaster, or human suffering. It
is all right to accept that there is randomness and serendipity in life as well as
purpose and divine intention. Depending on your viewpoint, randomness *has*
intention due to God's establishment of free will, resulting in both the possibility of human goodness as well as human folly.

I once heard Fred Craddock lecture that a preacher should carefully avoid
reading into the text what is not there or making an allegory out of a passage

that is simply good prose or poetry. As I have expressed his sentiment: not every rock or reptile is a symbol of God or Satan! Especially in anxious times—critical moments and times that people will never forget—may pastors offer a word of hope that those same folks will always remember: God is with us. We are not alone. Thanks be to God! Amen.

8

The Show Must Go On

JONATHAN MELLETTE

Sunday morning rituals are important to me. I'm not talking about liturgy. Liturgy happens to be important to me too. I'm talking about the things that happen each and every Sunday that help to make Sunday mornings feel like . . . Sunday. For instance, every Sunday morning when I arrive at church, I participate in a ritual. I pause by the table in the entrance to the sanctuary, pick up last week's unused bulletins, and drop off the new bulletins. Then I walk to the pulpit, pick up last week's sermon notes, and drop off the new sermon notes. So as not to confuse the old with the new, I rip the former documents in two and carry them into the kitchen with me to throw away. As I pass and use the wastebasket, I say hello to the people in their Sunday school class. After a few brief greetings, I prepare the elements for Holy Communion. I return to the sanctuary with the bread and juice, and place them on the table. That's my ritual; it's calming for me. To be honest, by the time I get to church, I usually need a little calming. See, the ritual actually begins long before I walk into the church. Well, I call it ritual. You'd probably call it chaos. Usually, it's manageable; one Sunday last summer, it wasn't.

The week before "Black Sunday," my ear-nose-throat doctor told me that I had "nasal polyps." Now, I still don't exactly know what nasal polyps are, but evidently they're not supposed to be there. So my doctor put me on ten days of a well-known drug called Prednisone. Prednisone has a few nasty side effects, the worst of which for me was severely elevated blood sugar. My wife informed me, more than once, that when my blood sugar was out of control, I was out of control. So, I thought that knowing of my Prednisone-induced predisposition toward a *poor* disposition, my children would have been on their best behavior. I was wrong.

The morning started out just fine. I was calm and relaxed; the children were quiet. There was no fighting, arguing, name calling, door slamming, or foot stomping. I wasn't upset at anyone and hadn't upset anyone, and I really was in a fine mood. But of course, I knew it wouldn't last forever. After all, we still had to get out of bed.

This particular Sunday morning, my eight-year-old daughter felt the need to find Waldo while she ate her breakfast. Instead of gulping down her cereal in three minutes like she normally does, she took over thirty to eat. Then, rather than a quick shower, she took her time and sang every Hannah Montana song she knew, not once but twice. Finally after much door-knocking-turned-pounding on my part, she stomped out of the bathroom in her towel, glared at me, went into her room, and slammed the door, leaving a trail of watery footprints in her wake.

Now, I'll admit that I probably wasn't very good to my children that morning, but in all fairness, they weren't very good to me either. My son decided to express his fourteen-year-old omniscience that morning by pointing out to me the many ways in which I had faltered in my role as a parent. The conversation ended with me yelling for him to get in the car immediately. As he stomped off, my daughter informed me that she wanted a daddy who didn't yell. I "suggested" that she go look for one in the car with her brother. Finally, fifteen minutes before the worship service was supposed to start, we left our home.

Silence boomed in the car on the way to church. I was fuming. Knowing that anything I said would do anything *but* improve the situation, I instead practiced deep breathing. We got to the church at about ten minutes before the service was supposed to start. Staring straight ahead, my fingers still clutched around the steering wheel, my palms sweaty, my knuckles white, I grunted, "Get . . . out."

They got out. My wife looked at me, arched her left eyebrow and said, "Does that mean me too?"

I took another deep breath, sighed heavily, and said, "Of course not." My wife, who was capable of moments of great compassion—especially when I was at my worst—petted my head, stroked my shoulder, and I nearly lost it. Tears began to well up in my eyes. "I hate feeling like this," I said, the dam bursting, tears rolling down my face.

"Shhhh. Just another hour. Just hold it together for an hour, then you can let it all go."

I knew she was right. I took one last deep, cleansing breath. I looked in the rearview mirror at my bloodshot eyes and wiped the wetness from my face. I noticed something in the mirror but couldn't focus on it. I blinked more tears away and checked the mirror again. "You've got to be kidding me," I said, my heart in my throat, as my recently appointed district superintendent (a judicatory official) and his wife got out of their sedan and started walking toward mine. Nothing brings you out of a medically induced self-pitying stupor quite like a surprise visit from your new boss.

It was now eight minutes before the service was supposed to begin. My wife bolted out of the car and ran back to greet them, hoping to give me just a few extra seconds to pull myself together. I wiped my nose on my sleeve—just as I had told my son not to do a thousand times—and got out of the car. I joined the group, big grin on my face, an obvious contradiction to my bloodshot eyes, and said, "I'm . . . I'm so happy you're here today."

The superintendent smiled, shook my hand, and said a few things that I probably didn't hear then and certainly don't remember now. What I do remember was his saying, "Why don't you go ahead and get into church? I'm sure you have some things you need to do." *Ah, you mean like prepare for worship, like a normal pastor would do,* I thought as I opened the door to the church, my chest thumping like a ten-year-old boy who had just been called to the principal's office for not doing his homework.

My congregation was not one that was concerned with starting or ending worship at any particular time, and over the time that I had been appointed there, I grew to enjoy rather than be disconcerted by this flexibility. However, with the superintendent mere steps behind me, I flew into a bit of a panic. These situations are where rituals can make or break you. I stepped into the entrance, sat down the new bulletins and picked up the old ones. I walked to the pulpit, set down the new sermon and picked up the old one. I walked into the kitchen, said hello to the class, ripped my materials in half, threw them away, and prepared the communion elements. I took the bread and the juice out to the table, lit the candles, turned on the audio equipment, and with thirty seconds to spare, was ready for worship.

I decided to use that thirty seconds as efficiently as possible and give my sermon one last quick look-over. I have often said that my call to ministry is focused on worship and centered on preaching. At a recent meeting with my district superintendent, in fact, I had bragged on my homiletical ability too much, wanting him to know that preaching was important to me and that I had enjoyed some acclaim in the field both in seminary and in other venues. It would figure, wouldn't it, that the one Sunday he chose to visit our church would be a Sunday for which I had not given quite the same level of sermonic preparation as I normally did. I'm sure the Prednisone was the interfering culprit; that's my story, and I'm sticking to it.

It didn't take thirty seconds, however, for me to notice that the pulpit was completely bare. Time stood still; my heart stopped beating. I replayed every step I had taken from the moment I walked into church. I watched myself as I dropped off and picked up bulletins. I watched myself as I dropped off and picked up my sermon. Then it hit me like a linebacker. The week before, I had preached without notes. In my panicked haste, I had set down, then picked up *this week's sermon*. Time moved again; my heart pounded as I gasped for air. Then I started to laugh. This was proof. Forget Anselm, Aquinas, Pascal, and Kant. Forget the cosmological, teleological, and ontological arguments. Forget reason, experience, and tradition. This was proof. Not only does God exist; God has an *incredible* sense of humor.

I put on the same contradictory smile I had previously given the superintendent, and asked my wife if I could have a word with her. A minute later, I was going over the morning announcements while she was in the church office Scotch-taping my sermon together. Outwardly, I reminded my congregation of the women's meeting that was to be held the next Saturday morning. Inwardly, I praised God that the finance committee had voted *not* to purchase a paper shredder.

You can probably imagine what happened next. We worshiped. We sang. We prayed. We opened our eyes and our ears and our hearts, and we listened to and for the Word of God. We hugged and passed the peace. We communed. We fellowshipped. We did all of the things that we had come to do, because as the old adage goes, "the show must go on." Now, I certainly don't mean to intimate that the singing, praying, and preaching are nothing more than a "show," but there is a truism at play here.

When people go to the theater, they don't care what kind of day the lead actress or the supporting actor had. They don't care whether or not the director has a cold, or the flu, or an itchy scalp. They don't care if the props guy had an argument with his mother, or his wife, or his teenage son that afternoon. They have come to witness something bigger than the actors, actresses, directors, and supporting staff. They've come to encounter the drama and experience "the show."

When our congregants come to church, they really don't care about what happened at our house that morning, or that week, or that month. They really aren't concerned with what obstacles stood in our way, because they're exhausted from overcoming the obstacles that stood in theirs. They aren't worried about all the meetings we have to attend and all the paperwork we have to finish, because they have meetings and paperwork of their own. They've come to witness something bigger than the pastor, the organist, the choir director, and the choir. They've come to encounter and experience God. It is our calling to help facilitate that experience. Which means that even when we've had a bad week; even when we've fought with our children or our parents or our significant others; even when we're not quite sure how *we're* going to go on, the show *must* go on. That means that we have a choice to make: lead, follow, or get out of the way.

Paul urged Timothy to "proclaim the message; be persistent whether the time is favorable or unfavorable; convince, rebuke, and encourage. . . . For the time is coming when people will not put up with sound doctrine, but having itching ears, they will accumulate for themselves teachers to suit their own desires . . ." (2 Tim. 4:2–3). It doesn't matter if it's a Sunday morning or a Wednesday night. It doesn't matter if it's at a retreat weekend or a revival or a summer camp. It doesn't matter if it's a simple conversation we have at someone's hospital bed or in our church office or at the post office. Our call beckons us to give our best.

Now, this isn't to say that our work—even when we give our best—will always be perfect, or even good. Professional baseball players strike out and MVP quarterbacks throw interceptions. Top CEOs buy the wrong companies, and heads of state make poor choices. Fortunately, we're not alone in our work. "Therefore, my beloved," writes Paul, "be steadfast, immovable, always excelling in the work of the Lord, because you know that in the Lord your labor is not in vain" (1 Cor. 15:58).

Someday we'll look back and know that we have fought the fight, finished the race, and kept the faith. Until then, although we may be sick, although we may be tired, although we may grow weary of the stumbling stones that are forever in our path, it is intrinsic to our calling that we stay the course, persevere, and give our best.

I also recommend staying clear of paper shredders—just in case.

PART TWO

The Congregants in Adaptation

This section of preaching and pastoring people through transitions begins with a change that preoccupies virtually all humans for most of their lives. If one does not consider his or her mortality, which includes the crawl toward old age, then that person fails to understand the theological notion of finitude. As Psalm 90:10 reminds us, "The days of our life are seventy years, / or perhaps eighty, if we are strong." As we explore issues that face individuals in our congregations, David Buttrick begins by addressing a burgeoning topic: "Preaching to the Elderly."

The elderly are regularly the highest percentage of a congregational age cohort. As we preach the gospel to the elderly, preachers recognize that we do not medicate them with a therapeutic message. Clearly the Bible recognizes problems of aging as Buttrick demonstrates by stories of Moses and the author of Ecclesiastes. As people age, we lose our power over the world. We also stare down the reality of death. The loss of power has implications for the lives of those who are aging.

Buttrick suggests that there are two parts of the gospel—the new social order preached by Jesus and the gospel of death and resurrection about who Jesus was. Which of these do we preach to the elderly? Most preachers, Buttrick avers, focus on death and resurrection. But Buttrick suggests that to the elderly we also preach the new order. Of course, Jesus loves me and wants to welcome me into heaven, yet Jesus calls all God's people to a new world and to be one of God's new people—and this call includes the elderly. What it does is give older folks a future. As Buttrick sees it, this perspective gives the elderly the capacity to see both their past and future. Even as God has repeatedly forgiven the elderly, their new vision of God's kingdom is future perfect, as it happens now. Preachers should not only speak *to* the elderly but speak *for* the elderly with creative solutions to problems such as poverty and the lack of health care. Buttrick wraps up by prompting us to remember that the elderly have many of the same problems as the poor—many are in fact poor—and that the church itself is the Preacher.

The subsequent essay, "Divorce and Marriage for Christians" by Ella P. and Henry M. Mitchell, is shrouded in sadness, for Ella died on Thursday, November 20, 2008, following complications of a stroke in September 2008. In fact Henry sent the essay just a few weeks after her stroke. The work is important as possibly one of the last articles she published. As they write it together, one might surmise that they had indeed just celebrated their sixty-fourth wedding anniversary.

The Mitchells write that conventional wisdom tells us that for two to be joined in a Christian marriage the two must have been trying to live in guidance and the will of God for some time. The authors then advise that the problem occurs when one plans on beginning to live within God's will "tomorrow." Single people should pray for God to bring them a loving partner. The Mitchells also recommend that young couples listen to the elderly regarding marriage—a specific appeal to the wisdom that can be found in the First Covenant.

The Mitchells write that the place and meaning for divorce is when one of the partners has a hardening of the heart toward God's will. Too often in these cases people decide to divorce too quickly and later regret their decision. Another reason for divorce is some form or another of abuse. The church should work to help abused spouses back on their feet and give them safe haven. We as the church should never condone the actions of an abuser in any circumstance whatsoever. The authors recommend marriage renewals on God's terms. Confession of sins is beneficial, but not just to God. If one can not confess to a marriage partner, then a pastor/priest should hear the confession. Pastors should help couples reconcile after they uncover or discover the "demons" in the relationship. Prayer should surround couples, and a good admonition is that they pray together as a couple. The Mitchells' approach to marriage and divorce may seem quaint to many, yet their sixty-four years together stand as a testament to the utility of their "marriage methodology."

Ecclesiastes is a teacher's advice for times of change. In the view of death's certainty, enjoy to the fullest the days God gives you. This is a piece of the wisdom that Sid Greidanus passes along in his sermon "Have a Good Day!" based on Ecclesiastes 9:1–12. In this sermon the contemporary preacher (Greidanus) reminds us of what the ancient preacher (Qohelet) tells his people: Change can rob us of the joy of living. This truth has been valid since the writing of Ecclesiastes.

The text, which Greidanus exegetes carefully within the sermon, addresses changes beyond human control and explores theodicy in helpful ways. No one knows why things happen, but Qohelet reminds his listeners that our lives are in God's hands. Although one can never know if actions are the result of God's love or anger, we do nonetheless all have the same fate—death. Greidanus then relates the ancient preacher's wisdom: We are to Go, Eat, Drink, Enjoy, and Do. Be joyful, for life is unpredictable, and death is uncertain, sudden, and unexpected. If we do not honor God's gifts, then we dishonor God. We should enjoy food and drink, our spouse, and work. We should not fritter our days with meaningless pursuits, frustrations, worries, anger, and so forth. Rather, God frees us to live as if our days are limited—as if each day might be our last.

In his homiletic reflection titled "Still Falling Short of One Hundred," John Holbert muses on Isaiah's vision for God's world as Holbert's mother celebrates her eighty-ninth birthday. The preacher, with this birthday in mind, contemplates the meaning of a long life and how it is a metaphor for God's intention for God's creation. The prophetic texts found in Isaiah and Revelation describing heaven are not simply intended as the stuff of dreams. Rather, for the faithful they are a vision of what God now wants for God's creation today!

Holbert, near the homily's conclusion, notes, "We still fall short of one hundred, because we do not finally live in the world God has in mind for us." In other words, when God created the world and us in God's image, it was this new heaven and new earth that God wanted for us now. God's desire for the creation is uncomplicated—peace, justice, harmony, and care. As faithful people who look to the vision for life, God frees us from our anxiety to change the world and work toward God's will of all living safely to a hundred.

June Alliman Yoder, in her essay titled "Preaching: The Role of Change and How to Get There," addresses the rhetorical function of persuasion. She begins by revealing why she thinks that so many preachers preach sermons that "do not do anything." Her question to such preachers is, "What are you trying to accomplish in this preaching?" She thinks that preaching should have a purpose. An element of that purpose is that a good sermon "should be proclamations that make us into new people." She clearly means that sermons should be powerful, and powerful sermons must be clear about what they do or accomplish. Yoder then ventures five reasons that she thinks preachers preach sermons without purpose. After this exploration she notes that "if it is misty in the pulpit, it will be foggy in the pews." The concept is, if the preacher does not know what is going on with the sermon, then it is unlikely that anyone else will either.

In this extremely helpful essay, Yoder establishes that in order to communicate successfully, the preacher must know the sermon's purpose. Next she explores the positive aspects of persuasion or rhetoric, which is a chief ingredient of preaching. The author uses three models for speaking/preaching. Each is useful to those who preach. Yoder illustrates what she means by persuasion and offers models from Monroe's Motivated Sequence, Loder's Transforming Moment, and Lowry's model of narrative preaching. (She footnotes each author for further inquiry.) What keeps persuasion from being coercive or manipulative, Yoder suggests, is that the speaker leaves the listener free to choose what to do with the material. She concludes that if the goal of preaching is transformation, using structures of rhetoric persuasion is both appropriate and necessary. Yoder's closing, hopeful comment to preachers is that people change in very tiny steps.

The always creative Thomas H. Troeger provides us with an essay titled "Long Enough at the Holy Mountain: Theologically Sound Spirituality for Change." He begins by noting that people often ask when facing the opportunity for change, "Why would I leave this?" They ask because, as Troeger observes, individuals or groups are in a place that is secure, reliable, cherished, or even holy. They resist leaving the holy mountain in response to God as did Moses at Mt. Horeb when God told him he had been there long enough. We cannot stay in one place forever, no matter how holy it is.

Yet a good question for those who contemplate a sojourn is, "How do we know when it has been long enough?" We can determine this by prayer, candid conversation, and critical analysis, and by recognizing that the first response to the change may need to be reversed. Although we leave the mountain, we need not forget the holy experience. When we realize we are fulfilling God's will, we receive energy for the journey. Troeger in my judgment makes a weighty statement when he writes, "Religious leaders need a theologically sound spirituality for change because the resistance to change is often rooted in theological and spiritual convictions about the sanctity of the way things are."

As a way to combat those who have eternally assigned themselves on the church's behalf to the ad hoc "Back to Goshen" committee, Troeger concludes that "implementing change requires engaging the poetry of the soul as well as the reasons of the mind and the emotions of the heart." Perhaps there are few texts that speak to our generation so thoughtfully as the text from Deuteronomy 1:6–7 (RSV), which reminds all of us, "The Lord our God spoke to us at Horeb, saying, 'You have stayed long enough at this mountain. Turn and take your journey.'" As a poet of note, Troeger treats us to one of his fine poems that fits the occasion and offers us singing directions. Selah!

In twenty-five years I have never read anything that Tom Long wrote that did not move me emotionally or challenge me rationally. Long does not disappoint in his essay "In Life . . . In Death: Funeral Sermons." One might label this topic, at least from the point of view of faith, as "the big transition." Preaching funerals in our culture has become an unfocused, often unChristian exercise, which Long tries to redeem in part through this essay. For a scrupulous treatment of this topic see Long's recent book *Accompany Them with Singing—The Christian Funeral* (Louisville, KY: Westminster John Knox Press, 2009).

Long writes here that Christian funerals are events of transition and action—taking the body from the place of death to the site of farewell. We human beings have now based funerals on human need. As most societies do this as an act of worship, Long reminds us that theologically the funeral enacted Christian baptism as part of life and death. Long spends time writing about the devolvement of funerals. In his view they have lost much of their previous, powerful gospel message about death and life. His essay offers a guide for what every funeral sermon/homily should have.

Long also provides a couple of excellent funeral sermons that in part illustrate his observations. These exemplars demonstrate how a preacher takes circumstances of death to help "get the dead where they need to go and the living where they need to be."

9

Preaching to the Elderly

DAVID BUTTRICK

Have you noticed, these days there are more and more ads aimed at the elderly? Ad agencies have targeted the "Golden Age." Most of the ads picture young-looking gray-haired couples teeing up on golf courses, dancing the night away cheek to cheek, or lolling by some sleek resort swimming pool. They are pictures of people having a great old age. But then who pays for the ads? Why, Zocor, Celebrex, Viagra, and, yes, Phillip's Milk of Magnesia. There you are, old age in America, on the one hand a fantasy vacation; on the other hard reality sponsored by pharmaceuticals. Every minister preaches, so here's the question: How do you preach to the elderly? How do you shape a Christian message for those who are growing old and who know they are growing old? There's our question.[1]

I

Yes, there are special occasions when preachers preach to nobody but the elderly—for example, speaking in nursing homes or retirement communities. But most of the time preachers preach to the elderly within congregations. In congregations, the elderly, their middle-aged children, and sometimes their children's children may all be worshiping together. But these days the old folk are apt to be a higher percentage of every congregation than ever before. Back at the beginning of the twentieth century, in 1900 to be exact, the average life

---

1. Previously I wrote a chapter on the subject titled "Threescore, Ten, and Trouble," in William J. Carl Jr., ed., *Graying Gracefully* (Louisville, KY: Westminster John Knox Press, 1997), 32–46.

span was no more than forty-eight years. But health care has improved stunningly, and now as the twenty-first century is under way, the average life span is more than seventy-two years. Forecasters tell us a decade from now the over-sixty-five crowd will reach more than 20 percent of the national population, thus straining Medicare and Social Security programs. But all those statistics must be doubled in most churches. Christianity in America has not kept pace: for example, the church baptizes a far smaller proportion of infants with respect to children born than it did two generations ago, so mainline congregations are mostly old and getting older. Did you know that in the Presbyterian Church (U.S.A.) the median age is now over seventy—that's the *median* age! Other denominations are not all that far behind. Look, like it or not, every minister almost everywhere is preaching to the elderly. To repeat our question: How does the gospel message speak to those who are growing old and, more important, to those who know they're growing old?

Now please notice, we are asking about the *gospel* message. How do we preach the *gospel* to the elderly? We do not begin with a therapeutic assumption, namely, that what we preach should be therapy for the aging. Christian faith may be liberating, but it is not primarily therapy. No wonder that again and again Jesus refused to be turned into a full-time faith healer—"You won't believe unless you see signs and wonders," complained Jesus (John 4:48).[2] No, Christianity is not therapy; it's faith. So we will not begin by asking what are the psychological needs of the elderly and then try to shape a modified Christianity to provide fulfillment of such needs. If God is defined by our psychological neediness, God becomes a great therapist strung up in the sky, with no more definition than our struggles. Such a God would not be the morally demanding God of Abraham, Isaac, and Jacob. Yes, we ministers should understand all we can about the special problems of the aging, yet we must preach the *gospel*. After all, if the gospel message is good news, then it is good news for the elderly as it is to the young. Ministers must somehow aim the gospel message at those of us who are card-carrying AARP types. What's more, they must do so without turning the gospel into a carefully designed comfort station.

II

Remember the ads, pictures of happy old-timers that were paid for by prescription drugs. There you are: a dream of a cheerful old age but at the cost of "Golden Age" pains. The Bible understands. The Bible also pictures a happy

---

2. All translations from the Christian Scriptures are my own.

old age but claims it's a special gift of God's grace. Exactly how old is biblical old age? According to the Bible, Methuselah lived to be 969 years, but we can write that tall story off as biblical wishful thinking. At the time of Christ Jesus, the average life span was probably in the late twenties. The figure was low not only because of the loss of life in childbirth but because of poverty, disease, and the lack of any kind of sterile medical care. The kings of Israel, who were well cared for, guarded, and treated beyond what an average citizen could expect, still averaged little more than forty years. So forty to sixty was a very old age in those days. Psalm 90 announces,

> The days of our life are seventy years,
> Or, perhaps eighty, if we are strong.
> Even then, their span is only toil and trouble;
> They are soon gone and we fly away.

The psalm is outlandishly optimistic. Few people ever made it to seventy; fewer still, to eighty. The days of everyone's years were toil and trouble beginning in the thirties. So anyone who actually survived to enjoy life in the sixties and seventies was regarded as triumphant. God had given them a priceless, quite exceptional gift: they had children and grandchildren, busy interesting work to do, and though they had white hair, they had a long, long prosperous life.

What about actual conditions? The Bible knows all about the troubles of old age. According to the Bible, Moses had excellent eyesight when more than a hundred, but most people were less fortunate. Qoheleth, the dour "preacher" of Ecclesiastes, describes losing eyesight metaphorically: "The moon and the stars are darkened," he writes, "and those who look through windows see dimly." As for hearing, listen: "all the daughters of song are brought low," he says, because he can no longer distinguish a full range of singing sounds. Can he get a good night's sleep; no, "We wake with the sound of a bird," says Qoheleth. When out walking he claims he is terrified, afraid to fall, even on a flat road. Listen as Qoheleth sums up old age: "The Almond tree blossoms white, the grasshopper drags itself along, and the aphrodisiacs fail." So his hair goes white, his movements are laborious, and as for sex, well "the aphrodisiacs fail." So Qoheleth sings of old age starkly, "Dust returns to earth, and life breath goes back to God, and vanity of vanities, everything is vanity."[3] In the Bible, God is old, God is a wooly haired ancient of days, but although ancient, God's vital signs are always excellent. But the rest of us are mortal. And with us mortals, bodies wind down, our skin loses tone, and after seventy, as my doctor explains, everyone should have a diuretic!

3. All citations are from Ecclesiastes, chapter 12.

But, at a deeper level, old age is a profound experience. For in old age, we lose our world—that is, the world in conscious awareness. Gradually, we lose our power over the world around us. We can no longer remember what we have to remember. We can no longer manage what must be managed. And, as an old song sings it, "'Don't get around much anymore!" Meanwhile, once in a while, we remind ourselves that we are not going to live forevermore. The death rate still runs around 100 percent. Do we hold up fingers on two hands and guess how many years we may have left? Do we laugh and ask, "Can we count toes as well?" Eugene Ionesco has a play called *Exit the King*. The king in question has been the ruler of his own universe, but now he must face up to dying. "Long live the king," his courtiers cry, and the king pratfalls flat on his face. Again and again, "Long live the king," and every time, pathetically, down he goes. Those around him suggest he would be wise to abdicate. But he can't bring himself to abdicate. As he begins to lose his powers—his memory, his eyesight, his hearing, his understanding—with each change, gradually the world around him falls apart or dissolves. Until at the end of the play, he and his world disappear altogether.[4] Most old people are quite honest about having to die. But death is not the primary problem. No, what's painful is losing the world, the world which is our world, the world in conscious awareness, the sweet, everyday-in-the-morning world. No wonder Dylan Thomas tells us to rage, "rage at the dying of the light."[5]

III

So now, what do we preach? What is the *gospel* message for the elderly? To get at the message, perhaps we had better stop and draw a distinction that, of late, has come to the fore. Jesus came preaching the kingdom of God, a message of God's forthcoming new order in which the poor would be raised up, the hungry fed, and the powerless empowered. God's new world is on its way, said Jesus, so let's join the future of God ahead of time. If you preach news of God's coming empire, announce a regime change, and ask people to join up, you're going to get in trouble with present-tense empires. Trouble in the first century was the Roman Empire. Perhaps you've noticed: superpowers (like our own) are nervous; oh, but they're nervous. Any potential insurrection must be stamped out at once, in Galilee or in Iraq. Jesus himself was strung up on a cross to prove that there was no power but Roman anywhere on earth.

---

4. Eugene Ionesco, *Exit the King* (New York: Grove Press, 1963).
5. Dylan Thomas, "Do Not Go Gentle into That Good Night," from *Selected Poems*, ed. Walford Davies (London: JM Dent & Sons Ltd., 1974), 131–32.

But then, then a wild, quite unexpected rumor spread around the ancient world. "Risen," they said; Jesus Christ has been raised by the power of God. Thus, gradually, another gospel message was preached, a message about Jesus. For if God raised him, then somehow Jesus was God's man—God's man in dying, God's man in living, yes, God's man in being born. Perhaps, in a way, Jesus Christ, was "God with us." Two gospels formed, a gospel of God's new social order that Jesus preached, and a gospel of death and resurrection, all about who Jesus was. So what do we preach to old folks? The gospel Jesus lined out about God's coming new social order, or the gospel about Jesus' life, death, and resurrection? What do we preach when we preach to old-timers?

IV

The big problem with the message Jesus preached is that it sets the new over against the old. Jesus announced God's new social order, claiming the old order was on its way out. Jesus himself started preaching in his early twenties. He chose disciples most of whom were as young as he, in their twenties and thirties. In many ways, the Jesus movement was a youth revolution. Jesus set God's will against old traditions represented by the older leaders of Israel—Sadducees, Pharisees, Herodians, and a group often labeled "Elders of the Jews." They were old clothes unfit for new patches, or old wineskins; Jesus and his followers were the new wine God was pouring into the world. The Beatitudes that Jesus shaped in the Sermon on the Mount denounced our world, a world where the poor are helpless, the hungry unfed, and the powerless trapped in huge human systems. But God's new world was on the way, and in God's new world the poor would be in charge, the hungry would banquet, and powerless people would be empowered. Those who now weep for the way of the world would laugh for joy.[6] In the Sermon on the Mount, Jesus followed Beatitudes with what we call the "antitheses." They all begin much the same way, "You have heard that it was said by the old-timers, but now I'm telling you. . . ." Unabashedly, Jesus set his message over against the traditions of Israel. God's new world is on the way, so come join the new humanity ahead of time. Thus Jesus invited those he called to party ahead of time. A kingdom feast for all comers! Celebrate, for the new order of God was a sure thing.

Well, Jesus and his disciples did not fare well in Galilee. The Jesus movement shook up that ancient province. Said Jesus quoting the prophet Micah, "For I have come to set a man against his father, and a daughter against her

---

6. Here I cite Luke's version of the Beatitudes, which may be earlier than the version in Matthew's so-called Sermon on the Mount.

mother, and a daughter-in-law against her mother-in-law" (Mic. 7:6). As a matter of fact, his words came true, for if sons went off to follow Jesus, they lost their family, home, and reputation. More, they were usually read right out of their clan. Said the disciple Peter to Jesus: "Look, we have left everything to follow you" (Mark 10:28). They did. No wonder that early Christians viewed communities of faith as new families, proving that blood was not thicker than water, at least not than waters of baptism. Remember when Jesus' mother and brothers showed up, and Jesus refused to see them and instead pointed to his followers: "Here," he said, "are my mother and my brothers" (Mark 3:34). Make no mistake, when quizzed by the rich young ruler Jesus quoted the Ten Commandments with approval, including the Fifth Commandment to honor one's father and mother (Mark 10:19). What's more, Jesus was sharply critical of a man who dedicated his wealth to God and then begged off having to support his parents (Mark 7:10–11). But nonetheless, Jesus preached the coming new order of God and turned on the old ways, the old traditions, because he regarded his movement as God's new wine!

When you flip past the Gospels to the letters of Paul the emphasis is the same. "Anyone in Christ," says Paul, "is of the new creation" (2 Cor. 5:17). Paul also underscores the new order, the new creation, the new Adam, and the new humanity. Paul is an apocalyptic thinker. He has divided the whole human enterprise into two aeons, the aeon of the old Adam and the aeon of the new Adam, namely, the risen Christ. The new aeon has begun with Jesus Christ and will conclude with the overthrow of all worldly powers and a full-scale resurrection of the living and the dead. Although we live in the old Adam world, a world ticketed for replacement, as Christians we are an advance guard of the new world; we are in fact the new people of God. So Paul has us live free from old forms of religious law, such as circumcision and kosher food regulations. For God is honored by the courage of faith and not by required legal obedience. What God does demand, according to Paul, is love, God's special brand of love. Sometimes we try to argue that Paul came along and complicated the simple teaching of Jesus. The argument is hard to sustain. Both Jesus and Paul celebrate the coming of God's new order, a new creation, says Paul, a new Adam, and, yes, a new heaven and earth.

V

Well, no wonder that in general churches preach a message about Jesus and his life, death, and resurrection to the elderly. What's the focus? We talk about what Jesus did, his miracles of healing, and his acceptance of sinners, and above all, we tell of his dramatic death and the glory of resurrection. To us who preach, such a gospel seems absolutely tailor made for those who are old and getting older. Yes, older citizens do seem to accrue medical problems, and the stories of Jesus showing concern for the ill, the handicapped, and the hurting should be a comfort. After all, HMOs are not nearly as compassionate! And the stories of Jesus reaching out to accept sinners, forgiving them freely, surely those tales are especially meaningful to us as we look back on our lives in old age. We single out what we did not do and, in particular, on failures to love as fine and freely as we should. We who are elderly know how to bow our lives and beg God's mercy. Above all, preachers figure that what the aging need to hear is news of death and resurrection. Jesus faced having to die as we all face having to die, and he willingly took the cup of pain and aloneness with courage. Jesus knew what we all come to know: the mystery of dying. "My God, My God, why have you forsaken me!" Surely the gospel message of Jesus who shared our humanity, our living and our dying, is a huge comfort to those who are growing into old age. The message links us person to person with Jesus the Christ.

What about news of resurrection? Resurrection is often preached as a promise of personal survival. On Easter Day, amid the lilies and the kids' new clothes, we are told we won't die. But "you won't die" is not the message of Easter Day, nor is it a sane message for the elderly. The elderly know perfectly well they're going to die; if they haven't figured it out they can feel it in their bones. If the elderly "rage against the dying of the light," it's because they love life; the beauty, the sweet loves, the friends, the partying. But we are not, underline the word "not," we are not immortal. No, we are dust-to-dust mortal, and we all die. So did Jesus—remember the creed emphatically recites "crucified, dead, buried." But resurrection is news of a social triumph: God, the God who raised up Jesus, will raise us all up in some new embodiment, for as W. H. Auden once put it, "I wouldn't be caught dead without a body!" Besides, how can we party with the "shout of them that triumph," and "the song of them that feast," unless there is embodiment and a table big enough for others? The news of Easter is that we can trust God with our lives and our dying—the one God, the God of Abraham and Isaac, of Sarah and Miriam, the same God who raised up our Savior, Jesus Christ. A message of Jesus, his life, his death, and his resurrection, is bound to be good news for the elderly.

VI

Now, let's turn around and be honest: What about the gospel of the new order, the gospel Jesus himself announced? Do we preach God's new order to the elderly as well? Absolutely! Otherwise the gospel message is reduced to the inward and the individual. Jesus loves me. Jesus wants to heal me. Jesus, my personal savior, wants to welcome me to heaven, and "Oh, that will be glory for me!" Notice not only can the gospel message be made personal, it can be positively embarrassing; just listen to our nineteenth-century hymnody! But Jesus came preaching future promises of God, news of a new social order. Years ago there was a newspaper for black Harlem in New York City, *The New Amsterdam News*. All through the fifties and sixties editor Roy Otley kept a banner headline at the top of every issue that read, "'New World a-Coming." So in a desperate season, when clanking armies marched through the province of Galilee, where 7 percent of the people had cornered 95 percent of the cash, where poverty was unsettling farmland and provoking banditry, Jesus marched through Galilee, saying, "'New World a-Coming.'" He pictured the future of God as a world where we will live for neighbors and neighbors for us, all fulfilling the law of God in love. Look, in old age our world narrows down and with our dying dissolves. But in our old age, Jesus still comes calling us to a new world, another world, a new creation. No wonder that when Christ was born old Simeon sang and the prophetess Anna, in her nineties, celebrated (Luke 2:25–38). You cannot live in God's new world without your neighbors, for God is never "my God" but always our God, our Parent, and our Savior. Jesus came calling us into God's future. Calling us, even in old age, to be one of God's new people.

Jesus' message of a new world coming gives us who are elderly a future. We are in God's social world. We who are elderly have a gift: we can look across generations; we remember grandparents, and parents, and our own lived lives. But also we picture our children, our children's children, and the future they will have. The elderly see the world, past and future. For the sake of children's children, we have a stake in the future of the world. What's more, elderly persons are often open to a changing world in ways that their children may not be. Good heavens, the rigid folk in every congregation are the forty-year-old set who've made a little money and still view themselves as moving ahead. They're apt to be the "neo-cons" these days! But the elderly looking back know they have been foolish and have been forgiven over and over again, as have their grandparents and their parents; as a result they have found a kind of tender tolerance toward themselves and others.

Some years ago there was a wonderful novel about a man who inherited property. He decided that he would build a new community for human beings. He set out to recruit people to work the project with him. He picked out a retired, limping contractor, and a old, one-armed carpenter. He found a wheezing, hypertensive nurse and a retired missionary priest who for the life of him couldn't remember the rituals he was supposed to conduct. Gathered together, he cheered them on. "With us," he said, "the world begins all over again."[7] Why did he choose such an elderly dysfunctional group? Maybe because they could dream dreams and see visions. The elderly know that the world is not what it should be, and it's certainly not the world God intends. They can catch sight of the world that ought to be, where warfare ends, and the poor are raised up. They can squint and see visions, maybe God's own dazzling visions.

Theologian Michael Welker calls the kingdom of God a "happening."[8] In a way, the kingdom is future perfect, an image of the world God wants. But Jesus' idea of a new order has been put together from prophet dreams in the Hebrew Bible. There's Isaiah's dream of a world where weapons of war will be hammered into John Deere tractors and combat fatigues, Pentagon issue, will be burned up, for as the great spiritual sings, "We ain't gonna study war no more." There's also Zechariah, who pictures a city of God with parks where old folk on canes can sit together and sun themselves while around them children play, filling the air with laughter. The Bible pictures the kind of world God wants. And we're allowed to add our own generations' dreams as well—a world free from nuclear threat, a world without terrors or terrorism. But though the vision of the kingdom of God may be future perfect, God *is now*, and is surely trying to bring the human enterprise into newness. Kingdom of God is a "happening," a happening in which we live right now. Somehow churches must enlist the elderly to join in the coming of God's new world, the reshaping of our future into a Holy City of God. Retirement should not mean stepping out of what God is trying to do. Nashville, the city I live in, has a citizens' organization called "TNT, Tying Nashville Together," dedicated to healing divisions and renewing the city. Guess what? More than half of its active members are over sixty-five.

VII

Are you ready for a P.S.? In the years to come we who preach will not only speak *to* the elderly but *for* the elderly, *on behalf of* the elderly. The Fifth Commandment is not addressed to individuals but to the collective soul of Israel. The commandment "Honor your father and mother" is more social policy than advice for children, urging them to be nice to parents. After Solomon's expensive military buildup, the kings who followed him cut funds for the care of the elderly, and God brought disaster on Israel (1 Kgs. 12). They had failed the Fifth Commandment. America may be facing a similar crisis. While the

7. A reference to Walker Percy's astonishing novel *The Second Coming* (New York: Farrar, Straus, & Giroux, 1980).

8. Michael Welker, "The Reign of God," *Theology Today* 49, no. 4 (January 1993): 500–515.

advertisements picture handsome elderly people on the golf course or loung-
ing in spas, consumer magazines note that retirement communities are so
expensive (as are nursing homes) that they only serve the top 5 percent of
the population. Incidentally, the report assigns many church-run programs
to the same category; that is, they are too expensive for most older persons.
Meanwhile in America we have 40 million people without health care, many
of them in poverty. We have corporate retirement plans, but they are often
subject to uncontrolled corporate profits. We have inadequate social security.
Yet these are things that all European nations provide. Obviously the church
must not only speak but also go to work to search for creative solutions.

The church is not a social service agency. We cannot let "faith-based"
initiatives force churches to assume the social responsibilities of government.
The church has a proper role. The church is a preacher that must speak out to
government and to a wider world, calling us all to obey the purposes of God,
which surely include a concern for those among us who are growing old with
fixed incomes and little money for investments or medications. So though
we've added a P.S., it is part of the gospel we must preach now.

10

Divorce and Marriage for Christians

ELLA P. AND HENRY H. MITCHELL

> What therefore God hath joined together, let not man put
> asunder.
>
> *—Matthew 19:6b KJV*

We were delighted to accept the invitation to write (and likely later preach) on the vitally important and complex topic of divorce and marriage for sincere Christians. Our delight arose from the fact that we had just celebrated our sixty-fourth wedding anniversary when the invitation came. Suddenly we had been blessed with an abundance of fresh insights from the Spirit and from the laboratory of life to enrich our exegesis and interpretation of that wonderful wedding text so often read and so seldom truly understood: Matthew 19:6b. For all too many, this text would seem to set an unrealistically strict standard. For response, we were given some of what seemed to us to be good-news answers to challenging queries. So please hear us old folks out. We dare to believe you'll be surprised and blessed.

> **Henry:** Just what do the words of this biblical text mean, as found in the mouth of our Lord himself? The first of our strange new insights was very clear: God's activity as joiner of couples does not begin and end with the ceremony. When God our Creator literally joins a couple together, it's because God has already been guiding their lives to a level of Christian maturity that makes a life-long bond not only possible but unspeakably joyous. However, one can't legally unite two adult brats, fully self-centered and immature, and expect that a proper ceremony will magically cleanse and bless this mess. God

91

unites us on *God's* terms, and these terms lock in long before the wedding, or even the proposal.

Ella: For God to permanently unite two people, they need to have been trying to live in the very guidance and will of God, for quite some time already. I love to sum it up in one of my favorite verses, Matthew 6:33 (KJV): "Seek ye first the kingdom of God, and [God's] righteousness, and all these things will be added unto you." So, living in such a mood as this, prospective partners ought to be self-giving rather than self-seeking; transparently honest and trustworthy; patient and understanding; and gladly doing what their hands find to do, to help each other.

That's not too much to ask, is it, especially if you intend to offer your same lifestyle to your beloved? The most common problem occurs when one person only plans to *begin* trying to live in God's will tomorrow, maybe, while seeking a partner who has been seeking all along to live in the will of God.

Henry: I can't recall the exact session on spouses matching God-given goals in life, but my church school teacher, when I was seventeen, had me praying for God to help me become worthy of a godly partner. Her lesson focused on Abraham's servant, whom he sent to find a wife for Isaac. The servant prayed (Gen. 24:14) to be led to meet a maiden of Abraham's family and faith, at a well. She was to offer drink not only for him but for his camels. That's an awful lot of water, but the maiden was at the well and did just as the servant had prayed. She said she'd be happy to draw water for him and his camels. She matched exactly the guidelines of generosity noted in the servant's prayer. She graciously invited the servant and his caravan to her home, and her parents were led to send her back with the servant, for marriage to Isaac. It's a beautiful story of love that was found by seeking a person of unselfish, gracious character. Such traits may not be very popular among marriageble young adults today. However, my teacher's insights were deeply unforgettable to my teenage mind. Her teaching methods were spiritually blessed, and so also am I because of them, over seventy years later.

Ella: Two more insights emerged during our sixty-fourth celebration, as we recalled that lesson. The first had to do with the choice of an *elderly* servant for the selection of Rebekah. He had prayed about this weighty responsibility in unusual detail. His prayer included a very wise choice of characteristics. Today, while old folks aren't thought of as infallible, their input will often contain far more long-term marriage wisdom than the opinions of most ecstatic young lovers.

Henry: I suppose I feel so strongly about this because my father first uttered the exact words of which God reminded me when I asked guidance in finding a wife: Dad had said, "What about that Pearson girl?" As a seminary senior, I had asked to be guided to a mate open to God's will—ready to serve wherever sent. And my dad saw my wise and wonderful answer to that prayer long before I did. I still think young folks need to consult "old folks" for wisdom in marriage matters.

Ella: Let me deal with the second insight, a matter too sensitive for most folks to dare discuss. It concerns the fact that the servant's prayer did not include a request for the wife to be pretty, yet the writer reported in verse 16 that "the damsel was very fair." However, the very mention of Rebekah's beauty raises the issue, showing the writer to be a creature of his culture.

I have strong feelings and insights about this issue of appearance. You see, I just *knew* I wasn't attractive. My own dearly beloved father called me "Ol' Big," and my younger sister was the campus queen of the family. When Henry showed interest in me, I dared not let myself believe it. I knew too many sisters who I thought were more attractive. When I finally let myself accept his interest, I phrased it far from the usual wording: "If God be for us, who can be against us?"

Once I was convinced that this was safely in the very will of God, love grew awesomely. I was blessed to realize that God gives beauty to *all* God's children. All babies are lovely, and every bride is beautiful. Henry was quite lovingly insistent that I had the countenance of an angel, and that this was the most important of all. I'm glad he kept trying to convince me. It takes years to overcome one's original feeling of rank in the primary family. So Henry has done his best to help me overcome all those negative self-images of childhood. He has worked at it all sixty-four of our years together.

Henry: And I don't plan to stop as long as I can see and talk. But I can't resist the temptation to copy the Genesis mention of beauty (v. 16) by mentioning the fact that today my wife is very striking, at age ninety-one. Rank strangers of all nations stop her to respond to the glow of her radiant countenance. The world has volunteered to help me convince her of God's fulfilled promise in Matthew 6:33: that "all these things will be given," attractiveness included.

There is a difference, however, in that her beauty is a radiance within the reach of all God's children. I have learned to watch for it in others. My casual notice convinces me that just as God gives genius-level intelligence to some people of all classes and castes, so also does God give some of the most important kinds of beauty to every single one of the human beings made in God's own image. One doesn't have to be a mother to admire something in whomsoever.

Summed up simply, then, our text is stating that they who seek to live by God's guidance in all things can fully expect their marriage to last for life, and that their living will be abundant indeed. This is what Jesus came to bring (John 10:10).

Ella: Further probing the issues in our text, we find that Our Lord follows his quote of Moses' on divorce (Matt. 19:8a) with this simple word: "But from the beginning it was not so." That is to say that it was not part of God's plan; neither Moses nor Jesus was giving carte blanche endorsement to divorce for believers. What, then, is its place and what is its meaning? The common practice of divorce among Christians needs more reason than the easy out of saying, "It's in the Bible, and Jesus definitely stopped short of declaring outright that Moses' law on divorce was wrong." And there's that other convenient out of conceding, "God didn't join us in the first place, so why not go ahead and get a divorce?"

Our first response to that question is that Jesus said that Moses' opinion came from hardness of people's hearts. We hardly dare expect a good outcome from such an unholy yielding to less than God's plan. When we cave in to this hardness, it's because at least one of these divorcers fully intends to remain hard and resistant to the very idea of a uniting on God's terms. Now I know we don't like the way that sounds, but hardness is hardness. And there is much better news later on.

Henry: Our second response to "Why not divorce?" is simply to report that too many children are shattered and too many adult partners' lives are laid waste emotionally, financially, and spiritually by a premature decision to quit trying to live together in peace. Altogether too many people awaken too late to the fact that divorce was a mistake. However, this is not by any means to label all divorcees as terrible sinners. I'm only reporting that, for many, the last word is, "I wish I had known then what I know now."

There are, of course, extreme circumstances that more than justify divorce. Some hardness of heart *requires* divorce; the necessity for it is unmistakable. I am reminded of an eight-and-a-half-year-old girl who looked at her mother's black eye and advised, "Mommy, we better break up this happy family, before somebody gets killed!" She was wise far beyond her years.

One may be sincerely trying to save a marriage cursed by violent abuse just because it is a trusted meal ticket. But this includes acceptance of risks to life and health. Battered bodies can't enjoy a meal. We may have to break out and trust God to feed us rather than to remain in real danger to life and limb. Churches need to be willing to provide emergency support for their own abused members, without embarrassment, even as they gladly aid strangers.

The disease of abuse is rampant, both in and out of the Church of Jesus Christ. We ourselves are involved in a crime of complicity when we cover up the harm suffered at the hands of a supposedly lifelong Christian partner. It doesn't matter how respected that abusing partner may be in circles such as the church. Regardless of how much one contributes, or how high the offices one holds, a violent crime is a violent crime. Period.

Ella: Not too long ago, we all heard the news of a bishop/pastor's vicious attack on his wife in a public parking lot! The fact that she was a famous preacher herself, and that their lavish wedding was nationally witnessed, was of no real protection from a crime more common than we Christians dare be humble enough to confront. God calls us to bite the bullet and launch serious ministry to deal with this no-longer-secret problem, just as we had to do with AIDS. God calls us to be a haven of safety for members as well as nonmembers.

We may honestly feel that we have no business meddling with the private affairs of abusive unions, but that's like the priest and the Levite in Jesus' parable. That's walking by on the other side, when the flow of human blood is evidence enough for us to act decisively, on the spot. There is no church meeting or other activity so important that a Christian ought not to pause and do whatever is needed to stop the bleeding right here and right now.

Henry: There are, of course, precautionary steps to be taken. The Samaritan no doubt watched, to be sure he wasn't attacked by the same robbers. In addition to obviously bleeding wounds, as in the parable, we need to find other ways to be sure of the facts of the crime. And we need to be covered with supportive witnesses, as Jesus suggested for the second approach, in Matthew 18:16. The first one-on-one conversation, which Jesus also suggested with offenders, should probably take place also, with these same witnesses for protection. Violent abusers can be violent with anybody. In any case, the Lord calls Christian churches and their members to bring the crime of violence out of the closet and under the influence of the redemptive mission of the church of Jesus Christ.

Ella: Thanks for these very practical warnings. It's time, now, to move on to the *good* news, which is why we came in the first place. Stated journalistically, the press release's headlines declare: "MARRIAGE RENEWAL OFFER STILL OPEN!" with subtitle "No Couple Hopeless." The offer is good for any marriage where both partners are willing to renew an existing marriage or begin a new marriage on God's terms. It does not matter how many times the applicants have tried and failed, or who the partners were then or now. They just need two people now who are serious about doing a marriage that seeks in partnership to do the will of God. Results are guaranteed for all-out efforts by both partners.

The biblical warrantee, as published internationally, applies to life in general, but has peculiar relevance for marriages. We paraphrase it thus, from 1 John 1:8–9: "If we claim to have committed no sins in a failed marriage, we are fooling ourselves. But if we confess our sins before God, God will forgive us those sins and cleanse us from those sins and all the others that threaten a marriage."

Henry: In the application of God's promise to marriage, we would feel justified in adding that in our confessions of sin and our repentance, the partners seeking renewal need to share their confessions with each other also. Supposed secrets, confessed to God only, are, with rare exceptions, not really or fully repented. (True confession of a sin not shareable with one's partner may be shared with a pastor or priest.) Unconfessed sins weigh heavy, and partners need each other's support and awareness to stay the course of doing God's will.

Ella: The story of Joe and Mary (changed names) illustrates the firm requirement of the full commitment of both partners. Joe and Mary had a lovely, romantic wedding. Corporal Joe and his buddies in formal uniform were one of the highlights. Fifteen years and three children later, they were so very divided that now-top-sergeant Joe had separate quarters, as they say. But a second household was far too expensive. They finally agreed to consult a ministry of known and trusted religious counselors to see if there was any hope.

It didn't take long to discover that when Joe retired, he had taken his sergeant stripes home with him. He had been increasingly overbearing all along as he rose in rank, but he was just too much after retirement. Once they agreed in candid confession on the source of their problem, the real question was simply whether or not Joe loved Mary and the children enough to surrender his stripes and become a humble, civilian, Christian husband and father. Mary hoped the answer was yes, but she feared it was no. How many tough sergeants did you ever see giving up their pride of rank? Mary was willing to stop her nagging criticisms and help him through his change, but did Joe really want to make the change?

The couple meditated on God's willingness to forgive, and Joe sweated through sessions of prayer, separate and together. His final answer was a resounding yes to God's offer. He moved back in and became the husband/father needed for them to become the family he and Mary had first prayed for. Their life together was so wonderful that they forgot to go back and thank the counselors. When the counselors did finally hear what God had wrought, they too rejoiced.

Henry: I agree that the story of Mary and Joe actually happened, but even so, I would like to be sure that we don't oversimplify our claim to this promise of God and make reconciliation and reunion in marriage look too easy. Let me ask this challenging question: "How does this promise relate to a marriage of grossly mismatched personalities?" In cases like this, doesn't one need to consult a psychologist or other healing professional? Don't we need to dig deep into ourselves to find out what makes us tick the way we do? You aren't putting these doctors and other certified practitioners out the window, are you?

Ella: Of course not! The counselors we just mentioned are a classic example of trained professionals. I'm just putting psychology into its proper, fruitful relation with faith and practicing Christianity. I look at it this way: You may learn all you need to learn about your own psychological makeup, and indeed you should know all you can of self-understanding. But this can only help you to know better what to pray for—what actual changes need to be asked for—and to have the spiritual power to make them happen.

Henry: I get your point: understanding that you have bad emotional habits isn't really changing them. A hot temper doesn't go away just because you now know when and why it started in childhood. I'm reminded of the story of Jesus and the legion of evil spirits that possessed the Gerasene demoniac (Luke 8:27–33). When the demons found out that Jesus knew their names, they recognized his authority over them and pled for mercy.

So it is with our evil emotional habits. If we can identify them, we can outgrow them by the power of Jesus. But the names of our bad habits would be all but useless without aid from on high. The main point was that Jesus had the power to cast out the demons once he knew their names. There is a sense in which this is still true: we may need help from psychologists to identify our demons, but we will still need the authority and power of God the Holy Spirit to help us to get rid of bad emotional habits. This psychological help isn't professional competition; it's preparing the way for the healing of the Spirit.

Ella: The good news in Christ for married Christians today is that those whom God has joined together can stay together in joy and peace, regardless of all the other changes in our society. And those who have made mistakes in marriage can be forgiven and assisted in Christ if their desire is wholehearted and their faith is strong. The power of Christ to build and preserve blessed families has never failed; when we see families fail, it is all too often true that the power of Christ just hasn't been fully tried by two sincere seekers.

It may often be that couples feel that they have tried when they have not really given it their all. This effort to build a family in Christ must come ahead of all other concerns. This means that jobs and education and even our church life must serve the purposes of the Christian home. This is where physical health, emotional maturity, practical wisdom, and the very core of living faith are born.

Henry: This is a great challenge, but let us be clear about the nature of that challenge. It may sound painful, like bearing a cross, but with all that's required, we still count every bit of it joy. Several friends have shared with us the fact that folks are always saying, "You must have tried awfully hard through the years to build a happy marriage." But that's just it: we agree—we didn't try. Love comes from God, and it just is. It doesn't have to try to be; in Christ it just flows. It's like motherhood; they don't have to *try* to love their babies. We certainly didn't have to grit our teeth and dig in, determined to succeed at marriage. Could it be a matter of letting Christ into the marriage and then doing what comes naturally? The togetherness is a present from God, on God's terms. To God be the glory!

Please permit us just one more story or case study, to illustrate what we mean in the real world of today. With names changed for confidentiality, let's look at John and Alice, who were six inches from divorce. They had nice cars and a lovely home, plus children in the best of schools and colleges. On paper, they showed better than average success in their two professions. It was a second marriage for both, but it had started as if they were far wiser than they were the first time around. So how did this happen? What on earth could be their problem?

Ella: They lived a busy, exciting life, including church activity. But close questioning revealed that they were not busy *together*. Even when they were at home, she was on the phone with her friends. When her work carried her out of town, it was never arranged so that the trip could be shared. His time at home was shared mostly with the youngest child, an early teen. They were father/son buddies, but Alice wasn't included in the ball games because of her other greater interests and priorities.

Unlike many families that have sought help, the load of responsibility for their plight stacked up higher and higher on the wife's side. John was very gracious, however. He avoided pressing his moral advantage. He even went so far as to applaud Alice's courageous honesty about her lifestyle. When they came back to joint sessions after separate ones, their prayers showed that both of them were serious seekers after God's will in their lives. They really meant it.

The acid test came when Alice confronted the foolishness of her luxury car. She frankly asked God's forgiveness, with husband and counselors listening to her prayer. She went to work changing hours on her job and her focus on her domestic chores. She promised to change her shopping habits, and actually did.

Henry: One might say, "Greater love hath nobody than this, that she gave up her nearly new Lexus in humility before our Lord." It was like a huge burden lifted from her soul, as well as from the budget. Now she was free to be fully family.

Ella: And there was a new and wonderful happiness in that home—joy unspeakable. Both partners used to stay out as long as possible. Now neither one could wait to get home. God had truly joined them together, and they were truly glad about it.

Both: Whom God hath brought back together, let nobody put asunder. No matter what it costs, it's worth all the other things you used to treasure, and much, much more. Hallelujah!!

11

Have a Good Day!

Ecclesiastes 9:1–12

SID GREIDANUS

I prepared this sermon at the invitation of Dr. David Mosser on the topic of "helping pastors preach congregations/individuals through change." In preparing a sermon for a specific occasion or need, as we often do, the danger is that the need addressed will drive and skew the interpretation instead of the interpretation leading to the need addressed. Fortunately Ecclesiastes 9:1–12 is a good fit for "helping pastors preach congregations/individuals through change." For the Teacher who wrote Ecclesiastes sought to guide Israel when it had undergone major changes from a rather isolated, agricultural nation to a people caught up in international trade and intrigue in the third century BC.

The sermon is designed as an expository sermon with inductive development from verses 1–6 to the theme revealed in verses 7–10; then again inductive development from the verses 11–12 to the theme revealed in the New Testament. Simply stated the sermon's theme is that in view of the certainty of death and the unpredictability of life, enjoy to the fullest the days God gives you! The sermon's goal is to urge the hearers, in view of the certainty of death and the unpredictability of life, to enjoy to the fullest the days God gives them.

Dear Brothers and Sisters,

Our society and culture are undergoing changes at an ever-increasing pace. The changes are coming so fast that Beloit College began to produce an annual "Mind-set List." The list reminds professors that references familiar to them may mean nothing to their students. It notes that students entering college this year "have lived their whole lives in a digital world—where GPS has always been available, phones always have had caller ID, and tax returns always could be filed online." These students have not used dial phones or IBM typewriters; they have not bought milk and Cokes in glass bottles; they have not asked the gas station attendant to check the oil and add some air to the tires. They don't know Viet Nam, Watergate, and Johnny Carson. "Every time the list comes out, the school hears from people around the world who say it makes them feel as though life is passing them by."[1] Life is passing them by!

The rapid changes rob people of the joy of living. Changes in our society, in our churches, in our work places, in our families are often upsetting and difficult to handle. They can rob us of the joy of living.

But we are not the first ones to go through rapid changes. The Teacher who wrote Ecclesiastes addressed this book to Israel when it had undergone major changes. For centuries Israel had been a rather isolated, agricultural people. But all this changed in the third century BC. Then Israel became caught up in international trade between Egypt and the rest of the world. People left their pastoral way of life and began to pursue riches. This led to fierce competition ("envy," 4:4), the loss of riches "in a bad venture" (5:14), corruption in high places and bribery (7:7), "the oppression of the poor and the violation of justice and right" (5:8). The Teacher writes about "the tears of the oppressed— with no one to comfort them!" (4:1). People began to complain that the former days were better than the present days (7:10). They wished they were back in the good old days. The changes had killed the joy of living.

In this particular passage the Teacher deals with changes that are beyond our control. He deals with the certainty of death and the unpredictability of life. In chapters 7 and 8 he has been struggling with the question why bad things happen to some good people. Why is it that some good people die young while some evil people live to a ripe old age? Why did John F. Kennedy die at such a young age? And Martin Luther King Jr.? How can a just God allow this to happen?

The Teacher ended chapter 8 with the conclusion that *no one* can find out all the work of God; "even though those who are wise claim to know, they cannot find it out." Then begins chapter 9, "All this"—that is, that the righteous sometimes suffer while the wicked prosper and that we don't know the ways of God—"All this I laid to heart, examining it all, how the righteous and the wise and their deeds are in the hand of God; whether it is love or hate one does not know."

No matter how much they suffer on earth, "the righteous and the wise and their deeds are in the hand of *God*." They are in God's care. Even the evil that befalls good people is not outside God's control. God is sovereign. God set the times: "a time to be born and a time to die" (3:2). God is in

---

1. *The Grand Rapids Press*, August 25, 2008. See www.beloit.edu/publicaffairs/mindset.

control. So when good people suffer, it is a perplexing yet consoling thought that "the righteous and the wise and their deeds are in the hand of God." They are in God's care.

The problem is, the Teacher continues, "whether it is love or hate one does not know." The righteous and the wise do not know whether their experience is an expression of God's love, God's favor, or of God's hate, God's anger. For example, when we become sick, is that a result of God's love or God's anger? When we are involved in an accident, is that a result of God's love or God's anger? We don't know, says the Teacher.

So he concludes, "Everything that confronts them is vanity [it doesn't make sense] since the same fate comes to all, to the righteous and the wicked, to the good and the evil, to the clean and the unclean, to those who sacrifice and those who do not sacrifice. As are the good, so are the sinners; those who swear are like those who shun an oath" (9:1–2).

The same fate, that is, death, comes to all: "to the righteous and the wicked, to the good and the evil." Death comes to all. Whether we have been good or bad, in the end we all die. When the mass murderer Saddam Hussein was executed in 2006, we probably thought that he received his just deserts. But nine years earlier Mother Teresa died. The person who had offered her life for the poor in Calcutta also died. Does this sound just? The same fate that comes to the wicked also comes to the righteous.

In 9:3 the Teacher bursts out, "This is an *evil* in all that happens under the sun, that the *same* fate comes to everyone" (italics in all quotes indicate my emphasis). It is an evil, isn't it, that good people as well as bad people suffer the tragedy of death? We can sense his outrage.

But the Teacher adds, "Moreover, the hearts of all are full of evil; madness is in their hearts while they live, and after that they go to the dead." When he writes, "the *hearts of all are full of evil*," he may be thinking of God's observation before he sent the great Flood: "The LORD saw that the wickedness of humankind was great in the earth, and that every inclination of the thoughts of their *hearts was only evil continually*" (Gen. 6:5). Because the LORD saw that the human hearts were full of evil, he said, "I will blot out from the earth the human beings I have created" (Gen. 6:7).

Perhaps the Teacher is thinking back even further, to Paradise, where God gave but one commandment: "'Of the tree of the knowledge of good and evil you shall not eat, for in the day that you eat of it you shall *die*'" (Gen. 2:17). Adam and Eve disobeyed God's commandment and God's judgment followed: "'You are dust and to dust you shall return'" (Gen. 3:19). Since we have all inherited this evil disposition of disobeying God, we all deserve to die. As Paul puts it in Romans, "Death spread to all because all have sinned" (Rom. 5:12). The so-called righteous as well as the wicked deserve to die.

The Teacher says, "Madness is in their hearts while they live." It is madness to defy our Creator God. "And after that they go to the dead." The life of all persons will suddenly be cut off, and they go to the abode of the dead—to the grave we would say. It's a somber picture of the destiny of each and every person.

Still, there are advantages to being alive. The Teacher writes in verse 4, "But whoever is joined with all the living has hope, for a living dog is better than a dead lion." The living have hope that they may still experience some of the joy that the Teacher repeatedly advocates. Today we express this hope in a proverb: "Where there's life, there's hope." The Teacher also uses a proverb to support his point that the living have hope. He writes, "For a living dog is better than a dead lion." In the ancient Near East a dog was not a beloved pet but a despised scavenger. Today we might think of a rat—a loathsome creature. By contrast, the lion, just like today, was admired as king of the animal world. Now the Teacher says that the living have hope, for a living scavenger dog is better than a dead lion. In other words, even a dog's life is better than death, for the living still have hope.

Moreover, he says in 9:5, "The living know that they will die, but the dead know nothing." The living have "consciousness"; "the living are self-aware";[2] they "*know* that they will die, but the dead know *nothing*." In addition, the dead "have no more reward": they have nothing to look forward to; they have no future. "And even the memory of them is lost": their past accomplishments are forgotten by those who live later. The dead, as the Teacher pictures it, have no future and no past. They have nothing at all. It's as if they had never lived.

Verse 9:6 says, "Their love and their hate and their envy have already perished. Never again will they have any share in all that happens under the sun." This is probably the starkest biblical description of the dead: they are gone; no more rewards; soon forgotten; their passions perished; no more share in life.

Against this dark background of death that awaits us all, the Teacher has some important advice for the living. Verse 9:7 says, "Go, eat your bread with enjoyment, and drink your wine with a merry heart; for God has long ago approved what you do." In this book the Teacher includes seven passages[3] where he encourages us to enjoy the life God gives us, but here he is most urgent. We cannot waste a day! So the Teacher here puts his advice in the most urgent form. He casts his advice in the form of commands: Go! Eat! Drink! Enjoy! Do!

2. Tremper Longman III, *The Book of Ecclesiastes* (Grand Rapids: Wm. B. Eerdmans Publishing Co., 1998), 228.
3. Eccl. 2:24–26; 3:12–13; 3:22; 5:18–20; 8:15; 9:7–10; and 11:7–9.

The first command is "Go!" It's a wake-up call. Stop complaining about the changes! Stop nursing your anger! Stop brooding about your problems! Get past your anxiety and frustrations! "Go!"

The Teacher's second command is "Eat your bread with enjoyment!" Enjoyment! Don't rush through your meals to get to the next task. Don't gulp down your food like a pig. God made us so that we not only need food in order to live but so that we can enjoy it. He has provided us with a rich variety of delicious fruit, vegetables, and grain. "Eat your bread with enjoyment!"

"And drink your wine with a merry heart." God has also provided a rich variety of drinks for us to enjoy. In Israel wine was a favorite. In other countries it may be coffee or tea. Whatever we drink, we should enjoy it. "Drink your wine with a merry heart!"

Some people think that this advice is the same as the pagan slogan "Let us eat and drink, for tomorrow we die" (Isa. 22:13; 1 Cor. 15:32). But this slogan is shallow and selfish. The Teacher's advice is much more profound. He writes in 9:7, "Go, eat your bread with enjoyment, and drink your wine with a merry heart; for [because] God has *long ago* approved what you do." Long ago God approved our enjoyment of food and drink. The Teacher is probably thinking of the creation story. God placed the first human creatures in a beautiful garden and gave them many plants and fruit for food (Gen. 1:29; 2:16). In other words, God not only created us with the need for food but provided food with great variety so that we can enjoy it. Psalm 104 proclaims, "[The LORD gives] wine to gladden the human heart, / oil to make the face shine, / and bread to strengthen the human heart" (Ps. 104:15). So if we enjoy our meals, God approves. God is pleased, for our enjoyment was the divine intent from the beginning. Our enjoyment was God's design. Our enjoyment is an expression of our gratitude to God for his good provisions.

The Teacher continues in 9:8, "Let your garments always be white; do not let oil be lacking on your head." In a hot climate, white garments would reflect the heat of the sun, and oil would keep the skin from drying out. Here the white garments and oil are symbols of joy. When people were distraught and in mourning, they showed their sadness by wearing sackcloth and putting ashes on their heads (see 2 Sam. 13:19). By contrast, when people were joyful they showed it by wearing white clothes and putting oil on their heads. In our culture we might show our joy by wearing colorful clothes, having a neat hairdo, and a smile on our face.

In 9:9 the Teacher becomes more specific: "Enjoy life with the wife whom you love, all the days of your vain [brief] life that are given you under the sun, because that is your portion in life and in your toil at which you toil under the sun." "Enjoy life with the wife whom you love!" Again, the Teacher may well be thinking of paradise, where God made the woman as a partner for the man. We read in Genesis, "Therefore a man leaves his father and his mother and clings to his wife, and they become one flesh" (Gen. 2:24).

Unfortunately, there have always been ascetic tendencies in the Christian tradition. In his day already, Paul found it necessary to oppose false teachers who, he writes, "forbid *marriage* and demand abstinence from *foods*, which God created to be received with thanksgiving by those who believe and know the truth." Paul adds, "For *everything* created by God [food, wine, marriage, sex] is good, and *nothing* is to be rejected, provided it is received with thanksgiving" (1 Tim 4:3–4). Enjoying God's good gifts is "true spirituality."[4]

In 9:10 the Teacher adds one more command: "Whatever your hand finds to do, do with your might; for there is no work or thought or knowledge or wisdom in Sheol, to which you are going." Sheol is the abode of the dead. So the Teacher reminds his readers again of death that awaits. "There is no work . . . in Sheol." All the more reason to "do with your might" "whatever your hand finds to do." For the Teacher, it turns out, hard work is part of the joy of living. Again he may be thinking of paradise, where God put the man "in the garden of Eden to till it and keep it" (Gen. 2:15). God created us to work. So purposeful work should give us satisfaction and joy.

In view of the certainty of our death, therefore, the Teacher urges us to seize the day: "Eat your bread with enjoyment!" "Drink your wine with a merry heart!" "Enjoy life with the wife whom you love!" And "Whatever your hand finds to do, do with your might!"

In 9:11 the Teacher moves on to the unpredictability of our lives. "Again I saw that under the sun the race is not to the swift, nor the battle to the strong, nor bread to the wise, nor riches to the intelligent, nor favor to the skillful; but time and chance happen to them all." Human life, he observes, is unpredictable. We would expect a race to be won by the swift. But the Teacher writes, "The race is *not* to the swift." Unexpected things happen in a race: the swift may trip; they may pull a muscle; they may be boxed in. In the recent Olympic Games, an American woman, Lola Jones, was expected to win gold in the hurdles. She was known to be the fastest in the world. But she tripped on the ninth hurdle and came in not first but seventh. "The race is not to the swift." Life is unpredictable.

The Teacher offers a second example: "Nor is the battle to the strong." At the Olympic Games we also noticed that the strong did not always win gold.

4. Ian W. Provan, *The NIV Application Commentary Series: Ecclesiastes, Song of Songs* (Grand Rapids: Zondervan, 2001), 185–86.

Sometimes they had to settle for silver, or bronze, or nothing. The battle is not always to the strong. There are exceptions. Life is unpredictable.

From these examples of physical abilities, the Teacher moves to three examples of intellectual superiority: "nor bread to the wise, nor riches to the intelligent, nor favor to the skillful." The wise could be either teachers or artists. You would think that teachers would have bread, that is a good livelihood. But there are exceptions. Life is unpredictable.

"Nor riches to the intelligent." You would expect that the intelligent, that is, the clever financiers and entrepreneurs, would be rich. But again there are exceptions. "Nor favor to the skillful." The skillful are those who know how to make things. You would think that people would appreciate the skillful. But there are exceptions.

Why is it that there are so many exceptions to our expectations? We expect the swift to win the race, the strong to win the battle, wise teachers to have a good salary, intelligent entrepreneurs to be rich, and the skillful to be appreciated. Why is it that there are so many exceptions to our expectations? Why is life so unpredictable?

The Teacher answers at the end of 9:11, "but time and chance happen to them all." The problem is "time and chance," that is, "timely incidents." We would say that the problem is "accidents." We cannot control accidents. Accidents happen: runners can fall; the strong can get a cramp; wise teachers can lose their jobs; intelligent entrepreneurs can go bankrupt; the skillful can fall out of favor. The point is that we are not in complete control of our destiny. Accidents can cause us to fall far short of our goals.

In 9:12 the Teacher ends with the most tragic accident of all: "For no one can anticipate the time of *disaster*. Like fish taken in a cruel net, and like birds caught in a snare, so mortals are snared at a time of *calamity*, when it suddenly falls upon them." He likens this time of disaster to "fish taken in a cruel net." You may have seen pictures of how they fish in the East. From their boats or even standing in the sea close to the shore, fishermen will cast a round net into the air. The net seems to hover in the air for a moment; then suddenly it plummets into the water on unwary fish. A time of disaster for the unsuspecting fish.

The time of disaster is also "like birds caught in a snare." You have probably seen pictures of simple snares: a noose staked into the ground or tied to a tree. The birds go about their business, feeding on seeds on the ground. Since there are no predators around, the birds are at ease. A bird casually sticks its head through the noose, and it tightens around its neck until it chokes him. A time of disaster. Caught in a snare!

"Like fish taken in a cruel net, and like birds caught in a snare, so mortals are snared at a time of calamity, when it suddenly falls upon them." All of a sudden, death can overtake us. We may not suspect a thing; we are just going about our business. Suddenly the net falls on us; we are caught in the snare—and life is over. With not only the certainty of death in view but now also its suddenness and unexpectedness, the Teacher urges us all the more to enjoy the life God gives us. Enjoy to the fullest the days God gives you!

The New Testament, of course, teaches us that death is not the end but a new beginning: our entrance into eternal life. But that does not change the message that we ought to make every effort to enjoy the days God gives us on this earth. Jesus himself enjoyed "eating and drinking" (see Matt. 11:18–19). On several occasions he provided bread for the masses to enjoy (Matt. 14:13–21; 15:32–39). He even turned plain water into "good wine" for people to enjoy at a wedding (John 2:9–11).

Jesus also teaches us not to worry about food and drink. Worry about where the next meal will come from kills any enjoyment. Jesus urges, "Do not worry, saying, 'What will we eat?' or 'What will we drink?' . . . Indeed your heavenly Father knows that you need all these things. But strive first for the kingdom of God and his righteousness, and all these things will be given to you as well" (Matt. 6:31–33). Food and drink will be *given* us.

Since food and drink are *gifts* from our heavenly Father, we should enjoy them. If we do not enjoy God's gifts, we dishonor the Giver. Then we are like children who receive gifts at Christmas, rip the wrapping off one, and toss it aside in order to grab the next gift. Our enjoyment of God's gifts is an expression of our gratitude to him. The early Christians understood this well. We read in Acts 2:46, "Day by day, as they spent much time together in the temple, they broke bread at home and ate their food with *glad* and generous hearts."

Not only are we to enjoy our food and drink; if we are married, we must also make a point of enjoying life with our spouse. Jesus honored marriage by being present at the wedding in Cana (John 2:1–11). And Paul enjoins, "Husbands love your wives, just as Christ loved the church and gave himself up for her" (Eph. 5:25). Husbands and wives should love, cherish, and enjoy each other.

And finally, we must also enjoy our work and do it with all our might. The Teacher motivated us to work with all our might because, he wrote, "there is no work . . . in Sheol," that is, in the abode of the dead. Jesus says something similar. He says, "We must work the works of him who sent me while it is day; night is coming when no one can work" (John 9:4). Jesus has in mind the night, the darkness of death, that will soon overtake him as well as his disciples. Unless the Lord returns first, each one of us will die. Before that hour strikes, Jesus says, we must work the works God has assigned us. Paul adds, "Whatever your task, put yourselves into it, as done *for the Lord* and not for your masters, since you know that from the Lord you will receive the inheritance as your reward; you serve the Lord Christ" (Col. 3:23–24).

Because Jesus died and rose to save us from our enslavement to sin and to reconcile us to God, we can begin to live as God intended at the beginning: enjoying our food and drink, enjoying life with our spouse, and enjoying our work.

Unfortunately, we so often fritter away our days with meaningless pursuits: frustrations about all the changes we encounter, worries about losing our homes to foreclosure or losing our jobs, anger, grudges, petty arguments— you name it. We waste our days as if there were an unlimited supply. You may have heard of people who were told by their doctor that they had only a few months to live. Suddenly their outlook on life changed. They lived each day as if it could be their last. They tried to live each day to the full.

When White House secretary Tony Snow returned to work after five weeks of cancer treatment, he said, "Not everybody will survive cancer. But on the other hand, you have got to realize you've got the gift of life, so make the most of it."[5] Tony died a year later at the age of fifty-three. "You've got the gift of life, so make the most of it." Each day *could* be our last. Therefore, enjoy each day to the full. We ought to remind ourselves every morning when we wake up, "This is the day that the LORD has made; let us rejoice and be glad in it" (Ps. 118:24).

5. Quoted in *Time*, July 28, 2008.

12

Still Falling Short of One Hundred

Isaiah 65:17–25; Revelation 21:1–4

JOHN HOLBERT

We just celebrated my mother's eighty-ninth birthday by moving her into a retirement village. Don't get me wrong. This place is very nice: it has round-the-clock care, a nice well-stocked library, a bright dining room with edible food, even a big-tiled ice cream parlor where Mom can indulge one of her life's great passions. No smell of urine, little obvious despair, happy staff wherever you look. My brothers and I are very happy, too, that she is safe and cared for. I would wish such a place for all those who find they cannot quite care safely for themselves. And so would God.

Mom is astonished she has lived so long. Her own mother died at age fifty-six, although perhaps my mother might have expected a longer life, since her father died at ninety-six. Nonetheless, she cannot believe she is still alive. My father died twenty years ago, and Mom has lived alone ever since. She worked at a paying job past eighty and fiercely maintained her independence. But after two broken femurs, her pace slowed, her vast energy waned, and finally she knew she could no longer live by herself, a hard fall during a fainting spell sounding the alarm. Every time she and I are together, she talks of her funeral and her desire for me to sing a favorite hymn. I laugh, saying she will prob-ably outlive me, or if not, when she dies I will be too old to sing anything at all. We have played this little game for over fifteen years now. It is not that my mother wishes to die; it is just that she wonders what her life now means. In her ninetieth year she reads *Guideposts* magazine, various devotional books, and prays faithfully.

I, too, wonder what her long life means. I wonder whether she reads Isaiah. I do not know whether she is aware that the book is a large compendium of prophetic writings, spanning some 200–300 years, from the fierce prophet of the eighth century, slamming his people for their sins, to the hopeful speaker of the exile, calling for "comfort" for the weary Babylonian exiles, to perhaps a series of writers with many far-flung ideas about what the great God of Israel still has in mind for the people of Israel and for the world. In chapter 65, this Isaianic author announces that God's will for the world is something fresh and new. He calls this place a "new heaven and a new earth" (v. 17), imagery borrowed years later by the composer of the New Testament book of Revelation. This Isaiah describes the new earth and heaven in the following ways: no weeping or cry of distress, houses for all, vineyards for all, children born whole and always loved. This is a place where God will answer even before the people call, a place where wolf and lamb shall feed together in safety, where lions shall be vegetarians, and all serpents, all who would destroy the harmony of the place, will eat nothing but dust.

But most importantly the place will be filled with a raft of very old people: "one who dies at a hundred years will be considered a youth, and one who falls short of a hundred will be considered accursed." Indeed, "like the days of a tree shall the days of my people be." And since some olive trees in the land of Israel are perhaps over two thousand years old, that will be a very old person.

Sounds like heaven, I suppose. Sounds like the sort of place my mother speaks of finding after her death. Sounds like the place so many Christians imagine will be theirs by and by, one fine day, Beulah land for certain.

But I do not think either Isaiah or the author of Revelation imagines this place as heaven, a land beyond death. Hebrew prophets and those who read them, like John of Patmos, are not in the business of buoying up their people with happy dreams of heaven. This has assuredly been a great confusion in the uses of these texts for centuries. Prophets are rather in the business of offering the visions of God in order to urge us to move forward toward the world that God wants for us now.

Isaiah knows that in his world very few if any people live to a hundred; infant mortality is ferocious, wolves eat lambs, and lions eat whatever meat their mighty jaws can grab. And the world's serpents eat caviar, foie gras, and avoid all sorts of dust, leaving that for the poor and the destitute. This unforgettable image of a new heaven and a new earth is not pie in the sky, by and by. This is God's will for our world, and the great portrait bids us cease our hapless gazing into the clouds, only awaiting some postmortem palace. We still fall short of a hundred because we do not finally live in the world God has in mind for us.

Isaiah is not speaking literally here; poets never do. He is saying that God wants more from us, more peace, more justice, more harmony, more care for one another, at last a place where "none shall hurt or destroy on all my holy mountain," a place where hundred-year living will be the norm.

So when I see my mother safe and secure in her ninetieth year, I see more than the woman who bore me, cared for me, nurtured me. I see a presage, a prefiguring of what God wants for all of God's creatures: safety, care, meaningful and purposeful lives. My mother may live to a hundred, and that may be a great blessing. But until all have that chance, until all are safe as they age, until wolves and lambs rest together, until serpents, even the two-legged kind, cease their hurting and destroying ways, we need to keep Isaiah's vision in our hearts. As long as we still fall short of a hundred, we have a long way to go to live in the world God wants for us all.

13

Preaching

The Role of Change and How to Get There

Jᴜɴᴇ Aʟʟɪᴍᴀɴ Yᴏᴅᴇʀ

As one who regularly attends worship and as a teacher of preaching, I have heard thousands of sermons. I have heard all kinds of sermons by preachers from many different countries and cultures. In the preaching arena, nothing irritates me more than a sermon that just sits there. What is the point of a sermon that doesn't try to do anything, a sermon that is a speech about a religious topic rather than a powerful proclamation of the desire of God to make us into new people?

So often when I talk to preachers in regard to a particular sermon they will be preaching the following Sunday, they tell me, "I am going to talk *about . . .*" and then they go on to name a general theme or topic. I try to guide the conversation by asking, "What is your sermon going to do? Or what is it trying to accomplish?" I firmly believe that a sermon that is not clear about what it wants to do or accomplish will usually do nothing. It will not move the hearts and minds of the listeners.

I want us to look at some of the reasons why preachers preach sermons that lack purpose because I think it is significant to be aware of the variety of reasons and which ones I might be given to. One reason is that some preachers think that deciding what they will accomplish in preaching is God's business, not theirs. They fear they will overstep the boundary between human and divine responsibility. These preachers seem to forget that they are collaborators and partners with the Spirit of God in the preaching process.

A second reason that preaching might lack purpose is that some preachers have lost their faith that preaching accomplishes anything. How sad this is. If the people who are doing the preaching think preaching is little more than giving a talk in the worship service, as a ritual that lingers due to tradition, it

112

is not likely that such sermons will nourish and motivate the congregation. Perhaps all the jokes about dull sermons and bad preaching have convinced preachers themselves that preaching is little more than a benign pastime.

A third reason that preaching might lack clarity about what it is supposed to accomplish is that preachers do not know what they want to accomplish with this particular sermon. This differs from the second reason above in that the preacher might be quite aware of the ability of a sermon to significantly change lives, but for this particular sermon the preacher is genuinely confused about what s/he wants to accomplish. So the preacher may preach about the topic hoping something of interest and value will be said that will connect with someone in the hearing congregation. Such fuzziness frequently connects with no one. If the preacher cannot figure out what the purpose of the sermon is, chances are not very good that the listeners will be able to understand. As someone said, "If it is misty in the pulpit, it will be foggy in the pews."

A fourth reason that a preacher may not identify a specific sermon purpose or articulate exactly what s/he hopes to accomplish with the sermon is that the preacher is unable or shy to admit the desire to influence the listener. Among Mennonites, for example, the strong teaching on humility deters some preachers from embracing the task of influencing the congregation. For these preachers, often the sermon barely dribbles over the edge of the pulpit rather than pouring out in rousing proclamation.

A fifth reason why some preachers lack a focus and clarity of purpose in preaching is that, in relatively recent times, in certain portions of the church, persuasion has been understood to be synonymous with manipulation and coercion. Certain branches of the revivalist movement were given to an evangelistic practice of scaring people into the kingdom with hellfire and damnation sermons that left the new believers quaking with fear rather than with the Spirit. These preachers had a purpose for their preaching, and all who heard understood what they expected to accomplish. But their evangelistic practice left a bad taste in the mouths of some preachers of future generations. Because these revival preachers abused their positions of influence in the pulpit, some who followed are unwilling to serve as agents of change. Shying away from acting as catalysts of transformation, they became teachers who merely try to inform their congregations about the content of the Scriptures.

I was trained as an actress before I was trained as a preacher and eventually a teacher of preachers. I hope this revelation will not scare off any readers. An actor must have a purpose for every line spoken. If a male character is supposed to enter a room and say, "Hi, Anne," the actor must decide if his motive is 1) to announce his arrival in the room; 2) to register his shock at seeing Anne in the room; or 3) to build a relationship. "Hi, Anne" can do any of these things and the actor must know which is the correct way to speak this line. The same is true for preaching. First and foremost the preacher must know what s/he intends to do in order to know how to speak the message in a way that will be successful to the intention.

It is time to redeem the word *persuasion* in the arena of preaching. It is time for us to better understand the full meaning of the word, to find its rightful place on the influence spectrum, and to bring it back to its central place in preaching.

One of the key elements in classical oratory is persuasion, and I believe it is one of the chief elements of preaching as well. *Rhetoric* is defined broadly as the art of speaking well or more narrowly as the art of persuasion. The goal of rhetorical training was eloquence, but in part eloquence is achieved by balancing one's style of speaking with one's aims. The ends of rhetoric were to teach, to delight, and to persuade.

Unfortunately persuasion has come into common usage with the connotation of abusive power, but that is a limited understanding of what persuasion is all about. I have found it helpful to think of influence as an umbrella concept, and persuasion as a form of influence. Freedom of choice heightens the degree of influence, and persuasion is at the center of influence and freedom. Here the listener is free to accept or reject the presented material. I am reminded of the preaching of Rev. Billy Graham in which he would lay out the gospel message and then invite the masses to decide, to make a choice. They had maximum freedom of choice, and many chose to make a commitment to follow Jesus.

Our ideas about persuasion have become confused because we associate persuasion with hard-sell marketing. I want to outline some characteristics of persuasion that will lead to a working definition of the concept.

- Persuasion involves at least two people whose joint actions determine the outcome. Persuasion is something you do with another person, not to another person.
- Persuasion is always a conscious activity; it is intentional. We can unintentionally influence others, but we cannot unintentionally persuade them.
- For persuasion to happen, one party must perceive another party as needing to change and must help the other understand the needed change. A need can be described as inconsistent, inappropriate, or ineffective thought or behavior. The perceived need must be based on a standard that both parties agree on. The Bible and the life of Christ could be the standard to which we all aspire.

In defining persuasion as a two-party activity, involving conscious intent, that seeks to reconcile thought or behavior with an agreed-on set of standards, it seems to me that persuasion is at the very core of preaching.

Many theorists have sketched sequences that outline how they think persuasion works. Of these, the Monroe Motivated Sequence[1] embodies most of the stages identified by other theorists and is particularly useful for preaching. The sequence includes five steps.

1. *Attention.* The task of the attention phase is to create interest or desire in the mind of the listener. The speaker attempts to upset the listeners' tranquility and begin to produce a desire for something. The primary task is to capture the listeners' attention to the topic at hand.
2. *Need.* In this step (commonly called the motivation step) the speaker outlines the problem in a way designed to create a sense of need in the listeners. Somehow the speaker must help hearers see the gap between things as they are and things as they should be. This step creates tension that the listeners will want to relieve if they care deeply about the matter.
3. *Satisfaction.* In this relatively brief step the speaker presents a proposal to alleviate the inconsistency or address the need defined in the previous step. A speaker who proposes several solutions at this stage will conclude with the preferred one.
4. *Visualization.* At this stage the speaker paints a picture of the tension relieved. If one applies the proposal of step 3 to the need of step 2, this is how things will look. Listeners begin to picture the difference between what is and what could be.
5. *Action.* The persuasion sequence ends with the visualization step. Now listeners seek appropriate responses. This step calls for action or commitment or change in response to the persuasion.

These five steps are the basic elements or substructure of influence, whether the persuasion in question is auto sales or political debate or biblical preaching. Somehow one has to bring the listeners along, and this structure gives good guidance for the presentation from start to finish if one wishes to motivate change.

Change can be in the cerebral or thought or belief area of the listener, and we might thus label it a call for "head" changes. Or it can be in the area of the "heart," where we are calling for affective or feeling changes. It can also be a call for changes in the "hands and feet," where the speaker is calling for an action. I think the differences between the words *convince* and *actuate* are helpful here.

James Loder's *The Transforming Moment*[2] follows a pattern similar to that of the Monroe Motivated Sequence, but Loder attempts to describe theologically what he calls *convictional knowing.* This knowing is influential and creates change, and its impact is deep and lasting because it centers on the very

---

1. Douglas Ehninger, Bruce E. Gronbeck, and Alan H. Monroe, *Principles of Speech Communication*, 9th ed. (Glenview, IL: Scott, Foresman, & Co., 1984).
2. James E. Loder, *The Transforming Moment*, 2nd ed. (Colorado Springs, CO: Helmers & Howard, 1989).

heart of what we believe. The result of conviction is transformation, which is any change in commitment or new understanding. Preaching is an influence mode that focuses on change in commitment and new faith understanding.

These are Loder's steps for transformation. Keep Monroe's sequence in mind as you read them.

1. *Conflict.* In this step we experience a rupture in the knowing context, and the more we care about the conflict the more powerful the eventual transformation will be. The initial conflict must be adequate to activate our attention and our concern. Often the deepest learning begins in conflicted, scrambled disequilibrium. Knowing comes out of the chaos or disorder.

2. *Interlude for scanning.* In this phase we scan through the problem, trying to understand it and all its components. This step also draws us into the process of seeking out possible solutions. We search for answers outside the problem, but we also scan the problem, differentiate its terms, and play possible solutions against various interpretations of the ruptured situation. In this phase the conflicted one holds together the problem, partial solutions, and the whole state of nonresolution.

3. *Bisociation.* Here two familiar but separate ideas merge to create a new entity. Bisociation brings two notions together into a relationship that creates a new construct. The ruptured situation is transformed, and we receive a new perception. Knowing occurs, and the knower will never be the same. This is the turning point of the transforming event.

4. *Release of energy and opening of the knower to the context.* The fourth step has two facets. The first facet, the release of energy, is our involuntary response to the fact that the conflict is over. This unconscious response indicates that we have reached a resolution. Opening of the knower to the context is the second facet. It is our conscious response to being freed from the conflict. In it we become aware of the expanded relationship with the context.

5. *Interpretation.* Here the knower is called on to interpret the imaginative solution in the context. Somehow the effects of the transforming event must be assimilated into the patterns of the past and into what will happen in the future.

Monroe's and Loder's theories differ in significant ways. Monroe deals in influence while Loder explains the patterned dynamic of transformation as a creative process. Monroe tries to create change while Loder looks to another source for change. In fact, Loder sought to demonstrate how the Holy Spirit collaborates with the human spirit for the sake of redemptive transformation. Thus Loder's contribution is especially foundational for preaching.

Eugene Lowry's *Homiletical Plot: The Sermon as Narrative Art Form*[3] builds on what we have learned from Monroe and Loder. His constructive model

3. Eugene L. Lowry, *The Homiletical Plot: The Sermon as Narrative Art Form,* exp. ed. (Louisville, KY: Westminster John Knox Press, 2001).

of narrative preaching is a motivational design to precipitate transformation. The following five steps describe the homiletical plot. Keep Monroe and Loder in mind as you read them.

1. *Upsetting the equilibrium.* Here Lowry brings together getting listeners' attention and creating ambiguity. Within us lives the deep need to resolve ambiguity, so in this step the preacher plants an itch to grab hearers' attention and get them to scratch until it is satisfied.
2. *Analyzing the discrepancy.* This step incorporates analysis and diagnosis. If we are to fully appreciate the resolution, we must know the complexity of the dilemma.
3. *Clue to resolution.* Pivotal to the sequence, the clue to resolution points and suggests. The full resolution comes later. This clue prepares the way for proclamation of the Word of God. Up to this point the sermon focused on ambiguities and needs. The preacher helped dig a deeper hole and thickened life's messy plot. Now, in the murkiness, light begins to dawn.
4. *Experiencing the gospel.* In this step, listeners discover how the gospel of Jesus Christ makes right the human predicament. The energy—experienced as gospel—intersects with the human dilemma. Listeners are free to open themselves to new understanding.
5. *Anticipating the consequences.* This final step takes listeners into the future. The climax of any sermon is step 4, experiencing the gospel. Step 5 focuses on the human response as those who appropriate the sermon experience grace and freedom. Traditionally we call this step the application.

As we look back and forth among Monroe, Loder, and Lowry, we see how each one helps us to understand the next.

It is interesting to note the references to persuasion in the Bible. The Acts of the Apostles is sprinkled with references to persuasion. Both believers and not-yet-believers are being persuaded. Paul, who was trained in classical methods, comes to mind most readily. King Agrippa asks Paul, "'Are you so quickly persuading me to become a Christian?'" (Acts 26:28). And the Jews and devout converts followed Paul and Barnabas, who spoke to them and persuaded them to continue in the grace of God (Acts 14:43).

A colleague once reminded me that Alan of Lille (c. 1128–1202 CE) was an early Christian church writer who rejected the persuasion or transformation motif and spoke more pastorally of "formation" as the goal of Christian preaching. His reasoning was that persuasion indicates a sudden change of attitude, and formation implies a lifelong process. One does not jump to the top of the ladder, but rather rung by rung, slow and gradual change occurs. If we embrace the life of the Spirit, I am of the mind that it can be both ways.

However, the careful communicator needs to remember that generally the change is made in very tiny steps. Our culture of hurry and instant does not lend itself to the small changes that move us close to the life of Christ. We tend to want to fix everything in one fell swoop. Seldom does it happen that way. But whether the change is dramatic and life changing, or whether it is pastoral and life sustaining, either way there is change. Each person comes to be pastored and cared for; each person reaches out to have his or her needs assessed and met; each person begs to be taken seriously as an entity to be formed in the image of Christ.

Individuals have needs, and the congregation has needs as well. Bringing change to the congregation is more complex, but the theory is still similar. A group of people gathered for a special purpose and absorbed for a period of time in a common interest has a new character that is not in any of the individuals who compose it.

No preacher stands in front of a congregation hoping that everyone will go home exactly as he or she was before the sermon. Every minister is dedicated to bringing the life-changing love of God into the lives of those who gather for worship. If the goal of preaching is transformation, if it is change-oriented communication, then using the structures of rhetorical persuasion is both appropriate and necessary. I believe that preaching is the public-address form of ministry in which a word from God intersects with human need and out of that meeting new life comes. Praise be to God.

14

Long Enough at the Holy Mountain

A Theologically Sound Spirituality for Change

THOMAS H. TROEGER

I wonder how many times I have heard people who were facing a decision about making a major change in their lives ask, "Why would I leave this?" The word "this" can refer to a number of things. Sometimes it is a house or a neighborhood or a countryside that is so filled with cherished memories and good feelings that they cannot picture themselves living elsewhere. Sometimes "this" is a satisfying job with appreciative colleagues and a reliable income and good medical benefits. Sometimes it is a stage in a long-term relationship where each has grown accustomed to the habits and rituals of one another, but now one of them wants to start a family or go back to school or try a new career path.

There are other times when not just individuals but an entire community raises the question, "Why would we leave this?" A social service organization that has been doing good work and running efficiently begins to consider heading in a new direction and expanding its clientele. A church that has settled into a pattern of worship that everyone feels comfortable with looks into expanding its repertoire of musical styles and ways of celebrating the sacraments. A group of scientists who have been successful in developing the application of a particular theory finds themselves drawn to following an entirely different line of research.

Whether it is an individual or a couple or a group, "this" refers to something secure, reliable, and often cherished, so deeply cherished that we might well call it holy. Why would we leave this holy place, this holy stage in our life and work?

"You have stayed long enough at this mountain; turn and take your journey" (Deut. 1:6, RSV). God gives this command to Moses at Mount Horeb.

119

We might easily understand God's words if the mountain were a place of debauchery and immorality. Then God would be like a parent coming home to a teenage party that had gotten out of hand and shouting, "You have stayed long enough. Now get out!" But that is not the case. Mount Horeb is where the Torah was given. It is the holiest place that the Hebrews have reached in their journey. It is the pinnacle of revelation, the high point of divine/human encounter.

Yet God says, "You have stayed long enough at this mountain. Turn and take your journey." You have stayed long enough at the holiest place, for even the holiest place you have known cannot contain the fullness of God nor the fullness of what God intends for us. There are always new territories, new realms of knowledge, new domains of truth, new ways of being and doing for us to explore. But so very often we hesitate to move on. The house where we live is too treasured to leave. The current job is too secure to abandon. The relationship is too stable to risk change. The social service outreach is too well established to venture expanding in new directions. The worship is too comfortable to tinker with. The established theory is too productive to consider new experiments and formulations. But none of these perfectly understandable rationales for avoiding change alter God's command: "You have stayed long enough at this mountain. Turn and take your journey."

As someone who has taught in theological education for over thirty years, I have observed again and again how people often resist leaving the holy mountain to set out in new directions in response to God. The pattern often manifests itself in people who have come to theological school as a direct response to a profound experience of God. The experience can take multiple forms. Some people speak of receiving a "call." Some tell about a profound tragedy or crisis through which they encountered the sustaining presence of the divine. Some recall a community of faith that was so warm and supportive they felt the presence of the living Christ. Some relate stories of working for a cause or a community service organization through which the word of God came alive for them. Some describe being overwhelmed by the sheer grandeur and beauty of creation when they visited a particular place. And these few examples do not begin to exhaust the variety of ways that people describe their encounter with God. But what they all hold in common is a degree of intensity and conviction that positively transformed their lives so that the experience became for them a holy mountain, a place sacred and beloved in the memory of the heart.

Whenever I hear these stories, I am moved by them, and I am convinced that something of holy significance indeed happened. However, the very experience that brings people to theological school can also become a stumbling block to their education and spiritual growth. They are sometimes reluctant to leave the holy mountain behind and to continue on the journey of faith that leads through critical scholarship about the Scriptures, theology, the church's history, the abuses and distortions of religious belief. They resist the disturbing new knowledge because it seems as if it devalues the holiest place they have known. Their resistance is theological: it feels as though they are leaving God behind. This pattern, however, is not limited to theological students. I have heard scores of stories from pastors and educators and community organizers that manifest in one way or another the same story line: the holy mountain becomes the holy One, the resistance to change is justified by a theological rationale.

What attracts me to these words from Deuteronomy—"You have stayed long enough at this mountain; turn and take your journey"—is that they point the way to a theologically sound spirituality for change. Since the mountain is indeed holy, there is no need to denigrate or devalue what it means. We affirm; we celebrate; we give thanks for what we have received upon the sacred summit. We understand that change in this case does not involve leaving what is bad for what is good, what is profane for what is sacred. We have in fact been at a holy mountain.

At the same time, the words from Deuteronomy remind us that we cannot remain forever in one place no matter how holy it is: "You have stayed *long enough*." How long is long enough? Sometimes the moment of departure has not yet arrived. There is still work to be done at the holy mountain, and what seems the prompting of the Spirit is simply the impatience of our own restless souls. But other times God is calling us to leave behind the sacred mountain. How long is long enough? It is not a question that lends itself to a swift and easy answer. It requires the rigor of prayer and candid conversation and critical analysis and sometimes even recognizing that our initial response may need to be reversed.

I can attest to this from my own experience. I recall facing a major career decision and being given several weeks to discern whether or not the Spirit was calling me in new directions. At the time, I was at a holy mountain with gifted colleagues and profoundly fulfilling work. First I decided yes, I will move on; then, no, I will stay; then, yes, I will move; then, no I will stay; and so the oscillations continued until the day I had to give a final answer. No, I said. Then for two weeks, I could not sleep. I felt as though I, like Jacob, were wrestling with the angel at the Jabbok River (Gen. 32:22–32). Exhausted, I phoned to say I would come if the offer could be reextended. It was, and I went. It turned out to be the right decision, but I have never forgotten the experience. Through all of these years, it has given me a keen appreciation for other individuals and organizations when I have seen them struggling to leave the holy mountain and *turn* and take their journey.

I love that word "turn" because it suggests that our gaze may have become fixated on one spot and that we need to refocus our vision and our energies in another direction. Turn from the holy mountain; turn from the place of revelation; turn from the experience that you hold so tight in your heart and mind. But "turn" does not mean "forget." In the biblical passage God does not want the people to forget what they have received at the holy mountain. God wants them to live the Torah they have received, and part of living what they have received is turning to continue on their journey. The journey places the holy mountain in a larger frame of meaning. Rather than diminishing the significance of the holy mountain, the journey deepens our understanding of its significance and expands the ramifications of what was revealed there. By turning and journeying—changing!—we are faithful to the God who was revealed at the holy mountain and who now calls us to new realms. When this insight fills our hearts and minds, we receive energy to undertake change, not begrudgingly but with a sense of adventure and faithful curiosity about what lies ahead.

Religious leaders need a theologically sound spirituality for change because the resistance to change is often rooted in theological and spiritual convictions about the sanctity of the way things are. Dismissing these convictions as wrongheaded or backward looking is seldom an effective strategy for change. It feels to those who are resisting the change that what they hold most sacred is under attack. Deuteronomy's imagery of leaving the sacred mountain to continue on the journey provides a metaphor for reconfiguring people's holy commitments. It invites people to remember and honor the holy mountain by extending its impact on their lives into a wider world. Their changing becomes a way of living out the highest and holiest desires of their hearts that were so strongly awakened at that sacred spot.

This model will not, of course, work for every kind of change. There are times when people are not stuck at a holy mountain but are mired in the "slough of despond," as John Bunyan named that place of disparagement and degradation in the human soul. But more often than we may have acknowledged, when people resist change, they often do so because they are not ready to leave their sacred mountain. When that is the case, it is helpful to listen again to Deuteronomy's words and to work out their implications for attending to the spiritual dimensions of significant change: "You have stayed long enough at this mountain; turn and take your journey."

Since the imagery of Deuteronomy is remarkably vivid and dramatic, I now share in poetry what I have already explored in prose. Ending with a poem is a way of reminding ourselves that implementing change requires engaging the poetry of the soul as well as the reasons of the mind and the emotions of the heart. The poem is a hymn text that sings easily to common meter doubled

(CMD or 8-6-8-6) so that a congregation might sing it at a service that marks the beginning of some significant change in its life and ministry.

How many times we start again
on faith's unwinding way:
we want, O Lord, to settle in,
to build a home and stay,
but then a dream, a voice, a light
disturbs our peace and rest
and sets before our straining sight
new stages on our quest.

Before we go, we look around,
surveying where we are.
Some ask, why leave familiar ground
for somewhere strange and far?
We know from all our startings out
each journey has its cost:
that sometimes faith gives way to doubt,
and sometimes we get lost.

But greater than the cost we find
is our expanded view
of what it means with heart and mind
to trust and follow you:
we hear a music never heard,
a different light descends,
and meeting strangers we are stirred
to welcome them as friends.

With eager hope we now depart
the places that we know
to travel regions in your heart
where you would have us go.
In you we live and move and dwell.
As close as breath and prayer,
you are our home: Emmanuel,
God-with-us everywhere.[1]

---

1. Thomas H. Troeger, *God, You Made All Things for Singing: Hymn Texts, Anthems, and Poems for a New Millennium* (New York: Oxford University Press, 2009), 20.

15

In Life . . . In Death

Funeral Sermons

Thomas Long

INTRODUCTION

"A good funeral," says poet and Michigan undertaker Thomas Lynch, "gets the dead where they need to go and the living where they need to be."[1] Indeed, when viewed historically, the Christian funeral was never intended to be what it has often become: a time of quiet meditation and introspection in which mourners are prompted to ponder the meaning of life, to reflect on the depths of grief, and to purify memories of the deceased. Christian funerals are, instead, events of transition and action. They are what the church does and says while on the move, picking up its feet and carrying the body of the deceased from the place of death to the place of farewell.

Funerals, Christian and otherwise, are built on a basic human need. Every society has recognized that corpses must not be left among the living, so whenever someone dies, the body must be moved, and fairly quickly, from *here*, the place of death, to *there*, the place of disposition—whether that be earth, fire, or water. But few societies have viewed this task of moving dead bodies from here to there as a bare necessity. Most have attempted, through ritual and religious expression, to interpret this movement, to name "here" and "there" in symbolic terms, and to allow the movement between here and there to be not just a processional but an act of worship that *pro*cesses the participants' beliefs about life and death.

1. Thomas Lynch in *The Undertaking*, PBS Frontline (http://www.pbs.org/wgbh/pages/frontline/undertaking/).

Early Christians gradually developed funeral rites that embodied the gospel affirmations about resurrection hope. When a Christian died, the body was washed and anointed and then adorned in the garments of baptism. In broad daylight, the family and others from the Christian community carried the body of the deceased to the place of burial, singing psalms and hymns as they went. At the grave, sometimes in the midst of a celebration of the Lord's Supper, the deceased was returned to God with thanksgiving for the life God had granted. Underlying this arc of action was a primary metaphor: the deceased is a saint traveling on a baptismal journey through life and toward God, with mourners walking with them on the last mile of the way, singing as they go. There was plenty of space for tears, but weeping was done as the mourners marched toward hope.

In other words, what we often think of as an afterthought, transporting the body of the deceased to the place of disposition, wasn't what early Christians did after the funeral. It *was* the funeral, and the whole ritual movement was seen as an enactment of the meaning of baptism, Christian life, death, and resurrection. Eventually funerals moved inside churches, but at first the church building was a way station, a place where the funeral procession paused for prayer in the midst of its journey to the place of farewell. Lately, however, we have come to think of what happens in the church (or funeral-home chapel) as the whole funeral. What was once a journey becomes a static experience. The image of the body of Christ carrying the body of the beloved to the place of departure fades, and the processional becomes optional, as does the presence of the body of the deceased. We would hardly perform a wedding without the bride and groom—what happens to the wedding couple *is* the wedding—but the fact that we are the first generation in history for whom the bodies of the dead are optional at their own funerals is a strong indication that funerals are no longer about the dead—not the real dead anyway—but about us, our grief and our memories.

Funerals are "for the living," we say, meaning "not for the dead" and mindless of the fact that we are the first people in the history of the world to think this way. Performing a funeral without the presence of the deceased is like performing a baptism at home, or behind a tree, or somewhere else out of sight, with everyone—except of course the one baptized—gathering at the church for a service in which we are urged to remember and think about what has happened. The metaphor of the funeral as the carrying of a brother or sister in Christ to the place of farewell with songs of lament and thanksgiving threatens to give way to a new metaphor: it is not the dead who are traveling anywhere but only the living, moving from sorrow to stability. The result is that funerals have become thinned-out ceremonies of light storytelling and self-reflection, rituals that have nowhere to go—much to the loss of powerful gospel meanings about death and life.[2]

FUNERAL PURPOSES, FUNERAL SERMONS

A reform of Christian funeral practices is called for—a recovery in our time and culture of the power of the baptismal metaphor underlying our rituals of death. A reform of the Christian funeral will, of course, involve a refocusing of the funeral homily or sermon. Elsewhere I have identified and elaborated eight purposes of a good funeral,[3] and while no single funeral sermon will express all of these, every funeral should embody one or more of them. Briefly, these purposes are as follows:

1. *Kerygmatic*—The gospel should be proclaimed at a funeral, not in the abstract but as refracted through the life of the person who died and our circumstances in light of this death. At a funeral, the promise that Christians are traveling toward the resurrection hope, toward the communion of the saints, is often the most salient aspect of the kerygma to emphasize.

2. *Oblational*—A good funeral affords an opportunity for people to offer to God what they have brought to worship. At a funeral, we primarily offer back to God the one who has died, but we also offer memories, emotions, and ourselves.

3. *Ecclesial*—Funerals involve actions of the whole church, not just private moments of grief. The church washes people at baptism and clothes them in the garments of baptism, and now washes the person in death and clothes them once again in the pall of baptism. Church members have walked alongside the believer, bearing one another's burdens all along the path of the Christian life, and now they walk the last mile of the way, bearing the burden and singing as they go. At a funeral, the church walks, sings, carries, and prays.

4. *Therapeutic*—A good funeral does help heal the broken hearts of the mourners, but it does so most powerfully by placing the fragmentation and disintegration of death into the context of the gospel story. Grief hungers not just for compassion but also for restored meaning.

5. *Eucharistic*—A good funeral sometimes involves a celebration of the Eucharist, but it always involves thanksgiving for the life of the deceased as the gift of God's own image, even when that life was exceptionally conflicted and difficult.

---

2. See a more complete discussion of the history and meaning of the Christian funeral in Thomas G. Long, *Accompany Them with Singing—The Christian Funeral* (Louisville, KY: Westminster John Knox, 2009).

3. Ibid., 137–39.

6. *Commemorative*—While warnings issued here and there in church history about the dangers of eulogizing the dead are sometimes well taken, the fact remains that a real person has died, a person who lived and loved, strayed and repented, in embodied ways in a particular time and place. A good funeral remembers this person and gives thanks to God for this real life.

7. *Missional*—As is true of all services of worship, a Christian funeral is a gathering of faithful people who are sent by God on mission for the sake of the world. While the circumstances of death and loss may seem to pull us away from service to the world, they must not be allowed to overwhelm our call to be Christ's people in the world.

8. *Educational*—The process of a funeral educates both the Christian community and those who have come as guests into the house of God. For the Christian community, the funeral is a ritual reenactment of the promises of baptism, a reminder of the hopeful shape of the Christian life. For those who have come to the funeral as outsiders to the Christian faith, the funeral can embody "hospitality to the stranger" and a welcome into a place where death is ultimately not feared.

A good funeral contains all of these purposes; a good funeral sermon, some of them. The funeral sermon is an obvious place in the ritual to proclaim the kerygma, to assure the hearers that the deceased is on a journey toward the God of resurrection hope, but the sermon is not the only kerygmatic opportunity in a funeral, and announcing the kerygma is not the only purpose that the sermon can accomplish. A helpful exercise for the funeral preacher is to review this list in the light of a particular occasion of death, asking which of the purposes it would be most helpful for the sermon to lift up.

For example, some years ago the Rev. Joanna Adams prepared a sermon for a funeral held for two members of her congregation—a thirty-one-year-old man who suffered from deep mental illness and was refusing to take his medication and his sixty-five-year-old father who, convinced that his son was now dangerous to others, shot and killed his son and then took his own life. Adams knew that the trauma of this terrible set of circumstances raised at least two aching theological questions: Why did this happen? Can God still be trusted? In her sermon, which is a moving example of excellent funeral preaching, she wisely chose to emphasize the kerygmatic purpose.

She first addressed the question of why, recognizing the urgency of the question but wisely refusing the temptation to craft an explanation:

> Because we are human, we want to know why; because we are only human, we cannot know why. The Scripture promises that someday we will know why, but that day is not today. God knows that what we need today is not an explanation; what we need today is faith.[4]

4. Joanna Adams, "The Only Question," in Thomas G. Long and Cornelius Plantinga Jr., eds., *A Chorus of Witnesses* (Grand Rapids: Wm. B. Eerdmans Publishing Co., 1994), 268.

She then turns to the question of the trustworthiness of God, telling the hearers,

> [We] are not dealing today with a God who comes around only when things are rosy and the birds are singing. There is a cross up there! . . . The God we know in Jesus Christ gets to the valley of death, of loss and grief, before we do, so that he can get ready to catch us when we fall blindly in.[5]

She closes the sermon by telling of visiting the grieving family and meeting Lauren, the three-year-old niece and granddaughter of the deceased son and father. She was sitting on her grandmother's knee and wearing a bib with a duck on it and a smile. "Tell Joanna what you say before you have your supper," her grandmother prompted.

> "God is great," Lauren said. "God is good," she said, and suddenly I could not wait to come to church today, so that I could tell you what Lauren said and what the Scripture promises and what faith knows even when the pain is piercing and the shadows fall. God is still great. God is still good. It is true![6]

A FUNERAL SERMON EXAMPLE

What follows is the full text of another difficult funeral sermon, this one for William _____, a forty-two-year-old man who died of a gunshot wound in an illegal drug deal that went awry. William, a small business owner, was married to Brenda, and they had two teenage children. William, Brenda, and the children were respected in the community, all active in the church, and William sang in the choir. When William was killed, everyone, including his wife, was stunned by the details. William, unbeknownst to family and coworkers, had developed a recent cocaine habit and was murdered trying to make a drug purchase on a seedy street corner. The local television station seized on this event and made it the signature story in an exposé series on drugs in the business world. William's picture and the details of his "secret life" and his violent death were evening news fodder for nearly a week, much to the humiliation of his family. The funeral was held at the church:

---

5. Ibid., 269.
6. Ibid., 270.

A Funeral Homily on the Occasion
of the Death of William _____

Psalm 139:1–18

We have come here today with many emotions—grief, perplexity, anger perhaps, maybe even a measure of embarrassment. Adding to our sense of loss and our shock over William's sudden and tragic death is the burden of watching as the newspapers and the television have offered up for public view every detail of his life and his sad death.

But we have not come here as those who view William as an outsider or as those who wish to join in the rumors whispered in our community. We come here as those who belong to God and who therefore consider William, no matter how troubled he was, as a brother in Christ. We come also as those who, every week in worship, confess to God that "we have erred, and strayed from thy ways like lost sheep." When another person's failings have become known to the world, we know that what we see in this person is but a visible reminder that we are all sinners.

In Psalm 139, we hear the testimony of the psalmist, who confesses that God has searched the lives of all of us and knows the thoughts of our hearts: "O Lord, you have searched me and known me. You know when I sit down and when I rise up; you discern my thoughts from far away." God knows all of us, knows all of the secrets of our hearts, knew William and knows William still.

Because we are human beings, we are often terrified to be fully known. In the company of friends and family, we can pretend to be who we are not, but it can be a discomforting thought to be in the presence of a God who knows all of our secrets. No wonder the psalmist tried to flee from God's presence, tried to hide in a place where his life was not exposed. But he could not escape God's presence:

> Where can I go from your spirit?
>   Or where can I flee from your presence?
> If I ascend to heaven, you are there;
>   if I make my bed in [hell], you are there.
> If I take the wings of the morning
>   and settle at the farthest limits of the sea,
> even there your hand shall lead me,
>   and your right hand shall hold me fast.

The reason God knows us so deeply—that God knows William so deeply—is not because God is some cosmic detective trying to get evidence to condemn us. No, the reason God knows us so well is because God made us. God formed us in the womb, lovingly fashioning us as God's very own children.

> For it was you who formed my inward parts;
>   you knit me together in my mother's womb.
> I praise you, for I am fearfully and wonderfully made.
>   Wonderful are your works; that I know very well.
> My frame was not hidden from you,
>   when I was being made in secret,
>   intricately woven in the depths of the earth.
> Your eyes beheld my unformed substance.

In fact, the psalmist imagines God as a loving parent, even keeping, as many parents do, a journal of all the things that God's children do, a scrap-book made by God before we were even born of all of our days, God's scrapbook of William's days:

> In your book were written
>   all the days that were formed for me,
>   when none of them as yet existed.

Not every page in God's scrapbook is a happy one. There are in every life times of darkness and rebellion. But God is there even in the darkness. As the psalmist says:

> If I say, "Surely the darkness shall cover me,
>   and the light around me become night,"
> even the darkness is not dark to you;
>   the night is as bright as the day,
>   for darkness is as light to you.

Even the darkness is as light to God. We cling today to that promise. *Even the darkness is as light to God.* There is no human darkness that cannot be illumined by the saving power of God, no place so broken that God cannot heal us. We cling to this promise. *Even the darkness is as light to God.*

In the days to come, our minds will raise many questions, some of them unanswerable. Why did William do what he did? How could he have lost his way so much? Did we miss opportunities to make a difference for him? Many questions. But today we cast ourselves and our memories on the mercy of a loving God who knows us deeply and well, the God who is our maker, too, who tenderly formed us, too, in our mother's wombs and who, as our loving parent, proudly keeps a journal of our days.

And we are bold to give William back into the hands of this God who can be trusted. Even when we do not understand everything, we give William to the God who has searched us and knows us and who understands all. Even when forgiveness may be difficult, we give William to God, whose mercy never ends. Even when the days ahead will be difficult, we give William to the God for whom the darkness is as light, and who creates resurrection hope in the midst of hopelessness.

Receive, O God, William. You formed him in the womb and knew the secrets of his heart. He was your child, and he was our friend, husband, and father. His life, as troubled and complicated as it was, was nevertheless a gift from you, and we give him back to you in confidence that you will receive him in your redeeming love and grace. "I come to the end," says the psalmist. "I am still with you."

In the case of this sermon, the preacher picked up on two key purposes of the funeral. First, there is the proclamation of the kerygma. The good news of a God who forms us all in the womb, who cares for us as a parent, who knows and forgives our sins, is emphasized. But the preacher also takes up the purpose of oblation. In a sense, the sermon "takes up the collection" of all of the angry, puzzled, guilty, saddened, and broken thoughts and feelings brought to this occasion, and also gathers up the person of William and offers all of this to the God whose mercy can be trusted. In the last paragraph, the preacher figuratively stands in the pews with the family and other mourners and, with songs of thanksgiving sung in a minor key, offers William's life back to God. The whole sermon, we note, is based on the conviction that the funeral is not simply a gathering of people to do grief work, but a community of faith traveling with a troubled saint on the last mile of the way. William is not just going to the cemetery or the crematorium; William is journeying to God.

Obviously, if the circumstances had been different, a different sermon would have been called for. When a person has died in loneliness, for example, it is good to invoke and evoke the ecclesial presence. When a person was a saint like the biblical Dorcas, "devoted to good works and acts of charity" (Acts 9:36), the preacher does not pretend that this person was not a sinner too, but the sermon can be deeply eucharistic, giving thanks for what we have seen of God's goodness in this life. Relating the essential purposes of the funeral to the circumstances of the death guides the preacher toward a sermon that will indeed help "get the dead where they need to go and the living where they need to be."

PART THREE

The Congregation in Crisis

This third part of this book's collection of essays and sermons focuses, as the title implies, on "congregations in crisis." Yet the title slightly misleads because in reality this section concentrates on methods that a pastor as leader and preacher can draw on to help congregations in the midst of the radical changes they face as a community of faith. Because many congregations have "built-in crises," this chapter helps leaders traverse circumstances such as pastoral changes, neighborhoods in transition, new economic realities, and similar issues.

The first essay in the section is painful to read because the crisis that Frank Thomas writes about is one in which he is at the very center. The text for what appears to be an autobiographical sermon (and therefore dovetails agreeably with Ron Allen's essay "The Minister's Story") comes from Numbers 14 and focuses on the eighth verse: "If the LORD is pleased with us, he will bring us into this land and give it to us, a land that flows with milk and honey." The first part of the sermon addresses the specter of a lost reputation—and no preacher can miss the implications of that crisis/trauma/disaster. As Aristotle wrote so long ago about the three persuasive appeals for public speaking (ethos, pathos, and logos) and as Augustine adapted via Cicero for Christian preachers, the credibility (or character) of the speaker is paramount. When the possibility arises that the preacher has lost "authoritative trustworthiness" in the household of faith, then that preacher is finished.

Thomas explores his own crisis of leadership and does so through the sermon. What he finally suggests is something of a new call to ministry as he relates to Moses' crisis of leadership as narrated in the book of Numbers. One of the important features of Thomas's work here is the pertinent fact of the importance of pastor self-care, because when the pastor is in crisis, then the whole congregation is in crisis.

The first two essays of this section are as different from each other as they can be. David J. Schlafer's essay "Paying Attention to Transitions" (written with Starsky Wilson) cleverly employs the idea of change and transition as part of a methodology of preaching. He knows that many of the sermon's listeners are perpetually anxious. Thus Schlafer demonstrates how preachers can use subtle sermonic transitions to help parishioners engage their own moments of transition. Wilson, an African American pastor in St. Louis, properly lays bare the homiletic points of Schlafer's essay in his sermon titled "Nazareth and the New Neighborhood." Wilson provides a snapshot of how sermon transitions can throw light on transitions within the community and the church. This preacher uses Schlafer's suggestions to take his congregation from Nazareth to north St. Louis and back again.

Ronald J. Allen's essay "The Minister's Story" discusses a topic that practically every preacher tackles at one time or another: how much can or even should preachers use their personal stories in proclaiming the gospel. Allen writes a quite thoughtful and well-documented essay, complete with substantial research from a Lilly Endowment study called "Listening to Listeners" also sponsored by Allen's seminary. Although Allen urges a certain caution, he also suggests that because preachers are unique leaders in congregations that they should use their stories, but in circumspect and strategic ways. Although many mainstream homileticians do not have one mind on this subject, Allen reasons that the personal experiences of preachers expedite and ease transitions for parishioners.

Carol Norén's sermon "Look Up; Draw Near; Reach Out" reminds thoughtful pastors that often in times of transition what creates anxiety is not so much what might change but what we may give up. This brings to the surface that much transitional ministry is in some respects important grief work. The best pastors/leaders remember that what they often do is tend loss.

Using an Ascension Day text from Acts 1 (as does John McClure below), Norén urges the pastor to invite the congregation to take part in the change. In some cases of change a pastor might treat a congregation as a spectator and leave listeners feeling like casualties of an ecclesial process. Her sermon engenders a sense of congregational unity as she moves "us" through the experience of saying good-bye to a pastor as we prepare to say hello to another.

Robert Stephen Reid's essay "Responding to Resistance during a Change Process" addresses the pastor as a leader in the process of change. The essay begins with a recognizable scenario of a pastor who leads a congregation through a difficult transition—in this case moving a congregation's physical location. As the moment of decision approaches, "the wheels come off" the pastor's good leadership methods. As an answer to this authentic church-life situation, Reid uses the story's circumstance to disclose some key insights between managing a complex situation while leading people as they cope with change. Reid also explores some implications of the differences between transactional leaders and transformational leaders. The seven "levers" for leadership that Reid provides may help pastors as leaders investigate distinctively effective leadership processes that they can bring into play. This essay is a rich journey through territory that every leader, whether of a large or small congregation, will benefit from surveying. Near the conclusion, Reid also offers some biblical models (Moses, Jesus, and Paul) to demonstrate to pastors how biblically principled these directional practices can be.

Although not original to him, in his essay "Preaching as a New Pastor in Times of Congregational Crisis" John S. McClure exposes a helpful distinction in terms of congregational transitions between what might be termed a "crisis" and a "trauma." The first is more or less expected while the latter usually leaves the congregation feeling out of control. An example of a crisis would be a change in pastoral leadership that although anxiety ridden is commonly expected in the life of a church. On the other hand, a trauma would entail something like an automobile accident that claimed a church leader as a casualty. As his exemplar, McClure uses a case of a pastoral change as crisis compounded by the trauma of a burning church building as the new pastor and family were arriving to the new assignment.

McClure clearly understands preaching and offers helpful insights in a process that could be emotionally fearsome for a preacher. He addresses issues of being a nonanxious presence and proposes several resources by which preachers can wrestle with issues of crisis and trauma. He also retrieves Paul Tillich's idea of "the courage to be" and counsels that regularly decisions navigate leaders toward danger. Indeed too often leaders goaded by anxious followers can make decisions too hastily. McClure's sermon on the ascension demonstrates many of his essay's guiding points by reminding us that like in Jesus' day we live in "in-between" times.

16

If the Lord Is Pleased

Numbers 14:8

Frank Thomas

> If the Lord is pleased with us, the Lord will lead us into a land
> flowing with milk and honey.
>   (Num. 14:8, paraphrase of NIV and NRSV)

On a typical fall, southern Memphis, Monday afternoon, I received a phone call that a group of members had filed a lawsuit against the church leadership and against me. It had been threatened, several times, but not in my wildest dreams did I think that it would become a reality. I immediately went into shock, and was even more dismayed when I found it and myself on the cover of the newspaper the next morning. There is a ministerial e-mail group in the city, where one person takes the responsibility to e-mail any religious news that is in the paper to every preacher on the list. By the next morning, every preacher in the city would have it, and it would not stop there because e-mail would take it all over the country. My phone, as the kids say, started "blowing up." Folks from everywhere began to call the church, my house, and my cell phone. At that point I was no longer embarrassed; I was in shock. People were kind; they were very kind.

Several days later the embarrassment hit. I was supposed to be a skilled pastor. This kind of stuff happens to people when they start out in ministry but not to someone who has eighteen years experience—and successful experience at that. I remember my first preaching opportunity, one week after the lawsuit. I turned the corner coming to the church, and it advertised my name on the side of the building—I broke into tears because I was embarrassed and ashamed. I was in the pastor's study, and I thought that no one would come that night. I thought no one would come to hear me preach. When I stepped out and the place was full, I was appreciative that they would come. I was dealing with all of the rumors and grapevines. You begin to hallucinate and you think that everyone knows—even when people do not know or do not care or do not believe what they hear, the enemy convinces you that everyone knows and everyone believes it.

We all live in fear of image—not everyone here has children, but some of us are afraid that our daughters will become pregnant, our sons will get hooked on drugs, our brothers will drown themselves in alcohol, and our sisters will show up on crack or crystal meth. We do not tell anyone that our uncle is in prison. We are afraid to tell people the truth about the realities that suggest our families or our ministries are not perfect. We are afraid to be honest about the conflict in our churches—the fact that it is there, that it is escalating, and that we do not know what to do. We are afraid other preachers are going to find out, and we're afraid of what they are going to say. We are afraid our brothers and sisters in the body of believers are going to find out. We keep up a desperate facade.

I told this story once—church gets real, you know. There are moments where we move past the ritual and really believe what the Bible says. A young man comes out of the choir stand and asks the pastor if he can have a word. The pastor gives over to the young man, who says that he has been a part of the youth choir, but he was experimenting with drugs. He needed to come clean and tell the church that he had a problem. He knew it was not right, but he could not stop. He did not want to embarrass anybody, but such was the presence of God that he could not keep up the facade any longer. He believed that this confession was the beginning of the healing process for him.

When he gets home, the parents jump on him for embarrassing and publicly humiliating the family. How dare he put that kind of stuff in front of church people? The parents are concerned with their image and how what their son said makes them look; they look like bad parents. They tell him how church people are and how they talk and that he is not ever to embarrass them. They are more concerned with their image than helping their child, and guess what? The kid goes back to drugs. If your image is more important than your child, then the child will get worse because the child is not the problem—the family image is.

Now, I agree the kid should tell his parents first, but sometimes we mouth all these platitudes. "It takes a village to raise a kid," and the kid believes it; but are we a village? The parents are at fault, but so often the church is too, because aren't the parents right? The church and fellow pastors can be petty, small, pretentious, and we will pass someone else's struggle as gossip—and God is not pleased. What if we worried less about our image and were more concerned whether God was pleased? *God help us to be delivered from the opinion of people.*

Maybe we do not know the deepest meaning of this text: "If the Lord is pleased with us, the Lord will lead us into a land flowing with milk and honey."

I know some of what these parents feel. I did not know it, but I was a deep people pleaser. It was very important to me what people thought about me. All of these things go back to episodes in our childhood, especially at the impressionable ages of eight or nine. I was spending some time with my grandmother and several of my cousins in Gulfport, Mississippi. We were living in Chicago, and as my eighth-grade graduation gift, they sent me south. My uncle in Chicago died when I was there, and we rented a station wagon to drive north for the funeral. In the back of that vehicle, my cousins were acting the fool. All of us could not get in the back, so they put me in the second row of seats between my grandmother and my aunt. The seat in the back was facing out the back window. The three of them were back there acting a fool—making faces at cars; being loud and stupid. Every time the adults would make them quiet down, they would act the fool again. I could not cut up because I was between two adults, so I was the perfect eighth grader. I wanted to cut up, but we had drawn straws and I lost, so that is how I got in the seat with the adults. My grandmother said it—and it stuck—"Why can't you be good like little Frank here—he is such a good kid, a perfect kid." And when she said that I felt so good. I translated the message that if you are good, then people will like you. So I did the good thing, you all. I did not drink, do drugs, two-time, or have sex. The father of my high school prom date begged me to marry his daughter. I was in church; I was clean, an athlete, a gentleman: I said "Please," "May I," and "Thank you." But secretly it created the need to be liked.

I was like that in college. I went into ministry; it was such a natural fit. But this need to be liked was still there. I became a pastor; the ministry started to grow. We bought land, then twenty-five acres of land. We built one building and then another. It was happening. I got a doctor of ministry degree, then another doctor of ministry degree. I got books and people, and the church was exploding, and we were having three services.

Let me make a whole long story short: I needed what happened to me. I needed to be sued. I needed to have my face plastered on the front of the newspapers. I needed to be an item on the television at 5 p.m., 6 p.m., and 10 p.m. on three stations. I needed the pain, the hurt, the disappointment, the doubt; I needed it to learn that the most important thing in life is *if the Lord is pleased*. I needed it because God delivered me from the opinion of people. If the Lord is pleased with us, the Lord will lead us into that land, a land flowing with milk and honey.

I want to look at the text found in Numbers 14. The people are out in the wilderness, and Moses and Aaron had sent the twelve spies out to the promised land. At the "church meeting," the exploratory committee submitted a majority and minority report. The majority report said that the people in the land were like giants whereas the Israelites were like grasshoppers. They said that we cannot go up and possess the land. The minority report by Joshua and Caleb said, "The Lord our God is able," and we should go up and possess the land. The people believed the majority report.

The people raised their voices in Numbers 14:1–4, wept aloud, and grumbled against Moses and Aaron. They said, "We should have died in Egypt rather than out here in this barren land." They threatened to choose a new leader. Moses and Aaron fall facedown in front of the whole people. Joshua and Caleb tore their clothes. Moses and Aaron pleaded with the people not to rebel against God. *If the Lord is pleased with us.* Just do not rebel and do not be afraid of the people in that land—if the Lord is pleased with us. We do not have to worry about anything if the Lord is pleased with us. It is not our money, intelligence, management skills—it is if the Lord is pleased with us.

What is the response of the people? They wanted to stone them. You are pleading with them to obey God, and they want to stone you. Deaf to mercy and blind to truth, they start screaming, "Stone them!" And as they were screaming, God got involved. I tell pastors, I do not care what happens, if God is pleased, they are not going to get you. They will howl, and they will threaten, and they will yell and scream, but if God is pleased, then God will show up. In the middle of the people's rage, God arises. The text relays a theophany in the midst of the rage of the people. That's a shout right there. God will show up. The people are raging and coming up with vain imaginations, but the glory of the Lord shows up at the Tent of Meeting. God interrupts their plans and calls for a meeting with Moses.

God speaks to Moses, and God is angry. God says, "How long will these people treat me with contempt? How long will they refuse to believe in me, in spite of all the miraculous signs I have performed on their behalf? You know, Moses, what I am going to do is destroy them and start all over with you. I will make you a great nation." What a chance at power, privilege, status, and position. I will make you a great nation. I will make you like Adam—the first of many born with power, privilege, status, and position. But Moses chose service.

If Moses had chosen power, privilege, status, and position, then he would have told God, "That sounds like a good plan. I am in on that. Just do not strike my wife, my kids, and a few of my family. And, oh yeah, Aaron, Joshua, and Caleb's family and the rest of them you can get."

Moses then pleads with God the way that he pleaded with the people. Here he is pleading for them, and they just wanted to stone him. Here he is begging

God for their lives when they have whined and complained and despised him and his leadership. He says, "The Egyptians will hear about it. They will get the report that you destroyed them. They know that you brought them out. They know that you go before them in a cloud by day and a pillar of fire by night. If you kill them, they will say that you were not able to do what you said and so you slaughtered them in the desert. What's more, God, you are slow to anger, abounding in love and forgiving sin and rebellion. Yet you do not leave the guilty unpunished and you punish to the third and fourth generation. In accordance with your great love, forgive the sin of these people." And because God is pleased with Moses, God relents. God forgives them; but even though God forgives, God does not release them from judgment. Not one of them will make it to the promised land.

But I am impressed with Pastor Moses. He loves God and the people; Moses pleads for both even when the people have wanted to kill him. How does Moses plead for them when they have just wanted to stone him? You cannot help anybody if you are not delivered from the opinion of people. If you are still trying to please them—after all you did for them—brought them out of a shack and built a virtual cathedral, and they're still talking about stoning you. You have your own blood on the walls of the sanctuary from what it has taken to move the ministry forward, and they do not even want you to put your son or daughter on staff without a fight. If you are into people pleasing, you will become angry. If you are into people pleasing, when they rise up to stone you, it will hurt so deep that you will hurt them. God will come up with a plan to destroy them, and you will not plead their case before God. You will take it personally, and the people will not have a shepherd. And in your pain, God will say, "I am going to destroy them," and you will have a list of the ones you want to keep, and the rest can go to hell. And then our friends will hear that we are having trouble, and to protect our image, we will reach out in unspiritual ways to crush the opposition—unspiritual management of conflict in order to protect an image. There is only one image to have: *if the Lord is pleased with us.*

In the midst of this, I had to call for help. Many churches are in trouble, but because of image, they do not ask for help. Half the battle is admitting that you need help. We admitted that we were sick, picked up the phone, and called Peacemaker Ministries, and they taught principles of peacemaking to the church and to me. And slowly, meticulously, as they taught and we practiced, I got past the image completely and now offer these lessons to any pastor or church in my hearing. If you are going to please God, you must get past the image—the opinion of people. I got through it with Peacemaker and God. and this is what I did:

1. *I remembered Jesus.* He despised the shame. God got a hold of me in Hebrews 12:2: "Looking unto Jesus the author and finisher of our faith; who for the joy that was set before him endured the cross, despising the shame . . ." He endured the cross. He had a choice; I have a choice. He endured the cross and despised the shame. The cross is embarrassing; it is a place for criminals. The cross was shameful—a public spectacle he despised. It is embarrassing, but he was not embarrassed by the embarrassment. God was pleased with Jesus. So I stopped being embarrassed. I despised the shame.

2. *I knew I had not done anything wrong.* If I had, I would have told the people and accepted the consequences; they would not have had to drag me to court to find out. If you have done what they have accused you of, come clean. I heard an old preacher at an ordination say, "Son, whatever you do, do not drag the gospel through the mud." I have personal integrity and accountability that is higher than both my friends' and enemies' estimation. God has to be pleased.

3. *You cannot take it personally.* It has nothing to do with you personally as a leader. You cannot keep this kind of stuff from happening in some of these places; the church has to die to live again. Do not eat other people's emotional garbage. God is pleased with the one who does not take the attacks personally but who pleads with God for the people and pleads with the people for God.

4. *There are no victims; there are only volunteers.* Many people counseled me to stay. One such person called me up and asked me, "Why would you leave people who love you to go to a land you know not of and where the people do not know Joseph?" I was not a victim; I volunteered for it. I am not a victim of my circumstances; I volunteered for it. God is pleased when we take personal responsibility and do not blame. I am not a victim; I volunteered for this assignment.

5. *Vindication takes time.* People can tear down in five minutes what it takes years to build. We like to see people fall in our culture and hear people make accusations; they can throw mud that takes years to clean off. I had to learn to wait and depend on God. God will vindicate, but it takes time, and you just have to wait. You can be so deep in some of this stuff that you cannot vindicate yourself. God is pleased when we can wait and trust God to vindicate.

6. *Do not fight battles with unspiritual weapons.* We do not fight with weapons that are carnal; they have no power to pull down strongholds. Our weapon is truth—and unarmed truth. God has to be pleased with my battle plan. Peacemaking is God's battle plan.

7. And finally, I am still learning to be honest about the fact that *I needed it.* I needed for it to happen. I was in counseling and the therapist asked me, "What lessons have you been avoiding that it took this kind of major calamity to reveal?" It took all this for me to learn that you cannot please people. It took all this for me to learn that what is important is "if God is pleased." I am not proud to tell you all this; I am not posturing myself as some hero. I am just a person who grew up in a family that has issues and problems that they could not handle, and I learned some things that

were not true, and I lived them for a long time, but God helped me and delivered me. God delivered me from the opinion of people.

I simply want to tell you that you cannot help your congregation if you have a need to please them. They will need you to plead with God for them and to plead with them for God. When God is pleased, God stays stuff like "This is my beloved son in whom I am well pleased." When God is pleased, God says stuff like "Well done, good and faithful servant." What better words could we want to hear than that God is pleased.

17

Paying Attention to Transitions

Passage Points and Preaching Strategies

DAVID J. SCHLAFER (WITH STARSKY WILSON)

Everyone knows transitions can be troublesome—in pastoring, in preaching, and in life. Healthy churches take serious hits if they don't negotiate significant changes successfully. Sermons well researched, well constructed, even well prayed over have minimal, even adverse, impact if their preachers can't handle sermon transitions well. And as for life—well—highly unusual are individuals and communities undergoing experiential sea changes that remain *un*-troubled at some stage or other by sea sickness of one sort or another. Since the whole of life is a series of unremitting changes, one might think we would learn to manage transitions better; yet troublesome they remain. What can we learn about preaching by reflecting on life transitions? What can we learn about life transitions by reflecting on preaching transitions? How can preachers effectively employ transitions in sermons to pastor people so that they are able to move with grace through significant transitions in their individual, communal, and cultural lives?

While predictable "stage-of-life" transitions can be accompanied by a sense of adventure (mixed with anxiety though they be), the instinctive default mode for most of us in the face of unexpected and unwelcome transitions (apart from denial or avoidance) is "coping" as best we can—hoping to God we get on the other side of the crisis as quickly as we can. The *Merriam-Webster Dictionary*, in fact, cites as the primary definition of *crisis* "a paroxysmal attack of pain, distress, or disordered function." The definition is revealing; its clear implication is that a "crisis" is something to be "managed," even palliated ("whatever it takes to stop the pain!"). How is this accomplished (apart from drugs)? What kind of resources do we offer one another in the midst of a crisis thus defined? We offer these, at the very least:

- Instruction for education on the nature of the transition
- Encouragement for endurance in the midst of the transition
- Empathy for reassurance in the stress of the transition
- Examples for emulation in the course of the transition

When we struggle with a major transition, we count ourselves fortunate if a wise counselor offers these (especially in combination). If our task is to offer such counsel, we consider our role successfully discharged if we provide such coping mechanisms (and we are often profoundly thanked for doing so). When preachers preach for "people in transition," they often take those objectives with them directly into the pulpit, attempting to do the following in one way or another:

- To explain and analyze the circumstances, conditions, challenges, and feelings associated with the transition
- To hearten or exhort those immersed in the transition toward faithful perseverance infused with hopeful expectation
- To calm and comfort those who experience the loss and anxiety in the throes of the transition
- To inspire and motivate those who may be temporarily immobilized by the transition with images and anecdotes of ideal role models who somehow managed to "make it through"

Those who receive such preaching counsel are often grateful for it, at least in the moment, and may well be assisted by it. Indeed, it is hard to imagine fruitful "transition preaching" that is completely devoid of any or all of these. Preachers, either self-assessing their performance or collecting "Good sermon!" comments from departing listeners, may feel that they have done their job if they have achieved these objectives—and perhaps they have. But all of this has been driven at some level by the sense of "crisis"—not by the particular transitional crisis being addressed but by the very connotation of the term: "a paroxysmal attack of pain, distress, or disordered function."

The place of primacy in the *Oxford English Dictionary*, however, goes to a different connotation of *crisis*: "a vitally important or decisive stage in the progress of anything, a turning point." If a "crisis" is essentially as the American dictionary describes it, then the "point" of a sermon on transition is to address—well—three points: 1) The initial *stasis* point—the point of past stability, 2) the present "stuck" point—the point where everyone is "hanging," and 3) the point of future *stasis* (where we will "all live happily ever after"). On the other hand, if a crisis is a vital or decisive *turning* point—a stage in an ever-continuing process—then preaching strategies designed (intentionally or unconsciously) to manage or palliate will not ultimately be effective. Any effectiveness that comes from instructing, encouraging, empathizing, or "exemplarizing" in the pulpit will only derive from understanding the "point" of transition preaching as the shaping of a journey that fosters a *turning* point through a series of *passage* points—all of which are critical *energy* points. As preachers among those who are in the midst of transition, we need *not* to preach

- *around* the transition—glossing over its crucial energy with pious abstractions.
- *about* the transition—accounting for the crisis from an objective distance.
- *at* the folks in transition—admonishing them regarding (or "pumping them up" for) it.

We need, rather, to preach them *through* the crisis of transition, shaping the sermon as *itself* a transition—a transition that will serve as an interpretive lens for an illuminating perspective in the midst of the process. Shift the metaphor in favor of a couple of others: preachers are not mere Web site designers constructing "virtual tours"; they are on-the-ground sherpas leading expeditionary adventures across perilous mountain passes. How can preachers undertake such a role? I will restrict my suggestions to four (and then offer an example from a respected colleague as to how that can play out in real sermon time).

1. *Pay close attention to the tensive quality of the transitions characteristic of the biblical dramas that comprise salvation history—and do the same with the dynamics at work in the current transition crisis under sermon consideration.* All too often the narrative materials in Scripture (or the narrative contexts implicit in Scripture) are treated (bluntly put) as exhortational illustrations akin to Aesop's Fables, complete with morals attached. ("It was a dark and stormy night on Lake Galilee, but it's always darkest before dawn.") It is important to dwell in the sequential details of narrative tension that are built into biblical stories rather than rushing right on to challenging, but reassuring, implications. The interplay of "then/there" tensions and "here/now" tensions can often be instructive as preachers attend "in slow motion" to the rich phenomenological features of both. Hidden elements in each can be revealed as they are attended to in light of the other.

2. *Resist the temptation to interpret "the end" of any particular biblical pericope as if it were a resolution to or a closure on the transition being depicted.* Israel's crossing at the Red Sea does not "end" with their safe landing on the other side. The pillar of cloud and fire leads them, inexorably, from one "transition" to another. The end result is never "happily ever after." The supposedly unchanging God is always on the move, never coming to a stasis point, always pulsing as an energy point, leading toward the next turning point. It is instructive, therefore, to look ahead in biblical narratives for the next crisis that is always created by the apparent resolution of the last crisis.

The book of Revelation may seem to be an exception to this interpretive rubric. Indeed, it has often been read as such—"It is done!" a line uttered by the One described as "the beginning and the end." Such a stasis interpretation, however, overlooks two other sound bites in the final chapters of Revelation—phrases that are in transitional tension with "It is done!": that is, "I am making all things new," and "I am coming soon." The latter promise from the risen Lord testifies to the reality of the "not yet"; the former suggests that transition is eternally inherent in whatever may be entailed in a "new heaven and a new earth" and a "new Jerusalem." Let's think of the implications! Preachers may well be called on to preach transition "forever and ever." If so, we better start getting in practice!

If such eschatological imagination is at all on track, then to preach toward resolution and closure on whatever happens to be "in transition" at the moment is seriously misdirected. Moreover, it invites preachers to attend to transitions, both in Scripture and contemporary experience, in a much more radical way than they may have realized that they are called on to do.

3. *Allow the energy of the sermon to be carried not so much by the observations, reflections, or affirmations that it makes but by rhetorical and linguistic elements that embody the dynamic, open-ended, tensive quality of transition.* The use of nouns and verbs, adjectives and adverbs is inevitable in preaching, of course. But whether the impact of their combination comes out sounding or implying a stasis-point stance or a turning-point stance depends, in remarkable measure, on how those "basic" grammatical elements are carried, propelled, diverted, and suspended by grammatical connectives. A preacher cannot compose by connectives, obviously; but preachers can be attentive, especially in revision and review, to how the process dynamic of transitions is manifested or mitigated by the presence, both literally and figuratively, of such seemingly insignificant words and phrases as *and, but, yet, so, if, then, thus, or, out of, under, over, into, by, through, moreover, although, however, perhaps, on the other hand, in tension with, unfortunately, in consequence of,* and *hopefully.*

Words and phrases such as these affect more than they appear to. They incorporate (indeed, require) bridging between what is and has been (grounding transition in situational continuity is essential for helping change to happen effectively). These words and phrases also point to what is not yet but may (or may not) be. Such connectives and the intentional rhetorical energy behind them convey the quality of fluidity in the midst of what seems to be either firmly fixed or fast failing.

Grammatical literalism is not the objective here. Inserting words and phrases is no guarantee of sermon success, and effective transition sermons need not necessarily employ these words and phrases per se. It is well, however, for a preacher to have the "spirit" if not the "letter" of these phrases well in mind during every stage of the sermon preparation process, which is itself, of course, a process of one transition after another. Most specifically, it is important for the preacher to perform a "connective check" during the final stages of sermon pruning and polishing.

4. *Ensure that the emphasis in focus and feeling tone is oriented more fundamentally toward understanding transition as a "crisis" that is "a vitally important or decisive stage in the progress of anything, a turning point," rather than "a paroxysmal attack of pain, distress, or disordered function."* Clearly the two definitions are not incompatible. It may well be "disordered function" that drives the need for a "turning point." "Pain and distress" may, in fact, be engaged and addressed by deliberately recognizing and undertaking stages in a process. It makes a world of difference, however, which of the two connotations of crisis is determinative in the preaching event. There is no list of rules to follow that will ensure a centering in the former rather than in the latter. But being duly attentive to transitions, preachers can consciously and listeners will unconsciously, if not overtly, recognize the difference when they encounter it.

Rather than further lengthen a list of strategy suggestions, let's let a sermon do the talking. The Rev. Starsky Wilson is pastor and teacher of Saint John's United Church of Christ in St. Louis, Missouri (an interracial, inner-city congregation). While the membership and neighborhood are primarily African American, they were both established in the 1850s by German immigrants. The church was integrated in the 1970s with the closure of a nearby congregation. Wilson is only the second African American pastor in the church's history. It goes without saying that like other similarly situated and constituted congregations, his is "a church in transition."

Notice in what follows how

1. the tensions in ancient text and contemporary setting are engaged and depicted.
2. the "end" of the text is not used as resolution or closure in the sermon.
3. the fluid quality of the discernment process that the preacher seeks to nurture is embodied throughout in sermon language and syntax.
4. the *turning-point* meaning of *crisis* is the centering energy, even though the *pain-and-distress* dimension is honored—and employed *in unresolved tension with* the "vitally important" and "decisive" progress toward which the sermon invites its listeners.

Notice also how the sermon *does* offer the four kinds of "counsel" noted at the outset of this chapter and how it preaches the congregation *through* the transition rather than preaching *around* or *about* it—or *at* the congregation.

Nazareth & The New Neighborhood

In those days Jesus came from Nazareth of Galilee and was baptized by John in the Jordan. And just as he was coming up out of the water, he saw the heavens torn apart and the Spirit descending like a dove on him. And a voice came from heaven, "You are my Son, the Beloved; with you I am well pleased."

And the Spirit immediately drove him out into the wilderness. He was in the wilderness forty days, tempted by Satan; and he was with the wild beasts; and the angels waited on him.

Now after John was arrested, Jesus came to Galilee, proclaiming the good news of God, and saying, "The time is fulfilled, and the kingdom of God has come near; repent, and believe in the good news."

(Mark 1:9–15)

There's No Place Like Nazareth

In those days Jesus came from Nazareth of Galilee . . .

To reduce the risk of looking too much like Dorothy in the *Wizard of Oz*, I will *not* click my heels together! But, I'll admit right off the bat, "There's no place like home." And for Jesus, that means there's no place like Nazareth.

Nazareth is the place where everybody knows your name, "and they're always glad you came." Daddy got all the business for craftsmen and carpenters in Nazareth. Nobody cooks like Mama did back in Nazareth. In Nazareth, everybody knew everybody 'cause we all got together on Friday nights for football. Good ol' Nazareth. Back in Nazareth, we had the best potlucks and fish fries. In Nazareth, the pews (I mean) the temple was packed because everyone lived faithful lives committed to the God of Abraham, Isaac, and Jacob. Although we talked funny in Nazareth (people from other parts were always making fun of our southern drawl), we all understood each other because we were cut from the same cloth. Man, you can't help but miss the good times we had (and still have every now and then) back at Nazareth. We were a thriving congregation back in Nazareth. We were the talk of the town in Nazareth. We had a strong Confirmation curriculum in Nazareth.

Why in the world would anybody leave Nazareth? In the case of Jesus, he leaves Nazareth and finds newness nearby.

There's Newness Nearby

[Jesus] was baptized by John in the Jordan. And just as he was coming up out of the water, he saw the heavens torn apart and the Spirit
descending like a dove on him. And a voice came from heaven,
"You are my Son, the Beloved; with you I am well pleased."

In this place, the old traditional practice of baptism initiates a newness in
the reality of Jesus. At Jordan (in Mark's telling of the story), Jesus' world gets
"torn apart" from above and (I can only imagine) his identity gets redefined
from within. I mean, what do you do? How do you respond when God says,
"You're special, and you make me happy?" I mean, in Mark's version, God
isn't making some grand proclamation to the community; God is talking to
Jesus. "Yeah, you standing down there in the water."

Great! No pressure. Now, I've got to go the rest of my life living up to
making God happy! And on top of all that, I'm not in Nazareth anymore. If
things get crazy, the folks I'm used to are not around. I can't call Mama. Dad
is back trying to keep the business together. My friends aren't here to witness
and worship with me anymore.

You and I are not that far from Nazareth. We're in the same building,
on the same corner, in the same denominational tradition. There are a few
familiar faces and there is some collective memory, but the environment
around us is new. This used to be an all-German community. Our members
(heck, we) used to live around the corner. That check-cashing place used to
be a locksmith. That Pentecostal church used to be a Lutheran church. That
vacant lot is where the house my grandfather built used to stand. I learned
to play soccer at that very park, and now nobody who hangs out there looks
anything like me!

We didn't travel that far from where we came from. All we did was integrate the church back in the seventies. We didn't tell members to leave; they
just did. All we did was follow the lead of our forty-year pastor who said
it was time for us to be the one really integrated church in our association.
All we did was vote a couple of times to keep our doors open when others
decided to close congregations in the city. We didn't go that far. But, now
we find ourselves in a completely new situation.

What now? Jesus didn't have to answer that question. Because . . .

There's a Network in the New Neighborhood

[T]he Spirit immediately drove him out into the wilderness. He
was in the wilderness forty days, tempted by Satan; and he was
with the wild beasts; and the angels waited on him.

This wilderness, although it seems foreign, and different, and other, and weird, and dark, and poor, and broken, and busted, and disenfranchised, and disconnected, and disengaged, and distant from the Nazareth I know, it is not disorganized. There is a network in the new neighborhood that has principles . . . and power . . . and purpose. As much as we would make "the 'hood" (I mean, the new neighborhood) an uncivilized, uninformed, uneducated mass of spiritual or social decay and depravity—a wilderness, of sorts—there is a system of spiritual formation in the neighborhood that nurtures the newness we have found. In the neighborhood

- the Spirit drives us.
- Satan tests and tempts us.
- the beasts accompany us.
- the angels serve us.

The God who so openly expresses and proclaims love to and for Jesus (to and for us) loves us so much that God recognized the awkwardness of new situations and developed a network in the wilderness to shape us. Let us be clear, navigating this network doesn't always feel good.

The nurturing neighborhood network includes *ha satan*—Satan. An adversary (or, as we read the story of Job, a chief investigator) in the court of God that helps God get a sense of the truth of our personality, commitment, and faithfulness. To be honest, on the north side of St. Louis there are many adversaries of peace, and justice, and personal security. The combination of high crime rates and the darkness of the night test our commitment to Wednesday-night Bible studies. The moves toward school reform without public input of constituents stuck in the city and thus in the public schools tests our desire to give voice to the voiceless. The adversary is in the neighborhood to test us.

But the network also includes a few beasts: the embodiment of dangers that we do not understand; creatures that we did not encounter in Nazareth. Monsters who speak a different language (perhaps broken English) are moved by different sounds (bangin' bass lines, mixing and scratching) and present themselves in a manner inconceivable and inconsistent with that with which we are comfortable (baggy jeans, big coats, and backward hats). But God has ordained their presence in the neighborhood to accompany us.

And so we don't begin to believe everything is negative or adversarial or awkward in the neighborhood; just when we want to write off our neighbors in the 'hood, God sends angels to minister to us. Perhaps they are the elders who lived through both waves of middle-class folks leaving the neighborhood. The first, German, and then the second, African American. Or maybe the fellas who sit on the stoop of the church all day, drinking the beer they purchased across the street, when they tell us (like they did for me in my first week here), "The people around here are good people. Man, they just need some help." When we think we've got it all down, the angels minister to us.

(Oh yeah, it's impossible to know the beasts from the angels without spending a little time in relationship, in the neighborhood.)

God Gives Newness to Nazareth through the Neighborhood

> After John was arrested, Jesus came to Galilee, proclaiming the good news of God, and saying, "The time is fulfilled, and the kingdom of God has come near, repent and believe in the good news."

When he sat amid a few beasts and angels of his own during the Lenten season in Birmingham (as a matter of fact on a Good Friday, I think), a young preacher with a little experience working in the neighborhood suggested that we are caught in "an inescapable network of mutuality." Somehow everything in the neighborhood is connected. And everything that happens in the neighborhood affects the reality in Nazareth. Fancy that, the neighborhood both affects Nazareth and is affected by Nazareth. It seems to me, God gives newness to Nazareth through the neighborhood.

This is what they in the neighborhood call the "remix." In a remix, you take a sample from something that was already there. You scratch what you don't need for the new moment, musical movement, and reality. Then you add your own new, creative element for the sake of discovering a new creation for a new community.

Jesus remixed John the Baptist's preaching for Nazareth. John preached baptism and repentance for the forgiveness of sins. Jesus sampled the repentance, mixed it with time fulfillment, and creatively added a word of newness for Nazareth that (I think) he came across in the neighborhood. It was that "kingdom of God" part.

It was in the experience of the network of the neighborhood that Jesus found the authenticity to preach the kingdom of God. It was the neighborhood of the desert that empowered Paul's proclamation of an *ecclesia*, a calling out for God. It was the neighborhood that inspired that preacher named King to speak of a beloved community. And that networked neighborhood, it seems to me, can embolden our witness to the world today. If, and only if, we remember that *the Spirit drove us here.*

18

The Minister's Story

A Resource for Helping Congregations through Transitions

RONALD J. ALLEN

The ancient Greek philosopher Heraclitus (540 BCE to 475 BCE) is famous for saying, "You cannot step twice in the same rivers, for fresh waters are ever flowing in upon you."[1] From this perspective life is itself constant transition. One moment passes immediately into the next. Transition is a part of the fabric of existence. Existence does not simply contain transitions but *is* continual process. When certain kinds of transitions cease to occur within the human body, life ends. To preach is always to preach during a time of transition.

SO MANY KINDS OF LIFE-SHAPING TRANSITIONAL MOMENTS

Nevertheless, some moments of transition rise above the everyday flux in personal lives, households, congregations, denominations, cities, states, nations, and Western and world cultures. Moments of transition can create force fields that shape and reshape perception and behavior. Examples of such moments in individual and household life include marriage, divorce, the multiple passages associated with children (such as birth, high school graduation, and leaving home). Changing jobs, retiring, and moving from a family house into a senior citizen complex are further examples of pivotal moments of transition.

---

1. Heraclitus, *Fragments* 41, 42 in John Burnett, ed., *Early Greek Philosophy* (New York: Meridian Library, 1957, orig. pub. 1892), 136. Plato reports that Heraclitus was known for this saying. Plato, *Cratylus* 402, trans. H. N. Fowler, Loeb Classical Library 4 (Cambridge, MA: Harvard University Press, 1926), 67.

Transitions regularly occur in congregations when people are immersed, confirmed, elected (or not elected) to congregational leadership. Congregations as communities often face key transitional moments, such as the decision to change styles of worship, to adopt a new approach to congregational organization, to launch a new mission effort, to move the church building from one location to another, to consider ordaining or marrying people who have previously not been eligible for ordination or marriage, to call a particular person as minister, or to terminate the leadership of a particular clergyperson.

In community, national, and international affairs, transitions are often quite public, as in the case of September 11, 2001 (the attack on the World Trade Center in New York City), the devastation of Hurricane Katrina, or the national economic catastrophe that began in 2008.

Transitions can result from a joyous decision (such as the desire to be immersed into the body of Christ) to a catastrophe that suddenly rearranges life possibilities. Whether sought or not, transitional moments disrupt previous patterns of life and force people to think again about values and behaviors.

THE MINISTER'S CALLING IN SEASONS OF TRANSITION

Ministers are called to help congregations interpret such transitions theologically and to respond to them faithfully. Congregations need to make theological sense of seasons of transitions, to figure out how their deepest theological values should lead them to live in and through the transition, and how transitional experiences might prompt them to rethink aspects of their theology. As a layperson from the study described below says, "I think this is what sermons are as much as anything to me: the ability to make some sense out of those things that are going on in life."

A recent series of interviews with people who listen to sermons finds that listeners report that the minister's own story can be an important resource in this ministerial task.[2] People often find it helpful when ministers describe

2. This study, "Listening to Listeners," was funded by the Lilly Endowment and carried out through Christian Theological Seminary. Interviews were conducted with 263 persons in individual and small-group settings in twenty-eight congregations from a range of racial/ethnic and denominational backgrounds. The major books to come from the study thus far include Ronald J. Allen, *Hearing the Sermon: Relationship, Content, Feeling* (St. Louis: Chalice Press, 2004); John S. McClure, Ronald J. Allen, Dale P. Andrews, L. Susan Bond, Dan P. Moseley, and G. Lee Ramsey Jr., *Listening to Listeners: Homiletical Case Studies* (St. Louis: Chalice Press, 2004); Mary Alice Mulligan, Dawn Ottoni Wilhelm, Diane Turner-Sharazz, and Ronald J. Allen, *Believing in Preaching: What Listeners Hear in Sermons* (St. Louis: Chalice Press, 2005); and Mary Alice Mulligan and Ronald J. Allen, *Make the Word Come Alive: Lessons from Laity* (St. Louis: Chalice Press, 2006).

how they got into transitional situations similar to those faced by the congregation, and how the ministers responded to those circumstances. Even when ministers have not dealt with the same phenomena as the congregation, people are often illuminated when the pastor tells about dealing with similar issues.[3]

This chapter sets out the main themes in the interviews regarding the minister's use of her or his stories in the pulpit as these stories relate to the subject of ministry in transition. As much as possible I try to let the listeners speak in their own words.[4] Along the way, the chapter lifts up several pieces of practical advice offered by the lay listeners themselves. In a spirit of candor, the chapter concludes by offering some cautions regarding ministers using their own stories.

While this chapter is particularly interested in how ministers can use their stories in preaching on transitions, ministers can make use of their personal narratives in many other congregational settings in which transitional moments come to the fore—for example, in pastoral calling, in decision-making bodies, in program planning, and in developing mission. Indeed, as insightful ministers know, the congregation is a system in which all parts influence one another.[5] Consequently, the minister's discussion of transitions in the sermon often has ripple effects in other parts of the congregational system. Likewise, the minister's leadership with regard to transitions in other settings affects how people hear the sermon.[6]

---

3. Many scholars of preaching have long urged preachers to make use of selected aspects of the preachers' autobiographies in sermons. Suggesting that preachers use their own stories as models for individuals and communities negotiating transition is more than asking for preachers to use their own lives as illustrations or other heuristic devices. The preacher's life can be a resource for theological reflection as I note in Ronald J. Allen, *Interpreting the Gospel: An Introduction to Preaching* (St. Louis: Chalice Press, 1998), 54–62. A seminal work is that of Edmund Steimle, Morris J. Niedenthal, and Charles L. Rice, *Preaching the Story* (Philadelphia: Fortress Press, 1980). For recent consideration and bibliography see the pertinent essays in Mike Graves and David Schlafer, eds., *What's the Shape of Narrative Preaching? Essays in Honor of Eugene L. Lowry* (St. Louis: Chalice Press, 2007). The new dimension to result from the Listening to Listeners study is that *listeners themselves* urge preachers to make use of the preacher's own story as a theological lens for helping the congregation make theological sense of life.

4. In order to maintain the integrity of the quotes and to help them retain their oral character, I have not edited them. Many of the quotes bear the marks of oral speech.

5. On the place of preaching in the congregational system, see Ronald J. Allen, *Preaching and Practical Ministry: Preaching and Its Partners* (St. Louis: Chalice Press, 2000).

6. This chapter does not set out a complete theology of ministry or homiletic for preaching through seasons of transitions. It highlights one aspect of ministry in such times: the use of the preacher's own story of navigating through transitions as a helpful approach for some sermons. While some of these ideas are not new, the fresh aspect is that they come from listeners themselves.

THE MINISTER'S JOURNEY THROUGH TRANSITION
AS A MODEL FOR PARISHIONERS

Interviewees are often quite direct in saying that they find it very helpful when ministers recount what happened to them as they made their way through a transition. They like for preachers to describe where they were at the start of a transition and then to sketch the process of going through the transition. What questions were on the preacher's mind and heart? What data or processes of reasoning were persuasive? Why did the preachers land where they did?

Several listeners directly say that the minister's way of handling an issue is a paradigm for how they might handle an issue: "[The minister] talks about . . . personal experiences and about how he might have had trouble with a person in his own life. He had to step back and think about it. He had to go talk to them and pray with them. That's something I've been trying to work towards doing." Someone else puts forward, "The other thing that has been helpful to me [in listening to sermons] in the past—I haven't seen it here but I've seen it in other places—is a pastor will talk about how he or she has had a personal crisis, and how they handled it, what they actually did." Again, we hear, "Lay it all out. This is what I'm about. I'm not perfect. I'm one of you." As someone else avers, "We should know what kind of struggles [the minister] has because [the minister's] struggles are our struggles."

Still another respondent recalls hearing the minister tell a story about something that had happened to the minister that had not happened to the respondent. The respondent questioned, "What if I found myself in that circumstance?" The minister's story prompted the respondent to consider how the respondent might act in the different situation.

After hearing how a pastor made a change of mind in regard to a controversial issue, someone reports what a preacher said: "This really is a new concept to me and here is how these people came about some of their ideas." For this listener and many others, learning about the minister's process of reflection and change is as important as where the preacher landed with respect to the issue. Such listeners can transfer the process to other situations, as we hear in the following remark: "If they [ministers] can take Scripture, and can find God faithful day in and day out, and it works in their lives, then we're more apt to listen to them and to say, 'If God did it for [the minister], God can do it for me, too.'"

In only a few words, one parishioner recounts such a word:

> Our former pastor talked one time about coming to know Christ for yourself and told of his personal experience when he came to know

Christ for himself and how he confessed not knowing. He was already in the ministry at that point, and for years had believed in [Christ], but had not had a relationship with [Christ] on his own. I will never ever forget that because that is the day I accepted Christ for myself as a preacher's child. I realized then, "You've got work to do," and I came down the aisle.

For this parishioner, hearing the preacher's story facilitated a life-changing self-awareness.

Many other people find that the preacher's life can be a model for them:

He always brings forth that he was not always a man of God. As a teenager he was brought up in the church, but he strayed, so he always lets you know, "I'm human. Because you're down, don't feel you can't be accepted and be saved and receive salvation. Some of us have been there. I've been there, and I know that."

One of the most poignant yet instructive discussions around this motif concerns a minister who had lost a child:

A particular sermon that I remember being very good was a sermon that [the minister] did in 1999 where he talked about his own son's death, and he talked about it in the context of Job and not understanding why bad things happen. The reason that it came to my mind is because after all the events of September 11, I got a copy of that sermon and reread it just this week and remember having heard it. One reason that I thought it was such a good sermon is that he didn't shy away from difficult issues. He faced them and talked directly about them. He was able to relate a meaningful personal story that added great emotional content to the sermon, and that was much more effective than when sometimes preachers start telling a story and as you begin to hear it you're not sure if it's urban myth, if it really happened, if it's some kind of illustration. That's not nearly as powerful and meaningful as [our minister] telling the story of how he dealt with his own son's death and his struggle in dealing with that and in relating it to Job. That's why I felt it was a particularly great sermon. [The use of the preacher's own experience] is appropriate, and in this case when you're talking about a very difficult issue. Most of the congregation struggles with why bad things happen. I wouldn't expect to or want to hear a personal story every week, but if it's appropriate to the sermon, it makes it more meaningful.

This interview took place in 2001, more than two years after the sermon. Yet the parishioner recalled the sermon and turned to a printed copy as a resource of making her way through the shock and grief of the destruction of the World Trade Center.

THE MINISTER'S STORY OF MOVING THROUGH
TRANSITION PROMPTS PARISHIONERS TO REFLECT
AFRESH ON THEIR OWN TRANSITIONS

At the simplest level, the preacher's story often helps the congregation identify with the sermon. Here are several listeners who speak for many others: "Great preachers have said, 'I have been there, and I know, and I'm still there. We're in this together.'" Or again, "[When our minister] refers back to his childhood and previous life, it is so similar to the people in the congregation that he can hook us that way. We've had similar experiences." Someone else recalls a preacher who would "relate some kind of personal story that tied the biblical message into everyday life. I think everybody can relate to that. They say, 'I know how it is.'" One member of the study group captures this sense especially well: "I think this pastor places himself there [in relating personal circumstances in the sermon], but in a way that the pastor draws us to that spot, too. I am speaking for myself. The pastor draws me to that spot, too." This point of view is reinforced by the following: "The [sermons into which I am drawn] are the ones with the personal experience of the pastor or someone that [the pastor] is close to. It can be so identifying that you put yourself in the situation."

To anticipate a section below, ministers increase the possibility of identification by speaking about difficulties they have had. "When you see that everyone has problems, it makes it easier to relate," one person said. Similarly, when asked for one or two things that the listener would tell a preacher that would be energizing, another person said, "Tell the truth and use your own personal testimony. You can talk a lot about what's in a book, but nothing is quite as engaging as when you talk about your own struggles and your own personal experiences." Another worshiper says, "There have been times when the sermon has seemed dry to me because no personal experiences have been brought into the sermon. . . . How can I explain? It's taking thoughts and ideas from the Bible and from other literary books and so forth and put them into a sermon, but it didn't seem to fit our human lives. It was just thoughts put together."

Another interviewee points to the preacher's story as prompting fresh perspectives on the interviewee's life: "But you know when the minister is telling a story; you know if you've been there or if you've done that. [You say,] 'Okay. You're right. Now I see a new way to look at what I did,' or 'I have a different feeling about this.'" Or as someone else says, "Whenever he talks about his youth, he has great stories about [the state in which the minister grew up]. They always seem to provide pertinent contextualization, like things you can relate to that help you link to the message of the gospel or the lessons for that Sunday."

Many respondents appreciate the minister's offering fresh perspectives on familiar texts, themes, and situations. This quote stands for many: "Just the different perspective that she offered, a different way of looking at a story that was familiar but causing one to think in a new way. Then the way she happened to link that up to experiences in her life that we encounter everyday—how we break out of our normal routine into the real presence of God. We talked about it afterward."

In a congregation in which three people preach regularly, a congregant points to a characteristic that all three preachers share: "They're honest, and they're that person's soul. They're very open. They show us this life that we're not used to realizing or feeling connected to."

This theme comes out as a member recalls a sermon that was engaging:

> I would say the first one to come to mind was the one that she preached after September 11 [2001] in which she confessed to the congregation how difficult that sermon was for her personally. As part of the message, [she said that] there was a real conflict as a spiritual leader between what she felt the government was trying to lead the people to do, rallying everyone, "Hey, let's go bomb the world." The spiritual leader [is supposed to say], "We're supposed to be striving for peace on earth. Is this the most effective way to get to point B?" The confession of that internal strife . . . I think she did a very good job of illustrating the inner conflict and after that points out each of those paths and where they would take for her. Using what she believed to be God's intention to help sort through that and come out and say, "I'm going to have to face that working for peace is the way we should go."

This parishioner joined the preacher in working through the options in the sermon.

Another listener reflects on self-disclosure from the pulpit and how it can provide a working model:

> You have to have the ability to say, "Here's a struggle that many folks have in marriage. Here's a struggle that I have as your pastor. Here's what I've learned from that. I'd like to share some stories with you." That's real. If you're just barking orders or if you're just telling fun stories, that doesn't work. I think self-disclosure is important within a parameter.

A ministers' use of personal material in the pulpit and classroom brings forth the following answer to the question, "What would be missing if there were no sermon?"

> Anyone can get up and read the readings. But when someone lends a personal experience to the teaching, to me that's what the congregation

takes away with them. If you think about a time in your life that may have occurred and start thinking about how you handled it, and you hear about whether you handled it correctly or not. If you handled it incorrectly, you're going to hear a way that you could have handled it differently. . . . I think that without hearing that in preaching, some of us would just leave and go on our merry way.

For this Christian, personal experience in the sermon and classroom prompts her to reflect on her life and to consider how she might live differently.

One of the most sobering reports comes in response to a sermon by a missionary from a nation with a brutal national government. "[The minister] would say, 'I met such-and-such an old lady who did such-and-such. She was a wonderful old lady, but all of a sudden, one day she wasn't there.' You're going, 'Whoa!'"

THE PREACHER'S NEGOTIATION OF TRANSITIONS AS A SOURCE OF ENCOURAGEMENT

It is important to note that the minister does not always have to come across as a heroine or hero. Indeed, many listeners feel a sense of solidarity and support when ministers speak straightforwardly about their frustrations and brokenness. For example, one person said, "In all three [of our ministers], you get a sense of striving, not a sense of 'I have arrived.' There may be a chance for you."

Here is an interchange from a small group visiting the same point. The question asked what listeners find engaging in sermons.

Listener 1:   "I think this morning when our minister told about how at one time they didn't go to church. It was just easier to stay in bed."

Listener 2:   "Her personal story."

Listener 3:   "Yes, and you're thinking, Oh, yes. Been there. Done that.' I'm sure that other people in the congregation were relating to that. She had been through that so she could relate to us how we would feel. That makes it better to me—if you've got somebody that's on your own level, and you know that they've lived that life."

Listener 4:   "They let you know they live that life. I think we've probably all done that, but it makes the application so much better when the preacher says, 'I have done this, too. I know where you're at. I know where you're going. I know how we can fix it.' I think that's crucial to any message. 'Hey, I'm a sinner here too. This is what I've done. This is

> how it can be fixed. This is why God has in place provisions that we
> can reconcile.'"

As noted in the introduction to the chapter, parishioners report that the
preacher's experience can be a guide even when that experience does not cor-
respond in a one-to-one fashion with the situation of the congregation. In
the following remark, we hear not only identification between preacher and
congregant but also the pastor's story functioning as a model for listeners for
their own versions of the preacher's experience and also for experiences the
preacher does not report.

> I think the story, whether it's the pastor telling a story about himself
> or herself, or an experience in his or her life. Something that makes
> it human because then I can say, "Yes, I've done that," or "I've felt
> that," or "I've been there," or "Sometimes I feel like I have to say,
> 'That's where I'm going to get. That's for a later day. I haven't been
> there yet, but hopefully this means that maybe if I have to go there,
> I'll know what to do.'" Or, maybe I'll never go there because I've
> heard what I should do.

In a small group, one interviewee says, "I think the effectiveness [of their
stories] is that they exhibit an experience you've had. You feel inspired by
their ability to see in life how they accomplish a spirituality or Christian devotion, or how they don't accomplish that and seek to improve themselves."

THE PREACHER'S HONESTY ABOUT LIVING
THROUGH TRANSITIONS ADDS AUTHORITY
TO THE SERMON

One of the questions asked in each interview was, "What gives a sermon
authority for you?" Not surprisingly, most people answered that sermons are
authoritative when the sermon has solid biblical and theological foundations.
Additionally, many people report that the preacher's own experience adds to
the authority of the message. "The minister lives in my neighborhood," said
one person. "We've all grown up together. When you use a personal story,
we're all pretty much in the same boat. That touches you." With respect to
what gives a sermon authority, someone in a rural congregation says, "It's
speaking from their own experiences so that you know they're genuine." In a
related way, someone recalls a preacher who "gets you involved usually by a
story or something that makes you feel that [the minister] has lived through
this kind of situation or knows someone personally that has. [The minister]
has a reason to know something about it."

When asked if a pastor needs "to go through something to be able to preach on it effectively," an interviewee recalls a minister preaching a compassionate sermon on HIV/AIDS. The minister had brought "a lot of research" into the pulpit that gave the sermon credibility, but the interviewee then not only commended this preacher but pointed to something that preachers can often do to add authority to the sermon: "You can go into the hospital . . . and just see for yourself. How would it affect you if it were one of your members? I'm not just talking about AIDS. I'm talking about drugs and all those things. [An effective preacher] should try to do your homework, [and, if possible] get exposed [that is, become personally familiar with], not bodily exposed but you've got to be personally exposed to the subject."

Many of the interviews concluded with the question, "If you had one or two things you could suggest to preachers to energize your listening, what would they be?" One of the most frequent responses to this question was that the preacher needs to be honest.

Perhaps no comment in the interviews more directly captures this emphasis on being real: "They have to be honest. They can't be trying to tell you something they don't believe. They need to be coming from the heart and from the mind and be honest about what they're talking about." Or, as someone else says, "Be honest. Approach life from an honest standpoint. Don't pull punches." Another parishioner remembers a preacher who dealt honestly with a situation of conflict in a congregation: "You could see this [person's] humanity come out in that sermon just as [that preacher] was trying to explain what was happening within this church body that was at times being less than Christian with each other."

In a candid moment, a lay participant in the study says, "I think listening to a minister every week is sometimes a hard thing to do. But I think the trait that I respect in any minister, wherever I've been, is that they can get across, 'This is me. . . . It's the truthfulness of the faith I have in Christ.' That makes a difference."

Along this line, a significant number of interviewees find it especially helpful when ministers describe their struggles. Someone says, "It was very, very refreshing to me to have a pastor who didn't have the answers, who struggled with some of the tensions that you would have in your faith, grace, and good works, or whatever. To be open enough to share that with the congregation, that just really means something." Recalling a sermon on marriage, a listener says, "The ability to say, 'Hey, here's where my wife and I struggle.' You don't have to go into intimate details, but at least highlight that, and it makes you more real. I think that makes a sermon more listenable as well." Another person muses, "You value [the minister's] honesty.

You value [the minister's] openness, and that [the minister] struggles, too, and has problems."

In the following quotation, a listener reports with particular clarity on how the preacher sharing her struggle is a model for the listener.

> [The sermon] was connecting with me because it's something I think everybody struggles with at one point or maybe at times in their faith growth journey. To listen to another person openly and honestly witness their own faith helps at times to connect and help me over a struggling point that I may have had that they have already gone through and can now help me go through.

For this listener, hearing the preacher's struggle is a source of encouragement. Another person who heard the same sermon—and did not know about the previous listener's remarks—expanded.

> What it was, was her struggle towards faith, the people that had helped her, and she really connected in that particular time with me emotionally. And she took a big risk. She took a risk to stand up there and bare her weaknesses and her struggles to the rest of the congregation, but that helped make a connection. . . . On the flip side, there are many ministers who feel that they have to have armor on, that they can't risk opening themselves up emotionally and exposing that to the congregation for fear that the congregation would think less of them.

For this person, vulnerability and risk enhance communication whereas armor frustrates it.

Many members of the congregations in the study also expressed appreciation for preachers' expressing their vulnerability in the sermon. When asked what a listener found engaging about a particular sermon, the listener replied, "[The minister's] honesty. [The minister's] brokenness . . . I think that's why it was engaging. Any time there is truth coupled with humanity."

A minister who had retired from a congregation returned to preach during the summer:

> [The minister] told us of the struggles he personally has in his own faith, or why the denomination or certain kinds of churches sometimes upset him. He was free to say in this [retired] time of life, "I don't think that's right. I don't do this. I struggle with this." I probably felt closer to [the minister] in those sermons he gave those two or three weeks in a row than any other sermon. I think it had to do with the fact that he felt he had the freedom to be in a point in his life and in the relationship with this church that he could just lay it on the line.

This listener regretted that the preacher had not shown such honesty when still serving the congregation full-time.

CAUTIONS WITH REGARD TO MINISTERS USING
THEIR STORIES IN SEASONS OF TRANSITION

As with all aspects of leadership in the congregation, ministers need to take a critical perspective on the potential use of their own life narratives during transitions. While the pastor's story can be useful, preachers need to consider carefully the degree to which a particular story can serve ministry in a particular transition and in the culture of the local congregation, especially regarding how that community receives and valuates personal stories.

While the first observation may seem obvious, the fact that it comes up a dozen times in the interviews suggests that it deserves consideration. *The story needs to relate to the sermon and to make a point.* This comment speaks for others. "Sometimes you can tell a story, and there's nothing there." Another remark resonates. "It's just that you don't want it to be all chit-chat. . . . It's still got to have a basis to it and a point. . . . I've heard talks in other places that it was just a cutesy talk. Entertaining." This person wants more.

Going a step further, an interviewee points out that when using a personal story, the preacher needs to be clear that the sermon "is not about you [the preacher]." Meditating on a preacher who uses a lot of personal experience in sermons, a listener says, "Sometimes I feel like the sermon is more about them than it is about God or trying to be a conduit of God." Preachers should use their experience as a way to help the congregation interpret the presence and purposes of God and a faithful response. "So when you're telling stories about your childhood, what's the difference between the person who is performing self in a sort of egocentric fashion and the person who is using that experience as a way of teaching others? That's a very delicate line." Another member of the study ruminated on a sermon that had a personal quality but concludes, "I felt [the minister] was working out [the minister's] own personal problems." Even more vividly a respondent advises, "You can't work out your own demons in front of the congregation." On the other hand, a member of another community says of a sermon that had a poignant personal story from the life of the minister, "Well, it was in the first-person singular, but it was not self-aggrandizing."

Moreover *the content of some stories is not appropriate for the sermon or for other public arenas of ministry.* "You value [the minister's] openness, that [the minister] struggles and has problems, too. But, that's not like you have to tell it all. . . . There are limits." More vividly someone remarks, "The more you can connect and expose yourself personally [is to the good], but that doesn't mean stand up and say, 'I'm sleeping with half the congregation.'" While acknowledging that sermons can sometimes voice some of the minister's transgressions, someone says, "Something like that, yes, but all the dirty laundry doesn't have to come out. It's not [the ministers'] job to wash their souls clean in front of us while they're talking."

Listeners frequently say that a preacher captures their attention when beginning the sermon with a situation from the preacher's life or with the preacher's own questions about a subject. One of the more extensive comments on this subject says, "I really appreciate [the minister's] stories. This preacher has a way of making everything relevant. [The sermon] starts with a story, and it gets you interested in what happens. Then the preacher leaves the story, but the story leads you into the sermon. [The sermon] engages you at the beginning with the story." Someone else remarks, "I like it when they begin with an experience, a story, and then elaborate on what the lesson of the story is."

However, while listeners can be engaged by a personal vignette at the start of the sermon, preachers need to *be circumspect about beginning the sermon with a personal story*. An autobiographical vignette at the beginning is sometimes the most vivid part of the sermon and is the highest (or deepest) emotional moment. From a dramatic point of view, the rest of the sermon is downhill, even anticlimactic. Furthermore, the sermon that begins with a personal story week after week can become predictable and repetitious. If the opening story is the high point of the message, people may get into the habit of diminishing their attentiveness as the sermon goes along. Rather than routinely placing a significant personal narrative at the outset of the sermon, preachers should consider where that story might have its greatest theological and emotional impact in the sermon. Placing the vignette in the middle or near the end of the sermon might give the story a better chance to serve the purposes of the sermon.

A preacher needs to *have a sense of a good length for a story*. One person said,

> For me, it's more about knowing when to stop. Like today's was very good, using the analogy of Dr. Seuss, but if it had gone on for two or three minutes more dealing with Dr. Seuss, [the cleric] would have lost me. It's more about getting to the point and having a relevant story and knowing when to drop that story and not belabor it.

It should go without saying that a minister should be able to tell stories so that people can follow them. However, ministers sometimes fail to connect a particular story (even a good one) to the actual drift of the sermon: "I don't always go with the preacher to where the story's going. I kind of feel sometimes over there in left field."

While members of the congregation often respond positively to stories from the minister's life, they caution that *the minister cannot rely only on autobiographical stories*. One parishioner said, "I know pastors that always pull from the same experience that they've had, or they pull from their family life or from another job they might have had or something like that. [Our current pastor] is good at balancing it. This pastor gets stories from everywhere." Another parishioner adds, "The other thing I especially enjoy is hearing about fellow parishioners. I don't have to have their names . . . but I like to hear about the person who's gone through this epiphany or resurrection in their lives or are struggling with some sort of death, spiritual or physical, somehow coping with it, a close-to-home story." A respondent wisely suggests that if the preacher uses material from people in the congregation, the preacher should get their permission before using it and should signal the congregation that it is used by permission.

When ministers have had *a profound personal experience*, we are often tempted to return to it again and again. However, the listeners in a study group urge ministers *not to go to that well too often.* One said, "Not something I want to hear every week, but it's comforting to know that [our minister] lost a child. I don't think I've heard him say that more than twice, maybe three times, since he's been here." The minister had been in that congregation for about seven years, and the listener found that the number of times the minister had referred to the loss of the child was about right. A member of another congregation agrees: "I can take one [a personal story from the preacher's life] every now and then . . . but I don't want them one right after the other."

And, the fact is, *some people simply do not like stories* in sermons, whether personal or otherwise. While few people in our survey voiced this sentiment, some did. "I really don't like a minister to bring his own personal life into a message," said one listener, who wants to hear the Bible: "Your experience? Your experience may not be biblical." Another person cautions that "false prophets don't really preach from the Bible. They preach from emotion. They preach from experiences."

MANY PEOPLE REMEMBER THE MINISTER'S PERSONAL STORIES ABOUT TRANSITIONS

Our study found that people seldom remember specific sermons. This should not dishearten preachers, however, because the same listeners report that the effects of preaching are cumulative. Over time, congregations become like the preaching they hear when they respond positively to that preaching. Nevertheless, the interviewees report that they do sometimes remember two kinds of sermons: (1) Sermons that they heard in crisis moments in life, when they were particularly in need of a word of theological interpretation, and (2) sermons that contain powerful stories, especially stories that come from the preacher's life.[7]

We hear this theme in the following remarks: "I think that the things I do remember are when a [minister] will personalize the sermon a little bit, disclose a little bit of something about him or herself that shows that person has grappled with the issues. . . . I think those things, when they are connected to the main theme or lesson, for me are really poignant, and often times those are things that I remember long after a lot of other material." Or again, "I think stories sometimes in the sermons are good because if it's a good story and relevant story, it's a good way to remember things. You'll remember the story, when you won't remember anything else he said."

One respondent provides an example of remembering a story from a sermon long ago:

> I always remember the stories. I was remembering [our minister's] story about when she was tracking down the truants, because she's a school counselor. She went into this horrible sort of crack house, and in one of these rooms there was a picture of Jesus. Her first reaction was "How do these people have Jesus' picture?" Then she realized. . . . That's the way she told it. That was her way of making the lesson clear. I'll never forget that.

Several times in the small group interviews, one of the participants would say to the others, "Do you remember a sermon . . . ?" Most of the time, the memory is of a story in a sermon, and most of the other people can recollect it.

CONCLUSION

One of the noteworthy characteristics of the early twenty-first century is a growing interest in community. We see less emphasis on individualism and more value attention focused on being in community. One might think that the use of the minister's own story would reinforce tendencies toward individualism. However, when ministers use their stories as lenses through which to

---

7. Sometimes people can remember the story but not the biblical text or the theological themes with which it was associated. Rather than be discouraged by this turn of events, preachers could rejoice that people remember a sermon days, weeks, and even months or years after they heard it. As one of the interviewees said, "What did she [the preacher] say? And you can remember the story. I can remember the story. I can always recall a story." The goal of particular sermons is not to be remembered but to contribute to the growing reservoir of theological awareness in the congregation much like drops of rain contribute to the pool of water accumulating in our driveway as I write this chapter.

help the congregation focus on broader patterns of theological interpretation, references to the minister's own experience can actually enhance the sense of community in the congregation. A listener sums up this phenomenon:

> I think the sharing of the pastor or pastors gives everyone here a sense of cumulative sharing of experience and narrative, as well as experience and worship together. . . . I think the fact that a preacher enables his listeners or her listeners to respond and to participate and to be a part of the experience of the sermon is very important. As people sitting together, sharing that experience and participation and response helps people feel part of one another.

19

Look Up; Draw Near; Reach Out

Acts 1:1–11; Luke 24:44–53

CAROL M. NORÉN

The following sermon is intended for a congregation in a pastoral transition. In my own tradition, the United Methodist Church, most pastoral changes now take place in late May or early June. The texts for this sermon are appropriate for post-Easter/Ascension, so there would be correlation between the liturgical season and the imminent change in leadership.

Where were you on February 28, 1983? I know exactly where I was: gathered with other seminary students in a dorm room to watch the final episode of *MASH*. My friend George had extravagantly rented a color TV for the occasion, and we all speculated what would happen in the series finale. Each person had a favorite character and generally knew the backgrounds of both the character and the actor portraying him or her. We could recount how the story line had changed over the years. More people watched *MASH* that night than any other series episode in television history. It was satisfying and bittersweet and much more enjoyable to view with other fans. But as the closing credits rolled across the screen, we all looked at George and one another as if to ask, "Now what?" Oh, we could watch reruns in years to come, and eventually, some bought tapes or DVDs of the series, but it would never be the same. There would be no new stories about the 4077th.

My guess is that some of us this morning feel the way *MASH* fans felt in 1983. All analogies have their limits, of course; we're facing the end of a particular pastorate, not the end of the congregation. We're dealing with real life rather than a fictional television series. But there are nevertheless some parallels. Some of us know the story line, the history, better than others. We will celebrate the event, even as we experience a sense of loss. Attendance will be higher than usual on the final Sunday. There have been events or episodes that make us laugh, and others that arouse very different emotions. There may even have been some scripts we wish we could rewrite, to work out a better conclusion. We know—even if we have trouble accepting—that things will never be the same.

Change is hard, God knows. The first followers of Jesus knew it, too. As we hear the account of the ascension in Acts 1, we may feel a certain commonality with them. Their leader was leaving after being with them several years. During that time Jesus had blessed them, taught them, been an agent of healing, and revealed to them the nature of God as they'd never known it before. They'd had good times and some awful times together. Now Jesus was going. So it was understandable that they had difficulty coping with the change. They tried to fit it into their more familiar, comfortable frame of reference, asking, "Lord, will you at this time restore the kingdom to Israel?" It sounds as if they were attempting to control the change, make it work for them, and meet their expectations. Then, once the Redeemer had vanished through the clouds, they stood gazing into heaven, focused entirely on his absence and giving little thought to what would happen next.

Change is hard. Endings are bittersweet. But if we stand in solidarity with the first-century disciples of Jesus, we will not be left wondering, "Now what?"—because God's Word speaks to us as it did to them. It reassures us. The angels who asked the disciples, "Why do you stand looking into heaven?" followed that question with a promise that God had not deserted them and Jesus would come again. Or if we turn to today's other reading, the encounter on the road to Emmaus, we are reminded that sorrowful and perplexed as the two disciples were, they were not abandoned by the Lord. It is true their eyes were blinded from seeing Jesus for who he was, but their "looking backward" over his life and ministry prepared them for the revelation that lay ahead. Hebrews 12 exhorts us to be oriented upward, not simply staring at an empty sky—fixated on the absence—but looking to Jesus the pioneer and perfecter of our faith, because there is a race set before us. We prepare for that race by recalling and reminding one another of the mighty acts of God in times gone by.

When the risen Lord accompanied the believers going to Emmaus, he talked about the past. They told him all about what Jesus had said and done, and he helped them understand what it meant as the fulfillment of all the prophets had foretold. Or think of Peter's sermon at Pentecost. Peter began by reminding his listeners what was spoken by the prophet Joel, and then explained who Jesus Christ was and is. Or remember the story of the apostle Paul's conversion; it's told not once but four times in the New Testament as a means of witnessing to the transforming power of God. Perhaps this tells us that we, too, are to look up in anticipation of what Christ is preparing for us as we recall God's faithfulness in the past and his promise "I will never leave you or forsake you" (Heb. 13:5).

Telling the stories and remembering God's goodness to this congregation are ways of living with change. Another strategy suggested in today's readings is for God's people to draw near to one another. If you think about the followers of Jesus around the time of his passion, death, and resurrection, "solidarity" is not the word that comes to mind. Peter denied Christ. Judas betrayed him. Thomas doubted. Only one of them was present at the foot of the cross; we can only imagine what the others did. In fact, John 20 depicts the only unity of the disciples, where it states they hid behind locked doors for fear of the religious authorities. It took the resurrection to bring them together, and even then, Jesus appeared to them many times over the course of forty days, reinforcing their faith and common purpose.

Before Jesus ascended into heaven, he as Christ told them not to depart from Jerusalem but to wait for the Holy Spirit to be poured out on them. Acts tells us that the apostles, plus some women, plus Jesus' brothers, in total perhaps as many as 120 people, went back to the upper room and devoted themselves to prayer. How crowded do you suppose that upper room was? Can you picture yourself there, without air conditioning or modern plumbing, not sure how long you'd be there? It couldn't have been pleasant or easy. The fact that it was a time of uncertainty, waiting, and change would only add to the anxiety of the situation, although we can assume they all knew one another and believed the same thing. You've experienced such stress if your family has ever come together to prepare for a wedding, or gotten ready to move, or anticipated another life-changing event. Even if the change is something you want, it brings with it human tension. Yet the drawing together, difficult as it can be, is necessary preparation for what comes next. The moving van pulls up, or the wedding march begins, and if you haven't all pitched in to make things ready—well, there's a heavy price to pay.

When there's a pastoral change, the congregation *does* draw together without being asked, in one sense. People who seemingly dropped out come back to say goodbye. It's a homecoming as well as a send-off. But it can be something even better if like Jesus' earliest followers, we devote ourselves to prayer. It is how we are equipped as a community for the future to which God calls us. We are changed ourselves even as we prepare for a change in leadership. Old grudges and resentments can be set aside when we await the promise of God. The Holy Spirit works in us and through us as well as around us.

The first believers looked to Jesus and preserved their memories of what God had done until now. They drew near to one another and devoted themselves to prayer, discovering unity as they awaited God's unfolding promise. When the big change came, and the Holy Spirit was poured out on them at Pentecost, it was a gift with a purpose. They spoke in other tongues so people of different nationalities could understand the gospel—not so they could impress one another. Others were given the gift of healing, not so they could compete with other healers of the day but to demonstrate the power of Jesus' name. The Spirit equipped others to preach and teach so that the gospel could be proclaimed and people believe it and be saved. In other words, change in God's hands is change for the good. Our Lord calls us in times of transition and uncertainty to rely on his grace and his strength, and then reach out in his name. Our mission is not to cling to the past, although we remember it with thanksgiving. It isn't to insulate and protect the congregation as a greenhouse plant but to spread the good seed of the gospel throughout the world. Look up to the Savior who has called you his own. Draw near to one another, praying for the unity Christ graciously offers. And finally, as the Spirit works within our church, reach out that all may know the transforming love of God.

20

Responding to Resistance during a Change Process

ROBERT STEPHEN REID

I

When he hung up the telephone Pastor Jim Dotson was stunned with the finality of Bob Jenkins's decision to withdraw support for the vote to sell the church property.[1] Bob had been one of the members of Grandview United Methodist Church who visibly supported key decisions in each leg of the move toward the vote to relocate from an aging facility to a new campus at the growing edge of Dubuque, Iowa. Pastor Dotson had counted on Bob's support of the vision for revitalization the move represented. The desperate need to have increased parking and lower heating costs were only the two most significant drivers in the need to relocate. New facilities would allow the congregation to expand the possibilities of reaching families with its day-care ministry. It would provide far more versatile worship space and a greatly expanded welcoming area for the Sunday worship events. The new educational wing would provide well-lighted, spacious classrooms rather than the existing musty basement rooms. The new location was needed if the congregation was ever going to grow. The cost was within reach, but it meant letting go of the historic facilities.

Bob Jenkins had been at the heart of the lay leadership of the congregation for three decades. He had been present at the initial meetings about moving

1. Grandview United Methodist Church of Dubuque, Iowa, is an actual congregation, and material for the case study presented here is derived from a December 2008 interview with Pastor Dotson. The case is derived from that conversation and inferences I made from it. It does not represent viewpoints that may be held by congregation members. Specific times, telephone calls, and other names in the case are all composite features of my creation, but the arc of his story in this essay is true to the conversation.

and had nodded his head yes about the need to make changes in order to permit growth. But now, with the key financial vote to sell the old facility only a month away, Bob had just presented his case for why the planned move was too ambitious, would cost too much money, and would cost the congregation too many of its faithful members who would not travel the four miles to a new facility. For these reasons, Bob indicated, he was unwilling to support the decision. If asked, he would vote against it. If asked for money, he would not give. In fact, he said at the end of the call, if the pastor knew what was good for him this whole "vote thing" should be postponed until someone had a better plan to help the church grow.

Pastor Dotson tried to imagine how the decision to make the move could go forward if Bob added his voice to the growing rebellion of those who were resisting the vision for change. Bob and Terry Jenkins were the second-largest giving unit of the congregation. Dotson looked at his schedule and saw the next two hours were blocked out for time to work on the sermon. Yet as he sat there and watched the cursor blinking on the computer screen, he knew that Sunday's sermon would have to wait. His mind was racing with questions. The church had been working on this plan for almost two years. They had hired an expert consultant, who provided the congregation with clear and compelling demographic data supporting the necessity for moving if the congregation wanted to thrive into the next decades. Membership had flat-lined for more than a decade in this midsized, landlocked congregation. Elected congregational leaders and ad hoc committee members had accepted that assessment and done the hard work of planning. The move was the right decision for Grandview.

Pastor Dotson remembered a private conversation with the consultant, who tried to prepare him to expect resistance. It was going to happen, he said, no matter how well the congregation planned and prayed about the change. He even provided Pastor Dotson with statistics on the number of people who's "No" vote on the sale of the property would likely mean they would leave the church. But the consultant had never told him that that it would be people like Bob and Terry Jenkins who would end up leading the resistance.

As he sat there, he couldn't help but wonder whether Bob Jenkins was right. Should he actually consider canceling the vote meeting? Postpone it? Or was that just caving to inevitable resistance? He sagged under the weight of it. How do you preach to a people about the possibilities of the promised land when the tribe leaders are heading up the resistance movement to return to Egypt?

He reached for the telephone to call his friend Don Abrams, a fellow pastor who lived in Southern Illinois. The tide of resistance was growing. If he was going to withstand its undertow, he would need some strong words of encouragement from his friend and mentor.

II

Is it possible for a pastor to *lead* significant change in the life of a congregation and not eventually be forced to leave because of residual resistance? Few pastors are adequately trained in how to lead change, and there is even less training in how to respond productively to the natural resistance that always occurs when proposing change in the life of a congregation.

Howard Gardner of Harvard's Graduate School of Education contends that resistance to change is an inevitable function of being human. Over time people naturally develop strong views and perspectives about how they want to go about doing things. These commitments represent patterns and perspectives that make humans "surprisingly refractory to change."[2] It is more reassuring for most of us to do what we know and stay with the same rather than take on the costs of risking the unfamiliar. Most of us know what our place is in the current situation, and our comfort with that was hard won over a good stretch of time. Change risks the beachhead of whatever power we have managed to amass. Why change things? It is at this point of change, emerging literature has established, that leaders matter the most.

Gardner maintains that "leaders almost by definition are people who change minds—be they leaders of a nation, a corporation, or a nonprofit institution."[3] This is why leaders are especially relevant when organizations need to engage in a change process. Management is about coping with complexity while leadership is coping with change.[4] During times of change or crisis, a leader plays a key role in helping organizational participants engage in the cognitive restructuring necessary to imagine ways to live into the new vision of what the organization must do or needs to become. When managers take on this responsibility for becoming the vision bearer for their unit or for the organization as a whole, they have made the choice to become a leader.

In fact, organizational theorists reflected for much of the last quarter of the twentieth century on what distinguishes a leader from a manager. In 1977 Abraham Zaleznik was the first to identify ways in which a leader's attitude about goals, conceptions of work, relationships with others, and senses of self differ from those of a typical manager.[5] The following year James McGregor Burns made a distinction between transformational leaders and transactional

---

2. Howard Gardner, *Changing Minds: The Art and Science of Changing Our Own and Other People's Minds* (Boston: Harvard Business School Press, 2006), 209.

3. Ibid., 1–2.

4. John Kotter, "What Leaders Really Do," *Harvard Business Review* 68, no. 3 (May–June 1990): 103–11.

5. Abraham Zaleznik, "Managers and Leaders: Are They Different?" *Harvard Business Review* 55, no. 3 (May–June 1977). Retrieved online at http://tppserver.mit.edu/esd801/readings/managers.pdf.

leaders, a distinction that Bernard Bass and Bruce Avolio have established as valid through the extensive use of their Multifactor Leadership Questionnaire (MLQ) developed in the mid-1990s.[6] Although some individuals argue that this distinction is unfair, that it treats the difference between the dual tasks of managing and leading as differences of kind rather than degree, the majority of contemporary theorists have accepted the distinction. Managers tend to operate with a *maintenance* orientation that keeps their focus on structures, systems, efficiency, and other operational elements. Leaders tend to operate with a *journey* orientation that keeps its focus on mission, vision, and strategies necessary to realize organizational effectiveness.

W. Warner Burke notes that definitions of leadership abound, but the best ones tend to focus on the relationship between the individual's power and his or her influence. Leadership becomes most apparent in any change process because it is in times of change that resistances will arise and the ability of a leader to influence organization members becomes apparent. Given this distinction Burke argues that "leadership . . . is the act of making something happen that would otherwise not occur."[7] Notice that the change process is at the heart of this definition. It is during a change process that we are able to see how leaders get persons who otherwise resist doing something to do it. This is why Burns argued that the real work of leadership is one of "inducing followers to act for certain goals that represent the values and the motivations—the wants and needs, the aspirations and expectations—of both leaders and followers."[8]

Leadership is less about managerial-role authority than the ability to influence people to follow who might otherwise naturally resist. Leaders must take people on a journey while also attending to the essential maintenance tasks that keep the change process moving forward. While leading an organization through a change process the effective leader copes with resistance by juggling three distinct communicative tasks.[9] They must

1. present a compelling and urgent vision for change in decision-making gatherings;
2. work closely and personally behind the scenes to involve managers and organizational members in the process of planning and continuous implementation of the new vision; and

6. See Bernard M. Bass, *Leadership and Performance beyond Expectations* (New York: Free Press, 1985); and B. M. Bass and Bruce J. Avolio, *Revised Manual for the Multifactor Leadership Questionnaire* (Palo Alto, CA: Mind Garden, 1997).

7. W. Warner Burke, *Organization Change: Theory and Practice* (Thousand Oaks, CA: Sage, 2008), 228.

8. James MacGregor Burns, *Leadership* (1978; New York: Harper Perennial, 1982), 19.

9. Burke, *Organization Change*, 109–10.

3. provide conceptual frameworks to help all people understand more clearly what is happening to them in the change and how to live into the new identity that change brings.

By engaging in these three communicative tasks leaders are able to *make something happen that would otherwise not occur.* In each communicative venue, the leader who takes on a vision-bearing role in an organization has different resources that can aid in overcoming resistances and change people's minds. Gardner gathers them together and calls them levers.

Every example of mind changing has its unique facets. But in general such a shift of mind is likely to coalesce when we employ the seven levers of mind change: specifically, when *reason* (often buttressed with *research*), reinforcement through multiple forms of *representation, real-world events, resonance,* and *resources* all push in one direction—and *resistances* can be identified and successfully countered. Conversely, mind changing is unlikely to occur—or consolidate—when resistances are strong and most of the other points of leverage are not in place.[10]

It is worth unpacking these means to leverage influence that serve as the leader's resources for overcoming resistance.

Reason

Reason, the first and primary means of leverage, is the bedrock of persuasion. We expect leaders to present good reasons for the "Why?" that requires organizational change. Reason is fundamental to belief. But too many people confuse it with rationality and a presentation of the *facts.* Actually, very few people are ever persuaded to change their minds because of the sheer logic of supposed *facts.* The inimitable John Henry Newman once wrote,

> Deductions have no power of persuasion. The heart is commonly reached, not through reason, but through imagination, by means of direct impressions, by the testimony of the facts and events, by history, by description. Persons influence us, voices melt us, looks subdue us, deeds inflame us. Many a man will live and die upon a dogma: no man will be a martyr for a conclusion. . . . Logic makes but a sorry rhetoric with the multitudes. . . . Logicians are more set upon concluding rightly, than on right conclusions.[11]

---

10. Gardner, *Changing Minds,* 211.
11. John Henry Newman, *An Essay in Aid of a Grammar of Assent* (Notre Dame, IN: University of Notre Dame Press, 1979), 89–90.

Harry Allen Overstreet said it more succinctly: "No appeal to reason that is not also an appeal to want can ever be effective."[12]

Leaders provide followers with good reasons to go on the journey, but they need to appeal to the heart as well as the head. Resistance will gain a clear foothold if leaders fall into the trap of assuming that facts speak for themselves. Resistance will also prevail if at any point a leader is challenged to prove why the change is really needed and fails to provide warrants already acknowledged and approved by existing decision-making groups in the organization.

Research

Whether the leader is struggling to overcome a compromised vision of the organization or to implement a clearly realized vision for change, that leader needs to have compelling research in support of the argument to make a change. Research needs to establish both the nature of the presenting problem(s) and the reason that among the possible responses to that problem, the current vision proposal for change is the most responsible set of steps to be taken. Decision-making bodies in an organization have first to agree to a clear description of the internal dynamics of the organization and the external pressures it faces before they are ready to hear a case for a prescriptive vision of what must change and why the new vision is preferable.

Research is needed to clarify the current reality and identify the likeliest prospects to help the organization move forward. Only then will people choose to change the rules and change the ways the organization has customarily conducted its work. Leaders know their facts. Resistance gains a clear foothold if it can ever dislodge the factual basis of whether change is really needed or whether the proposed change shifts the organization's core identity mission.

Resonance

Plans for change need to resonate with the majority of a leader's constituency. The plan needs to feel right and seem like a good fit for the organization. Its rhetoric has to resonate with the people. And while reason and research matter greatly, a leader must be *rhetorically adept* at presenting a call for change that is both compelling and appealing. The most important component of resonance is the belief by the followers that the leader is truly vested in the change. People are willing to change their minds if they believe their leader

---

12. Harry Allen Overstreet, *Influencing Human Behavior* (1925) as cited in Richard Shell and Mario Moussa, *The Art of Woo: Using Strategic Persuasion to Sell Your Ideas* (New York: Penguin Books, 2007), 137.

is willing to stake her or his future on the decision to take the journey. Resistance will arise if the leader falters at any point. Aristotle argued that the leader's character (*ethos*), leveraged in support of an argument, was always more persuasive than the reasons offered for the change (*logos*) and the ability of the leader to move followers with representational redescriptions of how the change would affect them (*pathos*).

Transformational leadership theorists James Kouzes and Barry Posner have repeatedly validated their research findings that above all else we as followers "want to believe in our leaders. We want to have faith and confidence in them as people. We want to believe that their word can be trusted, that they have the knowledge and skill to lead, and that they are personally excited and enthusiastic about the direction in which we are headed. Credibility is the foundation of leadership."[13] Resonance is about the ability of a leader to communicate the coherence of his or her own convictions regarding the change process. Resistance gains a foothold if the leader is perceived at any point to lack credibility or to step back from an enthusiastic commitment to lead people in their journey of change.

Representational Redescription

This lever entails providing constituents with multiple nonthreatening ways to imagine the opportunities a change process will make possible. The leader makes use of various forms of communication to help followers imagine living into this new vision. This may entail listing new opportunities, or it may invite people to imagine themselves living into a storied presentation of the new ways of being and doing after the change. Effective leaders are able to make appeals to different intelligences. While some people are convinced by more logical presentations, others may find themselves moved by the leader's ability to communicate effective images that help followers to envision the new reality. Gardner states, "A change of mind becomes convincing to the extent that it lends itself to representation in a number of different forms reinforcing one another."[14]

This form of leverage, which offsets resistance, is particularly relevant to preaching and to the second of the three tasks of vision-bearing leadership noted above. I will explore this connection later in this essay. Pastors need to be able to provide a clear biblical and theological justification for how living into the vision will continue to sustain the core identity of the congregation.

13. James Kouzes and Barry Posner, *Credibility: How Leaders Gain It, Lose It, and Why People Demand It* (San Francisco: Jossey-Bass, 1993), 22.
14. Gardner, *Changing Minds*, 16.

Failure in providing meaningful representational redescription that is linked to the congregation's core identity provides resistance leaders the means to reject the change process as an alien activity being imported into the spiritual community.

Resources and Rewards

Leaders must be willing to allocate rewards for productive efforts in realizing gains in the achievement of the vision. These leader resources are more obvious in for-profit organizations. For example, Jim Collins, the author of *Good to Great*, is famous for arguing that leaders of great companies have responsibility for getting the right people in the right seats on the bus. But in nonprofits it's usually only founding leaders who have any real say as to who gets to be in the key positions on the bus that leads the caravan. The ability of nonprofit leaders, especially pastors, is particularly diffuse because congregations often seek to reduce pastors to a role of manager of existing ministries and are reluctant to let pastors take risks that lead to change in existing structures.

I was in my first pastorate in a growing congregation when a wise lay leader explained why I was experiencing such resistance even in the face of positive congregational growth. Leo Moore said to me, "You have to understand, Bob. If you try and fail, then you'll just move on, and we are left to pick up the pieces. On the other hand, if you succeed, then the denomination or some other bigger church will tap you on the shoulder, and you'll be gone. Either way, we're left picking up the pieces." Leo's sobering words were my first real introduction to the reason that most congregations try to keep pastors in the role of a chaplain-manager rather than invite them to become leaders. Add to this the fact that the congregation is the pastor's employer, and it becomes immediately apparent that a pastor's power, especially in a democratically religious organization, is diffuse.[15]

Jim Collins has grasped the essence of this problem in *Good to Great and the Social Sectors* by pointing to the experience of Frances Hesselbein, the CEO of the Girl Scouts of America. Hesselbein responded to the question "What's it like to be on top of such a large organization?" by saying, "I'm not on top

15. On preaching and pastoral leadership see Ronald J. Allen, *Preaching and Practical Ministry* (St. Louis: Chalice Press, 2001); Craig Satterlee, *When God Speaks through Change: Preaching in Times of Congregational Transition* (Herndon, VA: Alban Institute, 2005). For a general systems theory approach to pastoral leadership see Norman Shawchuck and Roger Heuser, *Leading the Congregation: Caring for Yourself While Serving the People* (Nashville: Abingdon Press, 1993). For a mainline study of congregational leadership see Jackson W. Carroll and Becky R. McMillan, *God's Potters: Pastoral Leadership and the Shaping of Congregations* (Grand Rapids: Wm. B. Eerdmans Publishing Co., 2006). For an evangelical model of congregational leadership see Jim Herrington, Mike Bonem, and James H. Furr, *Leading Congregational Change: A Practical Guide for the Transformational Journey* (San Francisco: Jossey-Bass, 2000).

of anything." When asked how she got anything done without concentrated executive power she responded, "'Oh you always have power, if you just know where to find it. There is the power of inclusion, and the power of language, and the power of shared interests, and the power of coalition. Power is all around you to draw upon, but it is rarely raw, rarely visible.'"[16]

Just because pastors do not have the power to appoint and to remove people who are in the way of a change process does not mean that the pastor is without power. It simply means the lines of accountability for that power are more diffuse. A pastor who does not work the network of influence involved in "getting things done" in the congregation is a pastor who lacks influence and will meet stiff resistance if he or she tries to be anything other than a chaplain managing ongoing ministries.

Real-World Events

This lever is an acknowledgment of external factors that affect what a leader can influence. There are always factors beyond the control of the leader that impinge on the success of the leader's vision. The essential feature of leadership here is that the leader needs to be perceived as having acted with intelligence, good instincts, and integrity. Gardner maintains that "the most important trait for a leader to have is integrity."[17] When it comes to the passion to move them this trait is experienced as credibility. When it comes to whether the leader is viewed as grounded in reality, the necessary trait is integrity. Vision proposals and vision stories that do not resonate and lack integrity with reality will eventually meet resistance from small groups in the church that close ranks or groups that are concerned that changes will take away from their well-earned turf.

Resistance

Last, but far from least, Gardner argues that a leader "must take into account the power of various resistances."[18] The leader must be willing to challenge prevailing resistances that hinder the organization from realizing a new vision of change by leveraging the six other resources of leadership available to him or her. Reason and its buttressing resources should be employed to engage resistance to discover whether it represents substantive counterarguments

16. Jim Collins, *Good to Great and the Social Sectors: A Monograph to Accompany Good to Great* (Boulder, CO: Jim Collins, 2005), 9–10.
17. Gardner, *Changing Minds*, 112.
18. Ibid., 18.

why the change should not occur or just represents difficulty in letting the past go.

Pastors need to be prepared for the fact that resistance is going to occur when they try to lead necessary change. In *Managing Transitions: Making the Most of Change*, William Bridges provides excellent resources to help leaders determine "how to get people to let go" so that they can have closure with the past and be able to imagine the possibilities of the future. He argues that if resistance is to be met in a productive manner, it is the responsibility of the leader[s] to 1) identify who's losing what, 2) accept the reality and importance of subjective losses, 3) not be surprised at overreaction, 4) acknowledge the losses openly and sympathetically, 5) expect and accept signs of grieving, 6) compensate for losses, 7) give people information again and again, 8) define what's over and what isn't, 9) mark the endings, 10) treat the past with respect, 11) let people take a piece of the old with them, and 12) show how endings ensure the continuity of what really matters.[19] Endings must be respected if a leader hopes to see possibilities be given a chance to succeed.

III

Resistance generally emerges in three different forms: individual, small group, and systemic or pervasive (that is, resistances that indicate a system-wide failure of leadership). What follows are twelve ways, divided among the three forms, that people in congregations typically phrase their resistance, along with suggestions for responding to parishioners who resist change.[20]

Active Individual Resistance

1. *"These changes are stupid. We don't need change; we just need people to support what we have been doing."* Leaders counter **blind resistance** by determining what the real issue of resistance is and helping individuals move toward closure so they can let go of the past.

2. *"Why are we changing the way things are working? Instead of changing the way we do things we just need to do more. . . ."* Leaders counter **political resistance** by discovering why individuals believe they will lose power in the new reality and by helping them to imagine how they can model positive uses of power for the new future.

3. *"This change is just wrong! It is a betrayal of the faith and everything we stand for."* Leaders try to determine whether **ideological resistance** is real or

19. William Bridges, *Managing Transitions: Making the Most of Change*, 2nd ed. (Cambridge, MA: De Capo Press, 2003), 23–38.
20. Adapted from "Table 6.2," Burke, *Organization Change*, 114.

ideal; if the latter, then the task is helping the individual to let go of the hegemonic worldview that marginalizes the hopes of others. If it is real, it will likely lead to a parting of the ways.

4. *"You know what? They can do whatever they want. I don't care anymore."* It is rare that **apathy** can be countered since changing one's mind can only occur if there is sufficient passion to care about what happens in the organization.

Small-Group Resistance

5. *"These changes aren't fair. Why does our group have to give up . . ."* **Turf protection resistance** is always about a fear that there will be a loss of power, best redressed by helping participants reimagine the role of their group in the new reality.

6. *"The Women's Bible Study fellowship agree that these changes mean that we won't be able to . . ."* **Closing ranks/circling-the-wagons resistance** is a basic fear response; best redressed by providing conceptual frameworks to help people understand more clearly what is happening to them in the change and why the vision for change is needed.

7. *"Go ahead and make these changes and see if people will follow. We're not going to . . ."* **Changing-allegiances resistance** is typically best countered by having an outside agent hold a listening event with a goal to listen for the real issues at stake in the resistance.

8. *"We're no longer comfortable with where [fill in the leader's name] is taking us. . . ."* The **demand for new leadership** is an inevitable form of **resistance** that will occur at some point by a diffuse network of people who believe they are losing power. It will often be led by the people who have been ensconced in power for the longest period in the history of the church and recognize that the new vision will mean they will no longer hold the reigns that have kept the organization locked in its current operative orientation. Other leaders in the church who support the change process and are authorized by the central leadership need to meet with this group and challenge its efforts to make the decision to change about the pastor. If congregational leaders do not support the pastor when this type of resistance occurs, they set the pastor up to be the fall person for residual anger later.

Systemic or Pervasive Resistance

9. *"Yeah, we're adding that to the list. . . ."* When **revolution is reduced to evolution resistance,** it means that the organizational leadership has failed in its effort to communicate how the new organizational situation or culture will be different from how things worked before. A similar version of this is voiced as *"This too shall pass."* Here organization members *resist* by trivializing the change process, *treating change as yet another fad;* such statements may represent the resistance of the late adapters. But if it becomes system wide, it represents a failure on the part of the leadership

team to create the sense of urgency necessary to motivate people to see the need for change.

10. *"Our church just needs to focus on things that really matter."* When it seems that there is an **insufficient urgency experienced requiring the need to change,** it represents evidence of a leadership failure of the first communicative task—that of creating a sense of urgency requiring change.

11. *"We [choir members] don't think the pastor knows what he's doing. Look how badly he's treating [fill in a staff member's name who is sympathetic to the resistance]. Maybe it's time for the senior pastor to go."* When someone is able successfully to **fan the flames of a diversionary crisis and manufacture widespread resistance,** leadership may have failed to sustain the vision of change or failed to remove obstacles to realizing the new vision. This is a problem of complacency when it looks like the change has been accomplished. Other congregational leaders need to come alongside and support the pastor if she or he is the focus of the resistance movement's efforts at this point, and the vision needs to be rerooted in the system. Left unattended this resistance can sabotage the entire change process.

12. *"That's all well and good for [list the names of key parishioners supporting change], but we're not going to sit still and let them destroy what it has taken years to . . ."* This resistance usually reflects either a **lack of real followership** or **the efforts of an individual making a bid to lead significant division.** This failure arises for much the same reason as the previous resistance. Once again, other congregational leaders need to stop this effort to stall the change process. Left unattended this resistance will also sabotage the entire change process.

Obviously, not all dissent should be viewed as negative. Kassing has provided the most significant research that validates the voice of dissent in response to organizational power and organization change.[21] Applied to the larger church there certainly is a role for congregational dissent, especially in issues of inappropriate use of power, as in clergy sexual abuse or differences of belief regarding acceptance of homosexual clergy, and so forth.[22] But if you have ever been in a congregation going through a significant change process, you recognize many of these voices that mostly represent efforts to retain the old system. The fact that they occurred, especially at the level of individual

21. See J. W. Kassing, "Articulating, Antagonizing, and Displacing: A Model of Employee Dissent," *Communication Studies* 48 (1997): 311–32; Kassing, "Investigating the Relationship between Superior-Subordinate Relationship Quality and Employee Dissent," *Communication Research Reports* 17 (2000a): 58–70; Kassing, "Exploring the Relationship between Workplace Freedom of Speech, Organizational Identification, and Employee Dissent," *Communication Research Reports* 17 (2000b): 387–96. Kassing, "From the Look of Things: Assessing Perceptions of Organizational Dissenters," *Management Communication Quarterly* 14 (2001): 442–70; Kassing, "Speaking Up: Identifying Employees' Upward Dissent Strategies, *Management Communication Quarterly* 16 (2002): 187–209.

22. On the concern over the relationship between the power of magisterium and the responsibility of congregational dissent see Joseph A. Bracken, "Toward a Grammar of Dissent," *Theological Studies* 31 (1970): 437–59.

and small-group resistance, is natural and even inevitable. Leaders who know how these types of resistance will occur can actually turn resistance itself into a lever of change. On the other hand, when resistance becomes pervasive, it generally reflects a failure on the part of those responsible for vision bearing to sustain the original impetus for making the change. A standard leadership maxim in these maters is, *Leaving resistance unchallenged is like investing in savings bonds; it matures with interest.*

<h1 style="text-align:center">IV</h1>

I asked Pastor Dotson of Grandview Methodist Church how he saw the relationship between preaching and leading the change process: "Did it affect your preaching? What texts if any did you preach?" Pastor Dotson indicated that he did not vary from his commitment to preach the lectionary, but admitted he tended to choose the Hebrew Scripture texts rather than the New Testament: "You can always find something in those wilderness journey stories in Exodus and Deuteronomy. . . . They gave me an opportunity to speak to the people who were longing for Egypt and call them to journey with the rest of God's people headed for the promised land." As for other texts about changing one's mind, the most famous change of mind in recorded history is by a first-century rabbi otherwise known as Saul of Tarsus.[23] And the most famous leader who sought to change the minds of people was Jesus of Nazareth. The fact that Jesus employed teaching, parable, and testimony to challenge his community to reconceive their vision of God's purposes with humankind is built into the very DNA of Christianity. If preachers wish to deal directly with the issue of resistance in the pulpit, they can look to no more honorable heroes than Moses, Jesus, and Paul.

It is the third communicative task of leadership noted earlier that most directly implicates the pulpit: the task of providing a conceptual framework to help people understand more clearly what is happening to them during change and why the vision for change is needed. The pulpit provides pastors with an inherent congregational resource that their secular counterparts lack. Even when the president of the United States gives a State of the Union address, reruns of *Law and Order* on the cable channels often draw heavier viewing numbers. The sermon, on the other hand, is still central to the process of identity formation for most communities of faith. People look to a pastor to provide wise counsel about how to understand who they are as people of faith and how the changes they are experiencing in their personal life and in their

---

23. Gardner, *Changing Minds*, 186.

congregational life should be met. Warren Bennis and Burt Nanus maintain that "by focusing attention on vision, the leader operates on the *emotional and spiritual resources* of the organization, on its values, commitments, and aspirations. The manager by contrast, operates on the *physical resources* of the organization, on its capital, human skills, raw materials and technology."[24]

The work of conceptual reframing is at the heart of preaching's vision-bearing purpose. Gospel truth and gospel identity represent a timeless identity into which Christians are called to live. But how one lives into this identity in any given time, place, and culture is always different. Preachers are responsible for keeping Christian identity from devolving into a tribal identity by focusing on how the people of God must participate both individually and corporately in their communities of faith, thereby advancing the unfinished life of Jesus in their time and their place. When a vision-bearing preacher helps people reframe what is happening in their midst in terms of a gospel reality of something bigger than they are, that preacher is providing leadership in the most fundamental of human needs—"the need to be important, to make a difference, to feel useful, to be part of a successful and worthwhile enterprise."[25] Preaching is where this task is best realized in the Christian community. Preaching that effectively identifies the aspirations of a specific change process with the core congregational identity and gospel purposes of a specific community of faith will help the greatest number of people in that congregation make the transition into the new vision of who and how to be when the change is fully realized.

V

Two years into a new facility, where the old name based on a street location now identified the vista beyond the glass wall comprising much of the front portion of the sanctuary, Pastor Dotson was excited by the congregation's prospect of living into the new century. Younger leadership stepped up during the change, filling in for older leaders who chose not to make the transition. The fear that the congregation would not be able to make it financially seemed to be a thing of the past. Of course there were budget concerns, but new members and new leaders were stepping up to the task of meeting the

---

24. Warren Bennis and Burt Nanus, *Leaders: Strategies for Taking Charge*, 2nd ed. (New York: CollinsBusiness Essentials, 2005), 85. This quote is taken from the first of what Bennis and Nanus identify as four strategies leaders (as opposed to managers) embody: 1) attention through vision, 2) meaning through communication, 3) trust through positioning, and 4) a deployment of self through positive self-regard.
25. Ibid., 85–86.

vision of ministry the congregation imagined when it voted to take the risk to move. Of course there was residual sadness over the loss of the beloved members who had left the congregation rather than accept changes involved in moving, but the congregation now seemed poised for growth in many ways. New families were coming into the life of the congregation, made possible because of new facilities. Key to the growth was also the versatility that the new worship space provided. Worship experiences similar to those held in the former facilities still occurred in one service, but other services on Sunday and at other times were shaped by expectations of contemporary worship styles not possible in the original building.

Pastor Dotson believed they had weathered the change well. That confidence may account for some of his surprise with the level of congregational resistance that arose when he was compelled to make a staff decision that normally would have been seen as unfortunate but understandably necessary. Resistance to the decision grew, and it eventually became apparent that residual anger, likely anger that represented many of the losses in both style and substance that had occurred for some congregational members in the change process, was being tapped into and was playing itself out in the drama that unfolded.

A year after that decision it was apparent that Pastor Dotson's ability to lead had been dealt what he believed to be a mortal wound. He felt isolated from many with whom he had worked shoulder to shoulder to bring the change process to a successful resolution. It was clear to him that the congregation needed a different leader to take them to the next stage of growth. He announced his decision to retire from pastoral ministry a year out to permit the congregation to explore identity issues with the bishop regarding the next clergy appointment in June 2009.[26]

Extensive interviews with congregational members and additional analysis of the nature of Pastor Dotson's twenty-year ministry with this congregation would be needed to present a clear case study of his decision to take early retirement at age sixty-two. It is not atypical that a pastor ends up leaving within a year or so of guiding a significant building program or a change

---

26. During the six months I wrote this essay I visited the congregation's Web site numerous times. One matter struck me as odd from the first time I visited it in November 2008. Particularly telling of the congregation's ambivalence about its pastor was the fact that while all staff members are listed by name and role, the "Meet the Pastor" link led to the following simple message: "This page is under construction." The pastor's name appeared nowhere on the Web site and could only be discovered in archived PDF newsletters. Was it Pastor Dotson's choice not to submit anything or that of the congregational leadership to leave this link empty? I did not ask during the interview. The fact that the congregational leadership permitted this rather glaring lacuna on their Web page speaks more loudly than any explanation that might have been offered by either the congregational leaders or by Pastor Dotson.

process.[27] Diversionary resistance often occurs even after the first phases of a change process seem complete. More study is needed to determine whether such pastoral transitions represent a response to residual problems in dealing with resistance during a change process or simply represent leader burnout.

Leading change is hard, and it is hard on pastors. What is apparent is that pastors become leaders rather than congregational managers *when they take responsibility to become the vision bearer for "making something happen" in the life of the congregation and then take responsibility for preparing for resistance that will inevitably occur along the journey.*

---

27. Cf. Dean R. Hoge and Jacqueline E. Wenger, *Pastors in Transition: Why Clergy Leave Local Church Ministry* (Grand Rapids: Wm. B. Eerdmans Publishing Co., 2005).

21

Preaching as a New Pastor in Times of Congregational Crisis

JOHN S. MCCLURE

In the fall of 2003 I arrived in Nashville to begin working at Vanderbilt Divinity School. A few weeks after I began work, Second Presbyterian Church burned to the ground. As it turned out, the church burned while the new pastor, Jim Kitchens, was en route from California to Nashville. Thankfully, Jim had ample experience with church fires, having already seen a former congregation through this same tragedy. Jim brought steady leadership and a contagious optimism that helped Second Presbyterian Church weather the firestorm.

During the three years it took the church to rebuild, my wife, Annie, and I joined the church, pitched in, and did what we could to help. As a homiletician, this experience afforded me the opportunity to become a participant observer in a situation in which both congregational trauma and leadership transition were under way. In much of the literature on church trauma and crisis, leadership transitions factor in as an important dynamic. Sometimes, these leadership transitions are the cause of congregational crisis. At other times, leadership transitions are necessitated as a result of a crisis. Or, as was the case for Second Presbyterian Church, transition and congregational trauma simply coincide as a part of the natural order of events.

This essay seeks to hold both congregational crisis and leadership transition together. I will be writing primarily to pastors who are entering congregations that have experienced crisis or trauma. Some of what is written here will, of course, be easily generalized to long-standing pastors of churches undergoing periods of intense difficulty. My principle aim, however, is to make some focused observations on the things that new leader-preachers should be aware of.

Jill M. Hudson, in her book *Congregational Trauma: Caring, Coping, and Learning*, draws an important distinction between "crisis" and "trauma."[1] According to Hudson, crises are to some extent *expected* in the regular course of events. Trauma, on the other hand, is "the result of an unanticipated and sudden event and always involves significant personal loss, which leaves the individual feeling devastated and out of control."[2] Leadership transitions, therefore, usually operate more in the "crisis" category. We expect to lose our pastors as a part of the regular flow of institutional life. The burning of a church building, the revelation of abuse or incest by a pastor or lay leader, or the murder or suicide of a church board member function more in the "trauma" category. When the two of these are put together, as often occurs, the congregation experiences a tremendous number of simultaneous stressors. As if congregational trauma were not enough, normal patterns of leadership, some of which might have provided support and guidance, are missing or seriously compromised. A new leader and preacher in this situation, therefore, not only has to deal with the normal crisis of leadership transition but the additional stress associated with unexpected catastrophe.

Another helpful lens to focus on congregational crisis and trauma is provided by Andrew Lester, who divides crisis into two categories: *interruptive* and *eruptive*. An interruptive crisis has an external origin: a hurricane, a fire, a car accident, a murder. An eruptive crisis emerges from congregational life and is most often the result of the festering of systemic issues of conflicts that finally erupt and traumatize the entire congregational system, forcing the need for new leadership and direction.[3]

Still another helpful lens to put on a crisis or trauma is provided by Ronald Allen, who suggests that in situations of crisis or trauma there are, in fact, two levels of crisis under way that need to be distinguished. The first is a crisis of *understanding*, whereby people need to understand what exactly has happened, why it has happened, and how they can make sense out of it theologically. The second is a crisis of *decision*. Within this framework, people are struggling to understand what they are to do in response to the situation at hand. How are they to best organize their energy and resources in the aftermath of congregational crisis or trauma in order to move forward in life-sustaining and redemptive ways? Although preachers function largely as those who help congregations understand, they are also decision leaders in

---

1. Jill M. Hudson, *Congregational Trauma: Caring, Coping, and Learning* (Herndon, VA: Alban Institute, 1998), 16–17.
2. Ibid., 16.
3. Quoted from a lecture presented at Brite Divinity School by Joey R. Jeter Jr. in his book *Crisis Preaching: Personal and Public* (Nashville: Abingdon Press, 1998), 18.

congregations, helping congregations make decisions and choices that lead to new life.[4]

With these definitions and perspectives in mind, let me now move to a set of issues and dynamics that require new congregational leader-preachers' attention as they suddenly find themselves in congregations undergoing the effects of trauma.

ANXIETY

Peter L. Steinke, in his book *Congregational Leadership in Anxious Times: Being Calm and Courageous No Matter What*, points out that when a congregation's equilibrium is upset, one of the key immediate issues is anxiety. Adapting a definition from Murray Bowen's work, Steinke notes that "anxiety is an automatic reaction 'to a threat real or imagined.'"[5] Anxiety is a natural reaction designed for self-preservation and survival. Steinke notes that anxiety is contagious in congregations and can lead to a large range of reactive behaviors, many of which can be destructive of relationships. In this context he asserts that it is absolutely imperative that leaders "differentiate" in order to avoid being "triangled" as the lightning rod between people who are engaging in largely reactive behaviors. According to Steinke, "differentiated" leaders guide their behavior by

- thinking clearly,
- acting on principle,
- defining self by taking a position,
- coming to know more about their own instinctive reactions to others.
- learning to regulate those reactions,
- staying in contact with others, and
- choosing a responsible course of action.[6]

The goal is to become a "nonanxious presence," aware of what is happening within oneself while maintaining a clear sense of direction in a sea of chaos.[7]

For preachers, becoming a "nonanxious presence" begins with issues of voice. If you are new to a congregation, it is likely that you already lack some confidence, feeling within yourself and conveying to others a certain amount of healthy anxiety about proclaiming God's word in a new situation. In situations of trauma, you will experience increased pressure placed on the act of

---

4. See ibid., 25–66.
5. Peter L. Steinke, *Congregational Leadership in Anxious Times: Being Calm and Courageous No Matter What* (Herndon, VA: Alban Institute, 2006), 3.
6. Ibid., 19.
7. Ibid., 31–45.

preaching itself and the role of leadership from the pulpit. This can heighten your natural performance anxiety to new levels, exacerbating confidence issues. This anxiety comes from your innate sense that voice itself is dependent, to a large extent, on acceptance and belonging—two emotions often in short supply in congregations in trauma and transition.

In my introduction to homiletics classes, I have begun using an exercise encouraged by Mary Lin Hudson and Mary Donovan Turner in which I ask my students to remember a time when they've felt completely voiceless and a time when they've felt most voiced.[8] Inevitably, students feel *least* voiced in situations where they are under extreme critical scrutiny or when they are being shamed, avoided, disregarded, not accepted, or resisted. They feel *most* voiced when they feel acceptance, love, respect, and belonging.

When you are a new preacher, a great deal of the basic communicative tone and felt presence that exists between you and your congregation is defined by your (and the congregation's) belief that you are truly "voiced" in the current situation. As a small assist in this process, I encourage you to try what I encourage my students to do: to envision yourself in a "voiced" rather than "unvoiced" space when you preach—a task that requires both your positive memory and immediate imaginative powers. Like an athlete envisioning the race ahead, imagine yourself as differentiated, accepted, belonging, and *fully present*, claiming the new pulpit and this congregation as a space in which you are voiced. If you can operate from a voiced space, it is contagious and can encourage the same kind of open, direct, and voiced communication in the congregation.

Beyond the issue of voiced *presence*, Steinke's list encourages you to think clearly, act on principle, and define yourself by taking a position. This does not mean choosing sides but refers to the larger aspects of claiming *your voice* in the midst of the traumatized congregation. While remaining flexible, you need to be clear about your perspective and vision for the congregation—theologically, spiritually, and missionally. Anxiety can be diffused when you bring a consistent theology and an open-ended plan of action—not a blueprint—into the pulpit and are able to share these in direct but noncontrolling ways. In our situation at Second Presbyterian Church, Jim Kitchens was clear, consistent, and self-differentiated in his theology and vision, using it to interpret our situation in meaningful and helpful ways. He also managed to express and demonstrate genuine willingness to stay in communication with others with differing perspectives. The combination of his voiced presence, theological clarity, relationality, and commitment to an open-ended but stabilizing plan of action went a long way toward relieving congregational anxiety.

---

8. Mary Donovan Turner and Mary Lin Hudson, *Saved from Silence: Finding Women's Voice in Preaching* (St. Louis: Chalice Press, 1999), 99–104.

GRIEF

Once the emergency stage of trauma is over, the reality of what has been lost usually sets in. This loss can extend from physical loss to the pervasive sense of loss of personal or congregational control over one's destiny. In order for you to preach sermons that help your new congregation grieve adequately, several things are important. First, take the time to listen deeply to the congregation's interpretations of what has happened and to decipher what this crisis means to them. Be careful not to import meanings or to assume everyone in the congregation understands what has happened. As much as possible, determine what really happened and to whom it happened, as opposed to what members of the congregation think happened. This will help you accurately and adequately name the trauma from several perspectives when preaching. Naming is the first step toward gaining some small sense of control over a phenomenon of this magnitude. It is also important that you work to name the kinds of feelings, positive and negative, associated with what has happened. Knowing and naming these feelings can help the congregation adequately lament the loss they have endured. Lamentation always involves an accurate naming of a crisis and what has been lost, as well as an accurate identification of the feelings that accompany that event in the presence of God.

FEAR

Fear is the feeling that a trauma will continue, deepen, or lead to something worse—including death. In a situation such as a natural disaster or fire, adult fear typically focuses on finding the economic resources to sustain or rebuild the congregation and its facilities. When the trauma is eruptive and has come from within the congregation's life, the fear may be that internal conflicts are so toxic that the church will split and perhaps dissolve.

In the midst of fear, you can visibly demonstrate from the pulpit what Paul Tillich called "the courage to be" in the face of our shared finitude.[9] This courage is not grounded in our own adequacies or in other penultimate concerns (survival, growth, image, money, etc.), but in finding, once again, the congregation's "ultimate concern" in the person and work of Jesus Christ.[10] Tillich's framework, in my opinion, is one of the very best for dealing with fear. According to Tillich, when we are insecure, we cling to things (material stuff, insurance policies, political power, gossip, prejudice, etc.) that we think

---

9. Paul Tillich, *The Courage to Be*, 2nd ed. (New Haven, CT: Yale University Press, 2000).
10. See Paul Tillich, *The Dynamics of Faith* (New York: HarperOne, 2001).

will somehow secure us in the world. In your preaching you can help congregations see themselves within a larger transcendent frame of reference in the face of their fears, helping them realize that the only thing they can actually cling to in the midst of fear is the power of Christ's love, which is the power of God's eternal "Being" in the midst of the threat of nonbeing. It is only from this firm foundation that a congregation can rebuild its life together.

CONTINUITY

After any crisis within a congregation, questions linger: "Who are we now?" "What kinds of continuity can there be with our past?" "What do we do with our memories, good and bad?" "How can we maintain continuity with the good parts of our past while learning from what has just happened to us?" Within this frame, preachers can consider two things. The first is storytelling. As a new preacher, you cannot claim to have been a part of a congregation's past, so you cannot claim to be an adequate historian of the church in its proper sense. There are many people in the church who will be far better historians, and there are many helpful exercises that can be used (timelines, interviews, storytelling groups, etc.) to gain access to a church's history. Focus some of your preaching energy on letting the congregation see you working at becoming a faithful storyteller. This might include several things: One practice involves gathering the stories within the congregation and retelling them in bits and pieces. A second practice is to invite persons from the congregation to offer testimonies that tell the story of the church's past in terms of its impact on the lives of key individuals. This is another way to help the congregation envision the good surviving qualities of the church going forward. Longtime members feel respected through this process, and their spiritual leadership and wisdom are utilized. Testimonies by more recent members help the church realize its immediate and ongoing witness.

At Second Presbyterian Church in Nashville, Jim Kitchens instituted this kind of storytelling from the pulpit, inviting long-term and shorter-term members to speak about their own faith within the context of Second Presbyterian Church. This has had a very positive effect, helping the church maintain continuity with the past as it moves forward in a new sanctuary and building, with many new members who have no memory of the way things used to be.

Third, it is also comforting if you can preach in ways that show some continuity with what has gone before, at least in the immediate term. If, for instance, the previous preacher preached from the lectionary, you may want to avoid abandoning this practice in favor of topical sermon focused entirely around the congregation's immediate plight or your leadership goals. The lectionary provides ample opportunity for preachers to deal with the key issues in crisis situations. Other pulpit practices might also be carried forward, at least in the short term, so that the church doesn't experience more disruption.

VISION

If continuity addresses who we have been in relation to who we are, vision seeks to relate who we are to whom we will become. Most new pastors come into churches with some agenda or sense of where the church needs to move as a congregation in mission. The worst that can happen for a church in trauma is for these agendas to be imported entirely from the outside. A range of programs and models, such as those for becoming a "postmodern church," creating "church growth," or participating in the "emerging conversation," might be relevant, but when trotted out too quickly as blueprints, they might communicate that the immediate issues at hand are being either avoided or subsumed.

Although some of these larger visions and techniques may be helpful, it is extremely important in crisis situations that ministers work as inductively and collaboratively as possible in developing a shared vision within a congregation. The reason for this is that heaping large amounts of external expectation on a congregation that is already enduring forced change can lead to a certain amount of additional "push-back" between congregation and leadership. I encourage you to do something like the brief congregational study set forth in Nora Tubbs Tisdale's book *Preaching as Local Theology and Folk Art,* if only to determine the contours of the inherent theological genius of the congregation before attempting to correct or expand its vision. Allow a new vision to grow up organically out of the ashes of lament and grief as they are processed from the pulpit. God's new vision for a church should always take into account the ways that God has been at work in the past and helped the church through its times of crisis.

ACTION

The final frame within which the preacher operates is the action frame. This relates directly to Ron Allen's "crisis of decision" referred to earlier. Here the fundamental question for the preacher to address is, "What are we to do?" "What are the principal baby steps we must take as we move forward, and what are the larger issues in our midst and around us that we as a community of faith must seek to engage?" Congregational crisis has a way of focusing congregational action inward: "We must rebuild!" "We must act to get our insurance money!" "We must do damage control in the media!" "We must find a new building to worship in temporarily!" "We must act to keep our members!" "We must act to find a new member for the church board!"

Given this opportunity to have a significant impact on the church's infrastructure, processes, and procedures, it is tempting for preachers to turn the pulpit into a platform for church administration. "We need to do this next." "Let's take time out during the sermon to all take this survey." "Let's meditate this morning on the three-fold plan of action adopted by our board." The sermon becomes the place to conduct business or to fulfill the next thing on the minister's administrative punch list.

Rather than capitulating to this impulse, the preacher can work to keep the church's vision focused on deeper matters than administrative issues. In particular, preachers can focus on deepening the congregation's spiritual and relational life and helping the church maintain its sense of mission and outreach. One of the best antidotes to the way that a church in crisis can become internally conflicted is to help the church remember its mission to its members and to the world as its raison d'être. This should not be done in a manner that denies the need to work through internal conflicts or to avoid them. Rather, it becomes a way of healing relationships and connecting the best of the internal life of the congregation to its primary *activity* as the body of Christ in the community.

Every new situation bears within it new possibilities for participating in God's mission in the world. The preacher's goal is to work at the intersection of Scripture, theology, and the congregation's situation to discern these possibilities. One of the most helpful homiletic methods for accomplishing this during sermon preparation is what I sometimes call the "three story" method. Draw three overlapping circles on a blank sheet of paper. In one circle, titled "our story," enter notes focusing on a positive aspect of the current situation in the congregation. In a second circle, called "the larger story," enter notes focused on a situation or several closely linked situations within the community. It is helpful to have a newspaper in hand when considering the "larger story." In a third circle, called "God's story," enter the biblical text to be preached (this text does not have to be based on the other two stories but could be the lectionary passage for the day). Include in this circle any ideas from biblical commentaries as well as theological ideas within your tradition, making good use of the theological books on your bookshelves. In the middle, overlapping section, begin to observe ways in which these "stories" talk with one another, challenging, encouraging, critiquing, corresponding, or reframing one another. In most cases, new missional commitments and plans for action in the community will grow from this three-way conversation.

CONCLUSIONS

The role of preaching in the midst of congregational trauma and leadership transition cannot be underestimated. In many respects, the tone, style, and direction of leadership in all congregations are all set from the pulpit, and these matters are of utmost importance in congregations experiencing significant disequilibria. It is crucial that new preachers in congregations undergoing trauma are able to deal with anxiety, grief, fear, loss of continuity, lost vision, and the need for decisive action. You may not have all of the abilities necessary to meet these concerns. If not, it is possible to pray for the Spirit's help and to work hard at cultivating the abilities you need. Transitional leadership in times of trauma requires that we constantly open ourselves up to the leadership of the Spirit of God, whose presence and help can only be discovered through prayer and spiritual discernment. Here are some of the key abilities we can pray for:

- Voice (differentiation)—the ability to clearly and with confidence articulate a position that is not triangled by competing parties
- Openness—the ability to listen while developing a vision for the future
- Discernment—the ability to help the church name its grief and lament its losses
- Courage—the ability to access the power of God's Spirit, sustaining the church in the midst of their fears about the future
- Narrativity—the ability to help the church retell its story in a way that connects past, present, and future in positive ways
- Vision—the ability to preach a congregational vision that grows organically out of the ashes of lament, grief, and shared story
- Decisiveness—the ability to preach toward new missional commitments emerging in the new situation

These abilities, while not exactly "gifts of the Spirit," can go a long way in clearing the way for the Spirit's renewing power to gift your congregation with new life after experiencing trauma. What follows is a sermon addressing Jesus' ascension and how this story helps a particular congregation navigate through a treacherous channel of transition.

The End of the World As We Know It

Psalm 47; Acts 1:1–11

The ascension of Jesus Christ was deemed so important by our ancient forbears in the faith that they made it a part of the earliest Christian creeds.

Many of you will recall in the Apostles Creed that it says, "On the third day he arose from the dead, he ascended into heaven, and sitteth on the right hand of God the father almighty. . . ."

For the early followers of Jesus, the ascension marked the end of their earthly experience of Jesus, and it marked the beginning of the "in-between times" leading up to Jesus' "second coming," a time of between-ness that we still live in today. If Jesus' followers had been in my Sunday school class on the theme of music and religious identity last year, I imagine that they would have asked us to listen to REM's "At the End of the World As We Know It." Everything they had been living for seemed up for grabs.

And they couldn't help but wonder out loud, "Is this the time?" "Is this the TIME?" The time when God "will restore the kingdom to Israel"? When God will make the world whole once again.

Between-ness, living at the "end of the world as we know it," confronting an unsure future, may well describe the very essence of our society and institutions during this post-everything generation. After the modern (after the postmodern)—then what? After the gas-powered automobile, then what? After the polar ice caps are gone—then what? After global terrorism—then what? After churches and denominations—then what?

Think of all of those around us here and in our community whose lives are marked this day in very difficult ways by "between-ness," by sometimes difficult "passages": all those who are graduating from high school or college. This is the end of the world as they know it. Those whose government jobs are on the line across the state of Tennessee. This is the end of the world as they know it. Those whose homes are being repossessed as part of our mortgage crisis. The families of those whose lifeless bodies are on their way home from Iraq this day. This is the end of the world as they know it. And our longtime congregation members here at Second Church, as we have now finally begun worshiping in our new sanctuary, with two new pastors, and so many new faces, it is increasingly clear to us that this is the end of the world as we have known it.

Deep inside, these days, many of us are experiencing the end of the world as we know it. And we are asking like the church did on that ascension day long ago, "Now what? Is this the time?" SHOULDN'T this be the time? The time of God's great restoration? We wish for it. We long for it. We pray for it.

I'm sorry to say that in order to be faithful to this story in Acts, I have to repeat to you Jesus' words to the disciples; and they are words of delay: "'It is not for you to know the times or periods that the Father has set by his own authority'" (Acts 1:7). How frustrating! As if we didn't already know that! As if we weren't already living with the constant sense of incompletion and insecurity!

Well then, are we left hanging with this plea for help and the incessant delay: the seemingly omnipotent detour of healing and wholeness? "'It is not for you to know the times or periods.'" Is this all we have: our insecure, troubled between-ness and God's omnipotent delay?

Thank goodness our biblical story doesn't stop here! For the next thing that happens in the story is that we are given a purpose—a mission.

Jesus says, "'But you will receive power when the Holy Spirit has come upon you; and you will be my witnesses in Jerusalem, in all Judea and Samaria, and to the ends of the earth" (v. 8). Christ reminds us that we are not left in between worlds without spiritual power and purpose. There are very important things to do during these in-between times, as we work toward God's new day. We at Second Presbyterian Church are a "roll up your sleeves and get to work" bunch. We know what to do. And so,

> we visit and support those who are sick;
> we write our congressmen and women;
> we support the church's mission and programs for justice and renewal;
> we build houses for the homeless;
> we pray, and study the Bible, and worship together.

But this alone is not enough to sustain us during this in-between day. In fact, I think that I would simply feel worn out and weary were it not for what happens next in Luke's story. According to Luke, Jesus was "lifted up, and a cloud took him out of their sight," leaving them "gazing up into heaven" (v. 9). What can it mean that on this "in-between day" the disciples are given a vision of Jesus "taken up" from them into heaven?

Our first thought might be that this is an awful thing, a picture of God abandoning us only to send a phantom spirit later. This is because we like to focus on the divinity of Jesus so much. We like to see Jesus as God on loan to us, condescending to us, and then leaving us to go back to being with God again in heavenly majesty, leaving this mean old world and going home to be with God. We tend to see the ascension as a "homecoming" for Jesus after a long sojourn with humans on earth.[11]

But something in Luke's language hints at another perspective. Luke says that Jesus was "taken" up. He was "lifted" up. A cloud "took" him. The language sounds more like a home *leaving* than a home*coming*. And then the text goes on to say that he will "come" back or return, in the same way—that his home*coming* will be a *return to the world*.[12]

11. George Hunsberger, "'The Day When He Was Taken Up . . .'—A Meditation from Acts 2:1–9," *International Review of Mission* 86, no. 343 (October 1997): 391.
12. Ibid.

Pandipeddi Chenchiah, an Indian Christian theologian, says that this stresses the ongoingness, the permanence of the humanity of Jesus.[13] And I think he's right. Luke, the physician, is showing us a picture of the humanity of Jesus taken into the heart of God, and in that picture we see humanity itself taken more deeply into the heart of God than ever before. This, it seems to me, is profound good news on this "in-between day."

The world changes and we confront new forms of insecurity. We move from one place to another and wonder where we're headed. We experience oppression and sometimes violence. We confront suffering and death. We long for healing and wholeness. We work for justice and peace. But *through it all* we carry with us a vision of our humanity in Christ being taken up into God, sustained, valued, and belonging to God. The ascension of Jesus Christ is good news for our world.

At the end of this story the disciples receive a promise by two men in white robes that there will be a homecoming. This humanity that has been taken up somehow returns to us in a new way, certainly with a new and deeper grounding in the rhythm and beauty of God's life. This is grand, poetic language. I take this to mean that while in Christ the world as we know it is constantly *ending,* in Christ also the world as God knows it is constantly *coming.* Justice and compassion *are* rolling down. The knowledge of God *is* coming and will cover the earth.

On this "in-between day," I encourage you to remember the body and blood, the "permanent humanity" of the ascended one. This truly is the "body of Christ, the bread of heaven." Remember that our own very human lives, our "clay pot" ministries, and the world in which we live are taken up, held, and sustained, and are of great value to God. Remember that God meets us at the end of the world as we know it—meets us with a vision of the beginning of the world as God knows it—of our humanity and our frailty and our suffering and our longing taken up into God's heart, transformed, and one day coming home for good.

13. Ibid.

PART FOUR

The Community in Transition

The last section of essays concerns the idea of modes of change and how these changes influence communities. Sadly, the first writer in this section, Rod Wilmoth, died at the age of seventy-one on Wednesday, February 11, 2009, in Tucson, Arizona, where he was living after retirement. It is to both Ella Mitchell and Rod Wilmoth that this book is dedicated.

Wilmoth's sermon, "The Power of Disruptive Innovation," is based on Jeremiah 1:4 and Luke 4:21–30. By means of an idea he derived from Harvard professor Clayton Christensen, Wilmoth offers a biblical perspective on "disruptive innovation." Disruptive innovation is trying a novel way of doing business without the machinery of traditional organizational structures. Wilmoth then paints a picture of how the department store Sears bested Montgomery Ward by changing a few perceptions and launching into what was then experimental territory. Offering a few other compatible illustrations, Wilmoth drives home his point that sometimes major changes happen with the expanding of a few new insights. The point is that disruptive innovation can alter the way people look at things and therefore alter the way people either embrace or resist change.

Soon Wilmoth turns his homiletic sights on Jesus and shows how Jesus was a disruptive innovator. By accessing Luke 4:21–30 Wilmoth reveals any number of ways for people to understand Jesus. Yet seeing Jesus as a disruptive innovator helps Jesus become incarnate in people's lives. To be able to see change from a multiplicity of perspectives sometimes helps us adjust to our transitions.

Mary Alice Mulligan's essay "Embracing Our Neighborhood in Transition" will resonate with many urban churches and their leaders. As some of our contributors have pointed out, not all change is necessarily bad, but it often creates anxiety in any event. Mulligan addresses steps that a congregation can take to keep tethered to the neighborhood. She identifies the issues and offers some preliminary steps for engagement—much like tilling a garden prior to planting. In addition Mulligan provides some hands-on ideas by which laypersons can engage the neighborhood near the church—even if close-by members have long since died or moved away. One of Mulligan's points of emphasis is that refusal to change is a guaranteed kiss of death for a congregation in a transitioning neighborhood.

Mulligan aims the last part of her hands-on essay toward the preacher and how one might preach in this changing neighborhood circumstance. She furnishes some first-rate ideas on a preaching series that uses texts from the prophet Jeremiah. Over the course of several Sundays, Mulligan supplies texts and sermon ideas to help ease both the congregation and the neighborhood into relationship. In some ways she knows that each needs the other to survive and perhaps even thrive. Mulligan understands the "nature of this beast" because she knows that even after laying the foundation, reinforcing words need to come persistently from the preacher/pastor. The bottom line for Mulligan is simple: institutions must change or die.

Joseph M. Webb, long known as a researcher, teacher, and writer in the field of homiletics, uses Kenneth's Burke's 1935 book *Permanence and Change* to explore the idea of "hub symbols." The initial question Burke explores is what happens when our superstructure of certainties begins to topple. An example is what happened when the unthinkable reality of the Soviet Union's disappearing came to pass, and a hundred things no one ever expected to happen soon became everyday realities. "Hub symbols" are the realities we hold so tightly that we cannot imagine living without these cherished beliefs. They are our core beliefs, as others might call them.

Webb's fairly technical essay explores the meaning of hub symbols in the context of preaching and how some people's principal sources of meaning are so severely ingrained that without deep listening and persuasive preaching no change of attitude is even possible. One helpful Webb insight was that we leaders all need to recognize that some transitions are generational—it takes a long time, in other words, for some things to come to pass. Thus to change hub symbols for people may take a great deal of patience.

"What Has Not Changed about Preaching and Pastoral Care" is O. C. Edwards Jr.'s reassuring word that not everything is up for grabs. After delineating the many ways that human life is now played out, Edwards quotes from his excellent book *A History of Preaching* to show the astounding changes that have occurred in the last forty years. If I had to summarize his essay I would simply say that although the ways that human beings sin may be overtly creative, it is the same old human predicament or condition that causes people to do what they do.

Edwards plays his insights off an essay by Dorothy Sayers, "The City of Dis," which in turn opens up Dante's *Divine Comedy* and the circles of hell. Edwards via Sayers via Dante looks at the remarkable range of human behaviors in all their sinful glory. Edwards's point, of course, is that even with cell phones that can do almost anything and our ability to Google nearly any type of information, we still eat too much, gossip too much, and you-fill-in-the-blank too much. The more things change, the more they stay the same.

Our final essay in the collection comes from the mind of O. Wesley Allen Jr. and his extended title "From Crowded Stable to Empty Tomb to the Sunday Morning Pew: Preaching Transition through the Cycle of the Liturgical Year." This is a fitting essay to conclude because Allen's premise is that the liturgical year and worship help prepare congregants in some respects for the inevitable and unavoidable changes that will come their way. One of the helpful insights included is that of J. L. Austin's diminutive book *How to Do Things with Words*. Allen uses Austin's ideas to survey the concept of performative language, which is part of coping with life's transitions. The balance of the essay concerns some (negative) examples about how preaching language does not just refer back to something that happened long, long ago, but rather preaching language is language that does something now. These kinds of examples of performative language are what happens on Sunday morning (for Christians).

Allen reminds us that preaching and liturgy are powerful allies to help us navigate our congregations through the rough waters of change. Allen makes a compelling case for our referencing faith as a resource for those persons who have been destabilized by change.

22

The Power of Disruptive Innovation

Jeremiah 1:4–10, Luke 4:21–30

Rod Wilmoth

Rod Wilmoth preached the sermon that follows immediately prior to his retirement. In the original manuscript Wilmoth refers to Minneapolis' Hennepin Avenue United Methodist Church (UMC) and how it decided to become a Reconciling Congregation. Thus not only did Wilmoth reference this justice decision about congregational inclusiveness, but he also used the opportunity to attend to how the congregation might deal with a change in pastoral leadership.

In addition, after retirement Wilmoth served as interim pastor at First UMC, Colorado Springs. Wilmoth used this transition sermon to help the congregation tackle change. At the time he arrived there was considerable congregational unrest.

In his book *Seeing What's Next*, Harvard professor Clayton M. Christensen, world-renowned for his work on disruptive innovation, speaks of one of the great business concepts, of how some new, low-cost companies—with their new techniques and unencumbered by a lot of organizational structure, can cripple giant enterprises that are stuck in their ways and do not see the need to change. That business principle is called *disruptive innovation*.

According to Christensen, graveyards are full of businesses that ignored a competitive threat. Companies that remain arrogant about market share or product mix, about branding or price points, about customer responsiveness or market ignorance, learn painfully that they can be toppled. He writes, "If you feel you or your business is impervious to disruptive innovations or disruptive technology, you are wrong."

It was disruptive innovation that enabled steamships to replace sailing ships, transistor radios to supplant vacuum tubes, hydraulic excavators to displace steam shovels. It was disruptive innovation that enabled Mr. Sears to topple giant Montgomery Ward. Montgomery Ward had built a huge industry by building large stores by railroad centers so the trains could deliver the merchandise to where people were along the tracks. Mr. Sears had a different idea. Why not build stores where the people are in the first place? That way people could go to the store and purchase their merchandise without having to go through a mail-order house like Montgomery Ward.

It was disruptive innovation that enabled mainframes to move to mini-computers to desktop PCs to laptops and to handheld computers. It is happening right now as the book, music, and software publishing industries succumb to the Internet.

But here is the thing. We can see this business principle of disruptive innovation as a force for good because it can transform the mundane into the marvelous. But for that to happen requires some change. A wonderful example of this principle can be found with the famed Hanes brand of undershirts (can we talk about underwear for a few moments?), a division of the Sara Lee Corporation, which was willing to listen to its customers.

Customers were complaining about the tags around the neck of the T-shirts. They were an irritation. If they were cut off the sewing would unravel. So after much research and development, and much concern about retooling a product that has remained virtually unchanged for a century, Hanes went tagless in October of 2002. They have not only survived but have prospered because of the "power of disruptive innovation."

In many ways Jesus of Nazareth was a disruptive innovator in that he called people to change their ways of thinking and living. The disruptive innovation of Jesus was more than some folks could tolerate. Many of them simply would not change. Some flat-out ignored him. Others ran, as we heard in the reading of the Gospel of Luke this morning, ran him out of his own synagogue! Others plotted against him, and some eventually succeeded in taking Jesus' life.

So what does all of this have to do with us? Well, after two thousand years, Christians are still debating the identity of the Disruptive Innovator. Ever since Jesus asked, "Who do people say that I am?" the debate has raged. The early church struggled with the identity of Jesus. Was he divine or was he human? Or was he both? It is obvious that we are still fascinated with Jesus and his identity.

In February of 1804 President Thomas Jefferson sat down in the White House, and with two Bibles side by side and a straight-edge razor, he cut and pasted together his own Bible called *The Philosophy of Jesus of Nazareth*.

What Jefferson was left with after his cutting was a Jesus who was no more than a good ethical leader.

We may be somewhat amused by this, but in reality for the past two thousand years we have tinkered with the identity of Jesus. Look at some of the great masterpieces of artwork, and there you will often find paintings that depict Jesus according to how the artist sees and experiences Jesus. Much of the sacred music over the past two thousand years has been a variety of expressions of who Jesus was in the mind of the composer. Every once in a while something would come out of the music field, like the rock opera *Jesus Christ Superstar*. Some people thought it was wonderful; others thought it bordered on blasphemy. My father had a very difficult time with the content of the musical. For him, Jesus was divine and nothing less. He was not interested in Jesus being both human and divine. Therefore, my father could not possibly conceive of how a woman might love Jesus and found the song "I Don't Know How to Love Him" to be repugnant.

Look at the number of movies that have been produced through the years that have attempted to identify the "real" Jesus. Then there are groups like the Jesus Seminar that question just what Jesus might have actually said or done, which has often provoked the faithful to cry out, "Who do these people think they are? What gives them the right to tamper with the Word of God?"

Then there have been a host of books. *The Quest of the Historical Jesus* by Albert Schweitzer is one that comes to mind. Remember *The Robe* by Lloyd C. Douglas? And then more recently Marcus Borg's *Meeting Jesus Again for the First Time*, which has been a book that has been helpful to many people. Then came the gripping best seller, *The Da Vinci Code* by Dan Brown, which declared that not only was Jesus married to Mary Magdalene but that she was the first female apostle—a thought that has been existence for a long time but is only whispered in groups where there is complete trust.

Bishop John Shelby Spong has been advocating that thought for years, even suggesting that the story in the Bible of the wedding feast where Jesus turned water into wine was actually the wedding of Jesus and Mary. Oh, I am so glad that my father is not alive to read this! Both author Dan Brown and persons like Bishop Spong promote this thought because they believe that the early Christian Church, which was a male-dominated organization (and some would argue still is) never really knew what to do with women.

And so the debate goes on and on, with each generation rethinking who Jesus really was, as evidenced by the December 22, 1994, issue of *U.S. News and World Report*, featuring Jesus on the front cover with the words "The Jesus Code . . . America is rethinking the Messiah—again."

During my ministry I have had persons say to me in all honesty, "Sometimes I feel guilty being a member of the church because I am not sure who Jesus is. I have trouble with the thoughts of the Messiah as the Christ. I believe Jesus to have been a real person and one that I would like to follow, but not one who is divine." In contrast I remember an older woman in one of my Bible study classes who, when the discussion came around to the virgin birth, said, "If you take away that belief you take away my faith. I am nothing." I suspect most of us would fall between those two poles.

There is no way to return to the original Jesus, although that does not seem to keep many persons from trying to discover the true or authentic Jesus. Each new generation in its traditions and its perceptions have created their own understanding of the identity of Jesus. This is evidenced in the various theologies that are in existence and is certainly evidenced in various churches.

For example, take the three churches that sit in a rather straight line right here in Minneapolis. Just to the west of us a couple of blocks is the Unitarian Universalist Church. If you attend there, you are not going to hear about the Trinity nor are you going to hear the divinity of Christ. Just a few blocks to the east of us is Plymouth Congregational Church. As you sit in their sanctuary, you would note that the space is virtually devoid of any Christian symbols and that the pastor says rather bluntly that "our emphasis here is on God and not so much on Jesus." That brings us to Hennepin Avenue United Methodist, where the congregation is willing to struggle with the identity of Jesus. Simply put, we do not all see nor do we all experience Jesus the same way.

A few years ago a Chinese photographer took a black-and-white picture while flying over a snow-covered mountain range in Alaska. When he developed the photograph, he discovered something quite amazing. By looking at it carefully, he saw that the white of the snow contrasting with the shadow of the mountain formations created the face of Christ. It was absolutely amazing. One could see the forehead of Christ, the cheeks, the eyes, the nose, the mouth, and the outline of the beard. In a way it was an optical illusion because if you just glanced at it, you just saw the mountain range, but if you let your eyes focus on it, there was the obvious face of Christ!

I cut the picture out of the newspaper and put it in my weekly column and titled it, "Do You See Jesus?" Many people saw the face of Christ right away, but some didn't and had to work at it. One of my members was not able to see it at all. She told me that out of frustration she cut out the photograph in my column and put it on the refrigerator so that she could look at it on a regular basis. She said she finally recognized the face of Christ one night while serving guests. As she was removing some of the dishes to serve the dessert, she walked into the kitchen and startled her guests when they heard her exclaiming, "I see Jesus! I see Jesus!"

We don't all see Jesus, and we don't all see Jesus in the same way, and that is all right. What is important is that we allow the Christ, the *Disruptive Innovator*, into our lives regardless of our understanding of his identity so that we can come to grips with his message. So that we can think about who Jesus as Christ really is in relationship to our own lives.

The identity of Christ has been distorted down through the centuries. We may never know Jesus' true identity, but we do know his gospel message, and that is what we are called upon to trust. We cannot dismiss the message of Christ simply because we cannot capture his identity. It is his message that has withstood the centuries, that enables us to move freely in a world with many other religions. I often hear people say, "All religions lead to God." Well, there is some truth to that, but it's pretty shallow. That there is truth to be found in all religions is certain. What makes Christianity unique, however, is its gospel. The gospel of Christ contains the essence of all the major religions of the world. The uniqueness of the gospel of Christ is that it contains what is needed for a full life. The uniqueness of the gospel of Christ helps us to see and understand the nature of God in a way that no other world religion does. It contains a way for us to change. Its uniqueness is that it contains a way for us to be transformed.

We may not be able to trust our notions about the identity of Christ, but we can trust our notions about his gospel. And that gospel is disruptive. It forces us to move and change. It forces us to be more loving and forgiving. It pushes us to be accepting of others, especially those with whom we differ and disagree. It shoves us into saying things and doing things as individuals or as churches we thought we could never say or do. It changes the entire direction of our lives. Christ was and is the *Disruptive Innovation*. I invite you to affirm both your certainties and uncertainties about the identity of Christ, and let the Spirit of Christ disrupt you.

23

Embracing Our Neighborhood in Transition

MARY ALICE MULLIGAN

Rumor has it that following their eviction, as Adam and Eve ran from the garden, one turned to the other and said, "My dear, let's face it. We are living in times of transition."[1] Such a story reminds us: humanity is always in transition. Every congregation is changing and so is every neighborhood, all the time. Discomfort arises when transitions are dramatic (a highway slices through, a mall is built), or when changes appear for the worse (crime increases, pillars of the neighborhood move and are replaced by renters).

Congregations are not insulated from neighborhood transitions. In fact, narthex conversations (or Monday morning phone calls) often resemble canaries in the mine, first noticing change in the blocks surrounding the church building. The reality of transitions is irrefutable. The essential question is, How will our church respond?

NAME THE SITUATION

Congregations sometimes welcome change; they build an education wing as populations grow. More often, however, change upsets us, especially when it involves neighborhood deterioration. Members move to fancier suburbs, ignoring the reality of what it means when houses near the church become rental properties. Through the years neighborhood grocery stores, pharmacies, and banks relocate. Storefronts are taken over by payday loan companies

---

1. I am grateful to my father, the Rev. Dr. Robert A. Mulligan, for sharing this illustration with me. Ordained in the Methodist Protestant Church in 1939, he has successfully embraced many transitions.

and liquor stores. We have all dreaded the scene. Houses looking rundown; lawns full of weeds; litter in alleys and gutters. Inside the church walls, people are often racially homogenous and socioeconomically better off than neighbors. Members now commute on Sunday morning. No one seems to know the persons living just a few houses from the church building.

We move toward embracing the neighborhood by first articulating what is happening. People right around the building have never been inside or been touched by our ministry. Many of "us" think of the neighborhood as "them." Most of us are nowhere near the building six days a week. Describing our situation does not need a "program." Just speak the truth. More than forty-five years ago, two clergy sociologists warned, "The congregation which ignores its community cannot survive over a long term."[2] To assist the congregation in coming to terms with the community of which it is a part, leadership needs to offer language, concepts, and honest evaluations of what is going on. Alban Institute consultant Alice Mann advises, "Congregations generally cannot change any dynamic that they cannot name, discuss, and negotiate. . . ."[3]

Then, if pastors and lay leaders also imagine possible futures for the congregation as a normal part of church conversation, changes seem possible, theologically appropriate, survivable, and even embraceable. For instance, a leader may share a true story of a sister congregation whose building burned and the difficulty that arose because of the way the decision was made to rebuild in their deteriorating neighborhood. Sharing stories of decisions made poorly and others made well allows congregants to imagine their own reactions to new situations.

As the neighborhood changes, many church people will feel the need to "do something." Leaders may feel pulled into a new future of engagement with the neighborhood. Simultaneously, the past exerts a tremendous backward pull. In a study of twenty-three congregations in communities of transition, sociologist Nancy Tatom Ammerman discovered that "the most common response to change, in fact, is to proceed with business as usual."[4] The force of "what we have always done" locks us into habitual patterns of thinking and behavior. However, Ammerman finds repeating history spells disaster. She notes, "Of those [congregations] currently experiencing serious declines in membership and resources, all have either actively resisted change or have continued with existing patterns, apparently unable to envision how

2. Robert L. Wilson and James H. Davis, *The Church in the Racially Changing Community* (Nashville: Abingdon Press, 1966), 83.

3. Alice Mann, *Can Our Church Live? Redeveloping Congregations in Decline* (Herndon, VA: Alban Institute, 1999), 93. This entire text offers much helpful insight for congregations facing decline.

4. Nancy Tatom Ammerman, *Congregation and Community* (Piscataway, NJ: Rutgers University Press, 1997), 63.

things might be different."[5] This is a cold but important finding. Institutions must change. Turning toward the neighborhood is crucial.

When people panic, begin to "hunker down" during neighborhood transitions, they need leaders who honestly face the situation and communicate hope. Theologian Robert Franklin is painfully blunt about the role of leaders when the situation has become dire: *"We do not have the luxury of leaders who are not strategic and capable of leading change and producing results."*[6]

PRELIMINARY STEPS

If an organism is alive, it is changing. I remember my father saying, of churches he served during his sixty-five years of ministry, "Anytime you think you are standing still, you are really retreating." If congregations are to keep moving into the future where God is calling them, they need preparation and encouragement. Not only the clergy but the church council, the Sunday school classes, the women's circles, the youth group, and the aerobics class have to share in the conversation leading to congregational recommitment to the neighborhood. Of course it does not come all at once, but the eventual buy-in is essential.[7]

Some people in your congregation may never come along. Thus, they may leave. Let them go. Some people will change their understanding of what God is expecting of them now. Even with excellent leadership, some will not. There is an additional group that stays, wants to "protect" the congregation from the surrounding society, and venerates what used to be, hoping it may be recovered. Gregory Jones and Kevin Armstrong note that this group parallels the scouts of Numbers 13–14, who warn against entering the promised land. Better to return to Egypt. The familiarity of enslavement was preferable to taking a chance in the land of milk and honey. Jones and Armstrong claim, "Every church we've ever known has had a 'Back to Egypt' committee in it."[8] Leadership might redirect their energy by making them an actual archive or heritage committee. Using their energy, without letting it draw the congregation backward, blocks their ability to sabotage the move into the future.

5. Ibid,, 321–23.

6. Robert M. Franklin, *Crisis in the Village: Restoring Hope in African American Communities* (Minneapolis: Fortress Press, 2007), 25. His emphasis.

7. Wilson and Davis report reactions in churches where racial change came to the neighborhood. In findings reported from their study of over sixty churches, they state, "In no [all-white] church in this study did the majority favor receiving Negroes into the church in the beginning of the neighborhood change" (*Church in the Racially Changing Community*, 114). Preparation and fearless, open discussion worked hand in hand with strong leadership in those congregations, which eventually welcomed all neighbors.

8. L. Gregory Jones and Kevin R. Armstrong, *Resurrecting Excellence: Shaping Faithful Christian Ministry* (Grand Rapids: Wm. B. Eerdmans Publishing Co., 2006), 132.

To help the congregation's turn to the neighborhood, leaders should communicate the efforts to develop new understandings and mature in our faithfulness as the transitions occur around and within us. Whatever is being tried needs to be shared in board reports, newsletters, bulletin boards, announcements, and church calendars, but most importantly in the one gathering where everyone is expected to show up—weekly worship. The preacher should speak comfortably about God's presence in the neighborhood and in the choices the church is making and explain what God expects of us during this time of transition. The preacher can demonstrate how our belief in God shapes proper interactions with neighbors, how our becoming united with the neighborhood shows we take seriously our call to join in Jesus' ministry of reconciliation.

Preaching helps guide a congregation's journey. I am not so naïve to think that sermon suggestions make all the difference in the life of a congregation facing transitions. However, when Christian fellowships struggled during the early centuries, letters were sent to encourage, instruct, correct, guide, and offer spiritual support, because speaking our shared faith releases divine power. If we trust that God's *logos* (word) has power, we discover proclamation does in fact help shape congregational identity.

Another way to assist the journey is to devote the annual planning retreat to spending significant time looking at what has changed in the world, the congregation, and the neighborhood; and then considering how these changes need to influence planning for the next year. In addition, the minister and other leaders assist the congregation by modeling (being willing to try new things in their own roles, for instance) and by assisting the congregation's investigation of how decisions have been made in this congregation (determining if decisions made intentionally worked better or worse than decisions made by default).

IDEAS FOR LAY LEADERSHIP

Deterioration of urban centers and neighborhoods has been going on for decades. Concomitantly, mainstream Christian denominations and local congregations have experienced declining memberships.[9] Such changes have not

9. Jacob J. Hamman, *When Steeples Cry: Leading Congregations through Loss and Change* (Cleveland: Pilgrim Press, 2005), 11. He cites, for instance, that over a forty-year period the United Methodist Church lost 3.3 million, the Presbyterian Church 2.3 million, and the Episcopal Church 1.1 million members. Some observers argue that church membership has leveled out, with megachurches (often nondenominational) drawing a significant portion of those who leave smaller, mainstream congregations. Hamman's text offers helpful consideration of grief work in the congregation, although he probably overemphasizes the place of mourning in congregational life.

happened overnight, and they are not static. In church and neighborhood, if we are not actively working to reenergize the situation, decline will continue. Our efforts at renewal matter but will not cause immediate reversal. One "program" is not going to ensure the congregation is able to embrace the neighborhood or reverse years of congregational isolation. Situations twenty or thirty years in the making take real time to reverse.

Congregational leaders need to burn into their consciousness the critical finding that congregations unwilling to *try* change will not survive.[10] Leaders do not need "the perfect plan"; they need a contagious willingness to try new things, to embrace the neighborhood, to enrich the church, and to glorify God.

More important than denominational support or physical resources of buildings or property are members of the congregation able to imagine, share ideas, and plan for a new future. Lay leaders can identify and empower such visionary people. Ammerman notes, "Someone has to see the connections between the congregation as it now exists and the congregation as it might someday exist. Someone has to imagine that it might remain spiritually and socially rewarding for its participants."[11]

Here are some additional suggestions for assisting the congregation's embrace of your neighborhood in transition.

- Pray. Get your prayer warriors geared up immediately to start praying for your neighborhood and the church as a part of the neighborhood. In worship, pray for something specific in the neighborhood each week: the family who opened the second-hand store, the school around the block, people looking for work.
- Begin immediately eradicating "us-them" thinking. Communicate that you are all neighbors: church members who live twenty miles away, local high schoolers who throw rocks through church windows, and the owner of the liquor store with the "Booze to Go" sign in the window.
- Use every opportunity to welcome people from the neighborhood to worship. Make sure food-pantry participants receive written and verbal invitations every visit, and have folks ready to greet and sit with them on Sunday morning. Consider other opportunities. Congregants may sit on the church steps on Halloween night and pass out treats, which include an invitation to children's Sunday school.
- Get the congregation out into the neighborhood. Encourage members to shop in local stores. If a gallon of milk costs one dollar more than your megastore, consider the money an investment in making the neighborhood more solid. Have circle meetings in homes of people who live nearer the church. Mahatma Gandhi encouraged people to purchase only what was

10. Ammerman, *Congregation and Community*, 321–23.
11. Ibid., 326.

produced in India, nothing imported. He wrote, "*Swadeshi* . . . does not mean merely the use of what is produced in one's own country . . . there is another meaning implicit in it which is far greater and much more important. *Swadeshi* means reliance on our own strength."[12]

- Offer a study group focusing on engaging more with the neighborhood. Choose a book that will educate and challenge the group in one specific area.[13]
- Encourage early conversations and even training about how the congregation will deal with conflict. Tools for conflict management will be invaluable. Ammerman discovered that ". . . attempting significant changes will involve conflict, and congregations unwilling to engage in conflict will not change."[14] Evelyn and James Whitehead write, "Conflict is more often a sign of a group's health than it is a symptom of disease. The presence of conflict among us most often indicates that we are involved in something we think is significant. . . . Groups in which there is nothing important enough to fight about are more likely to die than are groups in which some dissension occurs."[15]
- Take time as a congregation to play and celebrate even small successes.

PREACHING IDEAS

Regular preaching that includes illustrations of communal change assists development of connections between congregation and neighborhood. Of course, change is not easy, but preaching reveals the power of the gospel available to us and the whole community. With the proper foundation, congregations can survive and even flourish during transitions. We can use the forces at work for God's good purposes and provide meaningful ministry that makes a difference in our neighborhoods in transition. Especially when people are feeling insecure or uncertain, sermons need to speak openly and often of our faith in God who brings abundant life. Sermons can offer listeners theological claims and method as well as moral reflection.[16] The preacher appropriately

12. Mohandas K. Gandhi, *Indian Opinion*, 2 January 1909 [found in *The Collected Works of Mahatma Gandhi*, vol. 9, 118], quoted in Judith Brown, *Gandhi: Prisoner of Hope* (New Haven, CT: Yale University Press, 1991), 90.

13. For example, to learn about using our power for community organizing, see Gregory F. Pierce, *Activism That Makes Sense: Congregations and Community Organization* (Ramsey, NJ: Paulist Press, 1984); to connect in ministry with the neighborhood, see Mary Alice Mulligan and Rufus Burrow Jr., *Standing in the Margin: How Your Congregation Can Minister with the Poor* (Cleveland: Pilgrim Press, 2004); or to get a renewed Christian perspective on money, see Michael Taylor, *Christianity, Poverty and Wealth: The Findings of "Project 21,"* WCC Publications (London: SPCK, 2003).

14. Ammerman, *Congregation and Community*, 335.

15. Evelyn and James Whitehead, *Community of Faith: Models and Strategies for Developing Christian Communities*, quoted in Pierce, *Activism*, 71.

16. L. Susan Bond makes similar claims in her *Trouble with Jesus: Women, Christology and Preaching* (St. Louis: Chalice Press, 1999), 3, 26.

describes how members are mutually accountable for actions and for inaction. People are looking to the preacher for assistance in knowing who God is and what God expects of them.[17] Of course the call for moral discourse and accountability is not always appealing. Robert Franklin reminds us, "One of the most important and potentially controversial rituals is the practice of holding each other accountable for doing what is needed."[18]

Below, I suggest a sermon series as an integral part of a whole church effort to embrace the neighborhood. Susan Bond explains, "[Preaching structures] a communally shared understanding of dynamic faith that is related to the tradition, to the daily life of decision making of believers, and to the ethical projects of the church."[19]

This sermon series uses Jeremiah, but many biblical options would work. Theological undergirding starts the work. We cannot expect the congregation to move without sensing who and where God is in the process. For the first sermon, we might use Jeremiah 1:1–10 to see God's constancy. YHWH is the One who attends to each person, who empowered the enslaved Israelites to walk out of Egypt. The same One called Jeremiah and became incarnate in Jesus; the same One whose Spirit filled the church in seasons of persecution; and the same One led our foreparents to plant this congregation. Congregants know these theological claims intellectually, but a sermon focusing on God's power and love for all reminds the congregation of its solid foundation.

In the second sermon, we can consider the inevitability of change. Preaching from Jeremiah 1:14–19, notice God's constant attention to all. God is aware of what is going on in our neighborhood, so spell out the neighborhood situation. What is changing, and how has the church responded in the past?

The third sermon might come from Jeremiah 2:1–7, 12–13. Consider what happens when people refuse to acknowledge God's presence in transitions. When we thirst for bygone times, our cities become like broken cisterns, which hold no life-giving water. When people carve out answers for themselves, ignoring God's guidance, they can die of thirst in the wilderness.

To offset this wrong-thinking response, we can note another option (either in the same sermon or in a separate one). Consider when the Israelites thirsted in the wilderness (Exod. 17:1–7). Moses releases water from a rock that was directly ahead of the people. Water gushed back to them from the very place they were going. We might say the water came from their own future. When our faith is strong, we can follow God's lead anywhere, even when we cannot see our way through. But when we falter, we abandon God's life-giving lead

---

17. See chap. 1, "Help Us Figure Out What God Wants," in Mary Alice Mulligan and Ronald Allen, *Make the Word Come Alive: Lessons from Laity* (St. Louis: Chalice Press, 2005).
18. Franklin, *Crisis in the Village*, 15.
19. Bond, *Trouble with Jesus*, 16.

and look for protection or meaning elsewhere. In embracing our community in transition, we have wonderful opportunities to deepen our relationship as a congregation with God and with each other. Resulting changes can bring exciting new growth. Since we aren't sure where we are going, we don't have preconceived notions of what success looks like.

For the final sermon, I suggest preaching from a single verse, Jeremiah 29:7: "But seek the welfare of the city where I have sent you into exile, and pray to the LORD on its behalf, for in its welfare you will find your welfare." We are intimately interconnected with the society around us, even if we feel exiled in it. Our survival depends on the survival of the surrounding community and vice versa. If the congregation is to flourish, the neighborhood must find sources of life as well. Since God has created all things, everything is interconnected. We need to be involved in our community's welfare. One of Dr. Martin Luther King Jr.'s most memorable sermons burns the idea into our consciousness: "It really boils down to this: that all life is interrelated. We are all caught in an inescapable network of mutuality, tied into a single garment of destiny. Whatever affects one directly, affects all indirectly. We are made to live together because of the interrelated structure of reality."[20] Cast our glance around the world; there is nowhere God is not. Look more closely at the deteriorating conditions of the neighborhood. Especially there, God is present.

In all the changes our congregations and communities face, by trusting that God can bring life in all circumstances, we can preach messages of embracing the transitions. When the surrounding neighborhood is deteriorating, with God's holy power, we engage in ministry with the neighbors, for we are co-responsible for the welfare of the community surrounding our church building. In fact, we are part of the community.

Once the foundation is laid, although it needs to be reinforced on an ongoing basis, you can shift to preaching suggestions for next steps. Any sermon can focus directly or mention in passing how we as a congregation and a neighborhood are moving into God's future. You might plan an additional series focusing on some specific suggestions for becoming more fully involved in improving the life and health of the neighborhood.

As you lead your congregation into a fuller sense of who you are as part of the neighborhood, trust Jesus Christ to continue to guide you, trust the Holy Spirit to continue to empower you, and trust God the Creator to continue to fill you with divine love for others.

20. Martin Luther King Jr., "A Christmas Sermon on Peace," in *A Testament of Hope: The Essential Writings and Speeches of Martin Luther King, Jr.*, ed. James Washington (New York: Harper-Collins, 1991), 254. Reading this and other sermons offers preachers continuing reminders of the importance of maintaining the prophetic element in our proclamation.

24

When the Center Doesn't Hold

A Working Orientation for Pastors Dealing with Transition and Crisis

JOSEPH M. WEBB

As I write this in the hard, frightening spring of 2008, the idea that America faces the specter of another 1929-style Great Depression is publicly, if gingerly, discussed. So maybe it is not so strange that, in my judgment, the very best book on the subject of coping with change—even serious, wrenching change—begins by saying that it was "written in the early days of the Great Depression, at a time when there was a general feeling that our traditional ways were headed for a tremendous change, maybe even a permanent collapse." That feeling has returned with a vengeance, particularly during the collapse in the final months of the George W. Bush presidency; and in churches everywhere (as well as in countless other places), the call is for leaders who can help people cope not just with transitions but with the major changes in life and outlook that appear inevitable.

That book, titled *Permanence and Change* and published in 1935, was written by Kenneth Burke, the great American social philosopher, rhetorical scholar, and communication theorist. It is still in print and well worth studying.[1] The book asks and proposes remarkable answers to questions about both social and individual transitions (as the title indicates), about why and what happens when, as Burke puts it at one point, our "superstructure of certainties begins to topple." How, in short, do we introspectively grasp

---

1. The book was revised in 1954, changed publishers a couple of times, and I am quoting from the third edition, 1984, published by the University of California Press. Some of the great Burke scholars of the twentieth century were at the University of Illinois, where I used Burke for the basis of my doctoral dissertation in the early 1970s.

what we are like—mentally, emotionally, and spiritually—in order for a "new structure of certainties [to] be erected?"

In this brief essay I want to indicate how Burke answered those questions—a matter that I have taught and written about for years—and in doing so suggest how his overarching answer can still provide a powerful working model for Christian leaders faced with helping parishioners, both individually and collectively, struggle through changes most never dreamed would ever come. Understand: there are no magic bullets here, and everything in Burke's proscription for confronting change can be adapted for preaching as well as for the larger purposes of counseling, teaching, and other forms of pastoral leadership.

The beginning concept for Burke is human "orientation," that is, every human being grows up developing an *orientation* to life, to behavior. One's orientation is one's learned and internalized way of naming, defining, feeling about, and making sense of the world. Despite our being part of a physical world, Burke contends, we actually live and move and "have our being" in a *symbolic* world, since everything of purpose and meaning that we do is done with and through a veil of symbols—mostly words, though the symbolic systems that shape us extend beyond words alone. We symbolize other people, places we come to know, kinds of music, objects, and so on. But it is in our "naming," in language, in what we call *things*, that for Burke our symbolic natures find their highest expression.

Moreover, he explains at length that our words and other symbols have no *inherent* meaning; they literally mean what we, in our various groups, say that they mean. As another of Burke's students put it,

> The meaning or value of a symbol is in no instance derived from or determined by properties inherent in its physical form: the color appropriate to mourning may be yellow, green, or any other color; purple need not be the color of royalty; among the Manchu rulers of China it was yellow. The meaning of the word "see" is not intrinsic in its phonetic (or pictorial) properties. "Biting one's thumb at" ('Do you bite your thumb at us, sir?'—*Romeo and Juliet*, Act I, Scene I) someone might mean anything. The meanings of symbols are derived from and determined by the organisms who use them; meaning is bestowed by human organisms upon physical things or events and thereby become symbols.[2]

Our growing up is a process of learning words, symbols, first from family units and the people, places, and groups to which parent or parents introduce us. We learn the language spoken around us. What is most significant, though,

2. See Leslie White, *The Science of Culture: A Study of Man and Civilization* (New York: Farrar, Strauss & Giroux, 1949), 25.

is that with every word, name, term, or expression that we "learn," we learn two things, not one. First, we learn a "meaning," something dictionarylike. This is the term's referent, if it actually has one. We always learn more than that, however. Virtually every word or term we learn carries with it an *emotional* quotient or content, which we learn as well. The emotional charge can be positive or negative, and it often carries one side overtly while implying the other. We digest and absorb the emotional loading of the words that come to make up our vocabulary. For Burke, the crucial dimension of what we actually *become* as human beings is found in the emotional dimension that comes tied to our language learning.

In other words, speech, as Burke puts it, "is not neutral. Far from aiming at suspended judgment, the spontaneous speech of a people is loaded with judgments. It is intensely moral—its names for objects contain the emotional overtones which give us the cues as to how we should act toward those objects." More than that, "spontaneous speech is not a naming at all, but a system of attitudes of implicit exhortations. To call a man a friend or an enemy is per se to suggest a program of action with regard to him."[3]

So how does one's "orientation" to life and living emerge from this? As Burke explains it, this tangle of words, names, terms—all with whatever emotional charges we have picked up from the variety of people and places during our growing-up years—all of this symbolic mix must be organized so that it will, at least within us as individuals, "hang together," as it were. Fortunately, we have within us a fundamental human principle by which this organizing takes place—the principle that ensures that whatever names or terms for things we have learned will comprise a more or less *unified* mental and emotional whole—what Burke designates as our "orientation."

For purposes of my teaching over the years, I have turned Burke's explanation into a crude but seemingly effective model: Envision the human being as a circle, a wheel, inside of which are all of the symbols—words, terms, people, places, objects, and so on—that one has learned (and will, to some extent, continue to learn throughout life). Innately, Burke says, our organizational principle takes over as this all collects. What is most important, though, is that this organizational principle works almost entirely with the emotional or feeling content, whether positive or negative, of the symbols we have "learned."

The organizational principle within our "wheel," that is, within us, is this— and I put it in italics to emphasize it: *The higher the emotional intensity of a given symbol (word, concept, object, etc.), the closer it is to the center, or "hub," of one's wheel. Conversely, the less emotional intensity each word or concept contains, the farther from the hub it is.* What results from this organization is a small collection

3. Burke, *Permanence and Change*, 177.

of symbols at each individual's center, at the hub, symbols that are extremely high in emotional value. Following Burke, I have come to call these unique, core symbols "hub symbols." Because of their intense emotional charge, they are the symbols that, overall, shape who we are, what we are like, and how we think, as well as how we interpret and respond to the world in which we live. This hub symbol system that shapes us is unrelated to where we live, to what culture is ours, or what nationality we represent. It is ours by virtue of our being members of the human species. Burke refers to these core symbols as "ur-symbols," ur being a prefix meaning the symbols out of which everything else about us arises.[4]

These hub symbols have special characteristics, characteristics that reflect their formative nature for every individual. First, these hub symbols, loaded with emotions and feelings, are the "sacred" symbols of an individual life. Sacred is not used in a religious sense, but in the sense that these are the symbols that we hold the most dear, that we will *not* allow to be derogated, and if someone does attack them, even verbally, we will usually do whatever is necessary to defend them. These are the symbols that we will fight for, if need be—the ones that give us enormous psychic and emotional pain and disorientation whenever someone actually does manage to undermine or tear one of them down.

Looked at another way, these are the symbols that embody our values, those things that we perceive ourselves to "stand for." They also represent our assumptions, the concepts and ideas that we hold to be nondiscussable, things that are never, under any circumstances, open for debate or compromise, as far as we are concerned. These are, in many ways, the symbols that, taken together, represent what some today would call a "worldview."

There are two other characteristic of our hub symbol systems that, together, go to the very heart of our concern here. First, our hub symbols form the glue that holds our very lives together. Second, this hub symbol "glue" hardens early and causes our outlooks, our "orientations," to become impermeable, often unchangeable, over the course of our lives. We believe intensely that our hub symbols are the "correct" ones, the ones *we* not only believe in but that we believe should be the hub symbols of *everyone else*. Ours are the "rational" hub symbols, despite the fact that such symbols are never rational. But the hub symbols of others, particularly when they run counter to our own, are held to be wrong, or worse. For most people, in fact, their own "hub symbols" came from God or some divine source; and whenever others

4. I have discussed this all in detail in two books. One is out of print, titled only *Hub Symbols*, published in 1983 by the Center for the Study of Christian Communication. The other is *Preaching and the Challenge of Pluralism* (Cleveland: Chalice Press, 1998). For anyone interested in exploring "hub symbols" further, I urge a reading of that book.

hold different hub symbols, they are just as sure that their hub symbols came from some merely human, if not some downright evil, source.

Moreover, we are powerfully drawn to people who hold the same hub symbols in the same ways that we do, whose hub symbols match ours. By the same token, our "enemies" are those who we are able to identify as having hub symbols that run counter to ours. Needless to say, those are the people whom we shout loudly against at every opportunity. Of particular importance, however, is that when our hub symbol systems are relatively undisturbed, when they are not under stress from outside forces or from other people, we tend to be happy, satisfied individuals. We are "comfortable" with ourselves and everything around us.

But—and this is the point—when our hub symbols are challenged, threatened, or subverted or, worse, when they are damaged by the words or actions of others, we react *in the strongest possible means at our disposal*. It is virtually an axiom of human interaction. We live by our hub symbols, and when things happen to punch them or prick them or derogate them, our defensiveness can take a hundred overt and often physical forms. Nor does it matter if the brutalizing of our hub symbols is intentional or not; or whether it is gradual or abrupt. When individuals or groups challenge each other's hub symbols—as virtually always happens during times of change from one way of doing things to another—the result is often a messy, combative, painful ordeal.

Some changes, of course, are slow, often generational. Take the change from a traditional form of worship, with hymns, organ music, and a preacher calmly reading a manuscript of twenty minutes in length, an accepted way of mainline worship for several generations. Gradually transition, then, to worship with a rock band, projected chorus lyrics, waving hands, and a lively preacher moving energetically in a sport short about the platform—two sets of hub symbols on a collision course unless one finds ways to keep them apart. In some traditions, robes for clergy, often elaborate ones, are positive hub symbols for congregants: it helps bring holiness into the liturgical setting; in other traditions, if the preacher should don a robe, a profoundly negative hub symbol is activated in parishioners, and the adverse reaction would be quick and more than noticeable.

Some hub-symbol violations are not gradual at all. They come in a moment, and the result can be as swift as a blade flying through the air. Some years back, I was the minister of a congregation of 130 regulars in an affluent section of southern California, a somewhat conservative congregation but one that seemed open to change. A woman of the congregation in her thirties, a Century City attorney, asked the all-male board of elders, of which her father was a member, if she could be more involved in the public life of the church. Without batting an eye, they all said "Yes," she could. The following Sunday, she was there as one of the four people, the other three being men, who served the Communion and took part in receiving the offering.

Several church members walked out of the service immediately after that, and the following Sunday the regular attendance dropped from about 130 to fewer than 70. The church divided in half over that issue. The role of a man versus a woman was a hub symbol for person after person in that congregation, although I simply had no idea that that was the case. It was a symbol that had been deeply violated for the half that left. A few returned after my repeated visits to them, yet nothing I could do, as it turned out, was going to change that hub symbol for most of them. We often change our behavior to conform to our long-established hub symbols rather than let our symbols be altered in any significant way. Gradually that church made the change to allow women to have increased roles in worship, and membership began to grow again, but it was clear, in retrospect, that the new people who came in already had hub symbols that included women as participants in worship.

I am very aware, too, that many of the crises in which church people find themselves are not those that arise from congregational or even religious life—but from the lives we are all living outside the church. We referred at the outset to the great financial traumas of today, which near Great Depression proportions. People are losing their jobs and their houses—both of which are firmly fixed for most people as immovable hub symbols. When these things are wrenched away, if not for oneself then for a family member, one's life can be shattered, a key "hub symbol" is destroyed, and the center of one's being simply is threatened with collapse. The house may be irreplaceably gone, but what must be fixed is the symbol of the house as life's great security. A new hub symbol for "security" must be shaped to replace the destroyed one.

What are the lessons here? There are many, and they are good ones. Only a few can be suggested in these short paragraphs:

First, it is absolutely essential for anyone working with others regarding their hub symbols or their responses to them to know what his or her own hub symbols are. It is not enough for one to say, "Oh, but I know myself. I have done a lot of introspection as part of my seminary education or whatever." That will not do; the focus of most such introspective activity is usually too general and doesn't ask the questions that are required. I often ask my advanced students to write a "hub symbol autobiography," meaning that they have to identify introspectively a half dozen or so of their own hub symbols, map out the "content" of each one, then track each one back in their lives to its source: that is, where did they pick it up along the way?

The easiest and quickest way to identify one's own hub symbols is to ask oneself, honestly and candidly, what another person would have to say to make one seriously mad, or upset, or verbally defensive, as we all know how to get. Research has taught us that most hub symbols are about five or six topics: religion, family, politics, occupation or work, possessions, or race/gender issues. Now and then something left over from a youthful trauma—for example, abuse or parental divorce—can leave a hub symbol behind, but most will be under one of those half-dozen topics. Search negatively, in a sense. It is like pricking yourself with a big pin: it will sting a bit, but you will learn a lot. And when you learn the negative side of a hub symbol, the positive will usually become visible just by turning it over.

The point of this is that about the only "defense" we have when someone attacks our *own* hub symbols, whether deliberately or not, is to know what they are. This makes us able to absorb the hurt and the defensiveness without striking back, which is the universal natural impulse. It is the inoculation effect, really. If you say something to me that really hurts my feelings or angers me deeply because you attacked one of my hub symbols, I am able to tell *myself* at that moment that that really hurt, but I am not going to let you know it. I am going to absorb it, knowing what you have done to me; and I am going to work with you as if that did not happen. That is why knowing one's own hub symbol system is essential in order to deal with others concerning theirs.

Second, there is great value in helping people who are in various stages of crisis to understand *how* their own "hub symbol" system works; and I say this after thirty-five years of working with both undergraduate and graduate students to come to terms with their own perceptual and communication systems. On numerous occasions I have heard from students from ten or fifteen years earlier who want me to know how an awareness of their "hub symbols" has helped them in their day-to-day relationships in all sorts of settings, formal and informal.

In 2003, after I arrived in Florida for a new assignment as a university dean, I got a note from the publisher of the *Palm Beach Post* asking if I would have dinner with him. When I did, I discovered that he had been a graduate student of mine at Cal State Northridge in 1971. The first question he asked me was whether I still taught students about "those hub symbols," and then he proceeded to explain how that idea and awareness had played a key role particularly in the business relationships of his successful life. All of us need tools, even strange, oddly named tools, to help us understand the complications within ourselves and with the relationships we establish and try to carry on with others.

Third, after the leader has something of a grasp of his or her own hub symbols, it is important to spend time just "getting to know" not just the people but the hub symbols of the parishioners among whom one works. This is different, and it doesn't do, again, to say, "I know them," or "I've been around them a long time." As with my Agoura Hills people, they had hub symbols

I did not grasp. How does one do this? One asks questions of parishioners. One "interviews" them without doing so, really. One picks key topics that we all have strong feelings about and asks them to talk about those topics. It is difficult to overemphasize how important this is, particularly as one sees crises or transitions looming up in the future.

Fourth and finally, as I also indicated earlier when I referred to the split in my Agoura Hills church, being *aware* of the vulnerability of our hub symbols and how strongly and unpredictably people can react when those symbols are threatened or destroyed is not the same as *fixing* them. One of the "defenses" we have when we are threatened or when our hubs have been injured is simply to run—to run away, to change churches, to move somewhere else, to find new people. That is easier, it often appears, than to stay and adjust how we "see things"; easier than to "change our minds" or the symbols that embody our long-held, most intense emotions.

But change we sometimes can if we find ourselves surrounded by others whom we trust and to whom we are willing to listen. And that, I think, becomes the challenge of the pastoral leader and preacher. Yes, we can and should preach about change, about making transitions. That is important. But not about change in general; no one can be bullied into it, and certainly no one will change just because we tell them to. Instead, this tends to work when we preach about specific "symbols," particularly the symbols that we share as "our hub symbols." Preach about a word, a concept, a term—and in a sermon move from its "old meaning," loaded with its old emotions, to a gentle redefinition of the concept, all the time refashioning it with an entirely new set of emotional charges. Preach consciously, gently, about old "hub symbols" giving way to "new ones."

Beyond that, live among the people. Be where they are. I indicated that some of the people who left the Agoura church came back. They did so because I sat around their tables and shared my hub symbol about women in the church with them. I talked about why I believed what I did, how my symbol was formed over time, and even the struggles I had had over it. I did that in sermons, but some only came to the sermons because I first did it in their houses, and over restaurant tables with some of the men, and in small groups where I managed to coax them together in someone's living room. Not all paid attention, but enough did to convince me that we do occasionally hear each other—particularly if people realize that we are speaking to them about those things that are deeply emotional and buried within us. It is then that we come across not just as pastors but also as real human beings.

25

What Has Not Changed about Preaching and Pastoral Care

O. C. EDWARDS JR.

If one thinks about the world in which the church lives these days, it is obvious that transition and change occur at several different levels. To mention but three, there is first the level of the life of the individual person. Next we think of all the rapid changes that have occurred in our culture in just the last half-century. But giving all thought of change an urgency it had lacked before is that which has recently occurred in world economic markets, including our own.

Change in one's personal life begins with those that occur at what are called the wonder moments of life, the times when rites of passage take place. Often there are religious rites connected with these, such as baptism at birth; confirmation around menarche, puberty, and coming of age; wedding ceremonies initiating matrimony; and Christian burial at the time of death. Somewhere along the way Christians receive Holy Communion for the first time. In the church we have the ordination of clergy, and we have their arrivals and departures in congregations, events that can be important for all the people of God in that place. Members of the congregation come and go. Parishes often take some official notice of high school graduations and are aware of youthful members who go away to college. Changes of jobs come in for pastoral attention. Certainly when communicants enlist in the armed services, when they are called to active duty, and especially when they are wounded and even die in battle, it is a matter of concern for their church family. And there are many other such transitions in people's personal lives; the list could go on and on.

The last five chapters of my *History of Preaching*[1] deal with changes in American society during the last four decades of the twentieth century. I cannot summarize those more succinctly than I did there:

> Movements for civil, women's, student, and gay rights, and for peace and the environment were developing simultaneously with the sexual revolution, experimentation with drugs, changes in standards of acceptable speech and taste in popular music, growing ethnic and religious pluralism, and a marked increase in the number of retired people in the country. During the same period the American people, like those of other nations, were having their consciousness shaped by the intimate medium of television. Computers became pervasive in every aspect of daily living.
>
> Along with the other changes occurring during this period was the disappearance of many of the common assumptions that made American life a culture. Trust was eroded on every hand. The Vietnam War, Watergate, and other evidences that national leaders had feet of clay undermined public confidence in government. The resistance met by the various rights movements that prevented their living up to their promises encouraged cynicism among those who had tasted hope. Meanwhile, church membership and participation were plummeting. Deep suspicion of the threat to human life posed by thermonuclear weapons, combined with the damage done to the environment through technology, replaced the awe and optimism with which the scientific enterprise had previously been regarded. This dethroning of the idol of science was abetted by a change in the understanding of its goal: from discovering laws of the universe, to merely devising models or paradigms that would enable a more effective prediction of performance. There was even a loss of confidence in the ability of language to describe reality or to convey univocal meaning. Eternal verities were vanishing right and left.
>
> A result of this erosion of trust in public institutions and loss of consensus in beliefs and values was a growing individualism and loss of commitment. Marriages were postponed or forsaken altogether, and those who married did not rush to have children. Many sought to find the meaning of their lives in their careers, only to come to doubt the worth of what they were doing and the integrity of the corporations they worked for. Consumption became the measure of success, and the hollowness of its victory was reflected in a bumper sticker that read: "The one who dies with the most toys wins." People seemed to live as isolated individuals, yearning for but achieving little sense of personal fulfillment.[2]

---

1. O. C. Edwards Jr., *A History of Preaching* (Nashville: Abingdon Press, 2004).
2. Ibid., 798–99.

The sour note on which this list ends was more characteristic of the earlier of those last decades of the twentieth century than of the later ones, but even that alteration of mood was but another among the overwhelming number of changes that were taking place. It was during that time that Alvin Toffler published his book *Future Shock*,[3] in which he said that change was taking place at a rate faster than the human capacity to adapt so that people would be left feeling disconnected and suffering from severe stress and disorientation.

That prediction was made forty years ago, and the rate of change has accelerated radically since then. The impact of two technologies on our culture can demonstrate that. The first is computers. The only ones that existed when Toffler wrote were mainframes that filled large rooms. Personal computers did not appear until the early 1980s. Yet now computer chips are in everything, including hearing aids. Who can imagine writing without word processing, communicating without e-mail, getting information without Googling for it, or even checking out at the grocery story without barcodes? The second technology is cell phones, which are fast replacing computers in many of their operations. The idea that one can simply reach any phone in the world by a device worn on the belt or carried in a purse would have appeared only in science fiction a short while ago, but now the phones almost seem glued into the ears of many people on the streets. Others, however, are using their hands to send text messages and even to Twitter—that is, when they aren't taking photographs, listening to music, or doing all the other things they can now do with cell phones.

But the most immediate and pressing change in our society right now is that it is in economic depression. Any statistics cited at the time of writing would be outdated before they could be edited, much less published, so the most that can be done here is to indicate some of the areas of American life that have felt the effects of this economic change. One could begin by looking at the way the leading economic indicators have plummeted and at how many major financial institutions and corporations have either collapsed or threaten to collapse unless the government provides massive bailouts. More poignant would be to look at the lives of individuals and families as they have felt the impact of these changes. Some of the highest unemployment rates of all times are being experienced. Breadwinners are without jobs; families are having to cut back drastically on expenses; mortgages are being foreclosed; and those who have not yet been personally affected are afraid to spend because they may be next. Even charitable institutions that have stepped up in times past to help in emergencies are themselves in trouble because funds have dried up as donors begin to feel threatened themselves.

---

3. Alvin Toffler, *Future Shock* (New York: Random House, 1970).

In all these areas of change many people turn to religion for guidance to help them negotiate the rough roads ahead. All of these experiences of change and transition cry out for good preaching and pastoral care to help people get through them.

My purpose in writing this essay, however, is to suggest that there are some things that have not changed and that some of these are perennial problems of human nature. In fact, it is some of these unchanging factors that lie behind the most threatening forms of change that our society is facing. This was brought to my attention by something I coincidentally happened to be reading when I received the invitation to contribute to this volume.

That this should be so is surprising because at the time I was reading what an author best known for crime fiction had to say about a work of medieval poetry. The author was Dorothy L. Sayers, whose mystery stories about Lord Peter Wimsey are regarded as classics in the field. She cannot be dismissed as a mere writer of thrillers, however, because she did much else as well. She had taken a first-class honors degree in medieval literature at Oxford. The first two books she published were collections of her own poetry. She was a playwright commissioned to create dramas for cathedral festivals, the London stage, and the BBC, most of which had religious themes. For instance, she wrote a cycle of twelve radio plays for the BBC on the life of Christ (based on the Greek text of the New Testament, of course), titled *The Man Born to Be King*; it was so popular that she was besieged with invitations to lecture on theological topics. The archbishop of Canterbury, William Temple (no slouch of a theologian himself), wanted to give her a Lambeth Doctorate in Divinity, but she refused it. Her translations of medieval poetry include *Tristan in Brittany* and *The Song of Roland* in addition to *The Divine Comedy* (the latter two being Penguin Classics that have sold millions of copies and are still in print after fifty years).

Since the medieval poetry she commented on in the article I was reading was Dante's *Divine Comedy*, fewer defenses have to be made for its theological and literary seriousness. What perhaps is needed instead is a demonstration that something written in the early fourteenth century could possibly be relevant to our technological age. Since that, however, is precisely the point that will emerge, I will leave that question for the moment.

What I had chosen for my Lenten reading this year was the three volumes of papers on Dante and related subjects that Sayers had presented to various learned societies and other groups while she was involved in making her translation of the *Commedia*.[4] The essay I was reading at the time was "The City of

4. Dorothy L. Sayers, *Introductory Papers on Dante* (London: Methuen, 1954); *Further Papers on Dante* (London: Methuen, 1957); and *The Poetry of Search and the Poetry of Statement and Other Posthumous Essays on Literature, Religion, and Language* (London: Victor Gollancz, 1963). All three of these volumes were reprinted by Wipf and Stock of Eugene, Oregon, in 2006. The article on which I will comment appeared in the first of these volumes. I follow in my discussion her use of

Dis," in which she explains the logic of the order of the descending circles of hell in which various sins are punished. In it she wrote about her own discovery that came about as a result of asking herself why Dante placed the Giants at the particular place in Hell where they are found. She writes,

> While I was looking for the answer, I quite suddenly saw a vision of the whole depth of the Abyss—perhaps as Dante saw it, but quite certainly as we can see it here and now: a single logical, coherent, and inevitable progress of corruption. . . . I saw the whole lay-out of Hell as something actual and contemporary; something that one can see by looking into one's self, or into the pages of to-morrow's newspaper. I saw it, that is, as a judgment of fact, unaffected by its period, unaffected by its literary or dogmatic origins; and I recognized at the same moment that the judgment was true. (128)

It should be explained that the truth she saw was not at the literal narrative level; she doesn't claim that hell is actually arranged like that. Rather, it is true at the allegorical level, which for Dante was its primary meaning, its description of the progress of evil in the human soul. Her reflection on her revelatory moment was amazement that none of the scholarly writing on the *Comedy* she had read shared her concern about whether the view Dante presents of reality is accurate or not. I will not attempt to argue for the validity of her insight, but only say that my experience of her discovery was the kind of "Aha!" moment for me that her discovery regarding Dante was for her. So I will only present what she saw and let readers decide for themselves whether this judgment is equally valid for them.

There isn't room to detail the whole complex structure of Hell in Dante's view, but neither is there need. Select sins along the way can illustrate the principles and reveal their contemporary relevance. The overall shape of Hell can be seen in its division into three main sections. Those who commit the sins of Incontinence (symbolized by the Leopard) say, "I know I am breaking the Law, but I can't help myself." Those who commit Violence (symbolized by the Lion) say, "I know I am breaking the Law, but I am justified." As they rationalize their choices, their wills become set on destruction. Those who commit sins of Fraud (symbolized by the Wolf) say, "I am right, Law or no Law," and the consequence is "violence against one's fellow-man" (140).[5]

---

capital letters to refer to the various sinful behaviors and the people who commit them. Hereafter references to it will be page numbers cited parenthetically in the text. Quotations retain the author's British conventions of spelling and punctuation.

5. This paper was written at a time when it was still thought that "man" could be a generic term for human beings, female as well as male.

In beginning with the sins of the Incontinent, we do not need to consider those of the Lustful because so many people in our society do not consider these to be sinful. And we are not in much better shape when we get to those of the Gluttonous, but Sayers gives us a good start with these, saying that such people are well respected because they have a high standard of living. But to set this in perspective she writes,

> If Dante has seen a civilisation that understood beatitude only in terms of cinemas and silk stockings and electric cookers and radiators and cars and cocktails, would it have surprised him to find it all of a sudden waking to the realization that, having pursued these ideals with all its might, it was inexplicably left cold, hungry, bored, resentful, and savage? (135)

She points out that in Lust there is a mutuality of indulgence, but with Gluttony one descends to the next lower level of sin, in which the indulgence is solitary: "The appetite, once offered and shared, has now become appetite pure and simple, indulged in for its own sake."

One could still wonder what is so bad about that, and, indeed, we are still in the upper reaches of Hell, dealing with the relatively least-serious sins. But Sayers goes on to show the downward direction we are going:

> Appetite cannot so indulge itself without encountering the thrust and pressure of other, conflicting greeds. So in the next circle the Greed of Hoarding and the Greed of Squandering are chosen as the types of those opposing greeds. . . . It is a community of opposition. The greeds of either sort combine in gangs; they roll great stones against the other party. (136)

Logically, the circle of the Wrathful comes next.

After that we leave the sins of Incontinence and move into those of Violence, thus leaving Upper Hell and entering Nether Hell. Obduracy has prompted Violence. The first circle there is that of the Heretics, which is surprising at first, because (a) Heresy is not considered a terrible threat in our society, and (b) the Violence of it is not immediately apparent. But Sayers astutely observes the psychological progression and says, "The Heretic, taken literally, is one who at the same time accepts the Church and defies it; for when he departs from the doctrine, he justifies his departure" (140). Thus we have entered the realm of those who say, "I know I am breaking the Law, but I am justified." It is this sense that "I am right, Law or no Law" that leads down to Phlegethon, a river of boiling blood where the Tyrants are. "Rapine, murder, oppression—these are the corruptions of absolute power." Next comes a wood in which the trees are the souls of Suicides and through this wood Profligates are chased and attacked by vicious dogs. With both sets of sinners, the Violent have been turned against themselves. With the Suicides, "self-disgust has led to despair." The Profligates are those who gamble away their resources "in a desperate thirst for sensation; they squandered, not for any pleasure bought with spending, but for the morbid thrill of ruining themselves." Their sin is certainly not foreign to our age, where gambling has been legalized all over the country and casinos have sprung up everywhere. And this is not even to mention gambling on the stock market.

The next (third) ring of the Circle of Violence has to do with the Violent against God, Nature, and Art: the Blasphemers, the Sodomites, and the Usurers. Of the first two I will say only that I thoroughly disagree with Dante's natural-law approach to homosexuals, and I am convinced that Sayers did too. In her mystery novels there are a number of couples of women who live together and who have contempt for men. She never says that any of them are lesbians, but the issue was hardly discussed in serious literature at that time, much less in writing for entertainment. While one woman of this type turns out to be a murderer, all the others are sympathetically presented. Thus in her own writing Sayers's treatment of homosexuals seems more like attitudes today than Dante's. By contrast, Dante's treatment of the Usurers as presented by Sayers sounds very close to today's headlines:

> The nineteenth-century commentators, brought up in the tradition of financial autonomy and the sacro-sanctity of banking, were aghast at this astonishing listing in one doom of unmentionable vice and irreproachable finance. . . . To us, pondering upon the "End of Economic Man,"[6] and looking at a world full of dust-bowls, unemployment, strikes, and starvation, yawing hideously between over- and underproduction, the connection between usury and the barren and burning sand does not, perhaps, seem altogether too far-fetched. (142)

Christian morality has often been perceived to consider the sins of the flesh as the worst if not the only sins, but, truthfully, moral theology considers those of the spirit to be far more threatening to the soul. Dante reflects this by having warm-blooded sins punished at the top of Hell with cold-blooded ones reserved for its deepest pit. Thus the worst sins are seen in the Circle of Fraud. Describing the "black funnel of the Abyss," Sayers writes,

> At the bottom are fire and stink, and the ten circular pits of Malebolge, carved in the eternal rock, and bridged by radiating spurs of

---

6. I assume this is an allusion to an article Peter Drucker published in *Harper's Magazine*, May 1939, 561–70, and later expanded into a book.

stone. Far below the circles of appetite indulged and appetite self-justified lie the circles where the appetite is exploited. (142–43)

The "ten circular pits of Malebolge" then are the eternal destinies of the worst sinners of all. And who are they? The Panderers and Seducers, Flatterers, Simoniacs, Barrators, Hypocrites, Thieves, Counselors of Fraud, Sowers of Discord, and Falsifiers. What a shocking contrast this list exhibits to that of the vices considered the most serious in popular thought today!

The prominence of fraud in our society makes it relevant to look briefly at all ten of its manifestations. The Panderers and Seducers indicate the nature of the evil. Like those of the Lustful, the sins of this group are related to sexual activity, but here the motive is not one's own appetite but is instead the calculating decision to profit from someone else's urges, to exploit someone else's weaknesses for one's own gain. When we move on to Flatterers we see the seriousness with which Dante takes what the average person who considered this activity would regard as the merest trifle. Dante saw Flattery as the "prostitution of language." "Words are falsified for gain. Flattery—wheedling (for the word *lusingare* means that too)—shall we go on to say advertisement, journalism, propaganda?—this is the filth and ordure of the falsifying intellect" (143).

Concerning the Simoniacs, I think Sayers could have said more than she did, but that is perhaps because they abuse my profession—or, rather, vocation, because if those who sell and buy church office have been called by God, they have served themselves rather than God and God's children. She writes, "The consecration of these Simoniac priests is a true consecration; the sacraments they administer are valid. But they are fraudulently exploited by the lean Wolf whose maw is never filled" (144). Sorcery does not strike our generation as evil because we and those who practice it know that it is not real magic: it is merely entertainment. But like all the other sins, it has a number of manifestations, and Sayers's list of them allows us to see the evil that Dante detested:

> Here are the fortune-tellers, here are the witch-wives. The image is of the twisted magical art, which deforms knowledge to an end outside the order of creation; the image of the abuse of all psychic power and of all scientific knowledge—it includes the "conditioning" of other people to selfish ends by the manipulations of their psyches, as well as the vulgarer forms of spirit-rapping, and the more disgusting excesses of Satanism. (144)

To me one of Sayers's most contemporarily relevant observations is to say, "When religion is discredited, men turn to wizards who peep and mutter; and if they have been put at the mercy of words, and so have lost the gift of tongues, they will not easily retain the gift of the discerning of spirits" (145).

It seems to me that some of the most gullible people around today are those who have decided that they are too enlightened to believe in Christianity.

When I see references to Barratry I usually have to have recourse to a dictionary to remind myself that it is to offices of state what Simony is to church offices. Sayers was as surprised as I to see that Dante regarded it as an even more sinful act than Simony, but she goes on to reflect,

> There is a sense in which the State, which is of the natural order, lies at a deeper level of man's being than Religion, which is of the spiritual order. This the Lord Christ recognized: "If you cannot be honest about worldly riches, who shall trust you with the true?" (144)

In our day this sin may seem even worse because we are too aware of those who use governmental power to feather their own nests rather than to care for the needy. A political leader who sees public office as a way to further enrich the wealthy at the expense of the suffering would surely be deserving of one of the lowest berths in Hell.

Sayers thinks that Dante had a very subtle reason for his placement of the Hypocrites, recognizing that most of us are not too upset about Barratry until we are personally inconvenienced, and then we cry out with indignation about corruption:

> Between our admiration and our indignation, between our recognition that Barratry is worse than Simony and our strong disposition to countenance and practise it so far as is reasonable, there might appear to be some contradiction. Is it possible that *we* are hypocritical in these matters? The Ditch of the Thieves is the place where "no personal rights are respected." (145–46; emphasis added)

Next comes the place of the Thieves of Personality, the Counsellors of Fraud "who filched away the integrity of those they counseled." And in the Ninth Ditch are the Sowers of Dissension:

> Religious schism, political sedition, family dissension: the fomenters of discord split the State at every sensitive point. Their will is to distintegrate; by this means they achieve their personal power. . . . All groupings, all centres of union, must be split up, because they are centres of resistance, in which justice and truth and other positive and divine things may find a refuge and a rallying-point. (146)

A final surprise is that the lowest ditch in hell is reserved for Falsifiers, who falsify their persons and their speech, and they counterfeit money.

> Why is that so important? It is important precisely because it is the means of exchange. In the other circles everything is bought and

sold—sex and religion and government, and art and speech and intellect and power: now the very coin for which they were sold is itself corrupted. That no state can hold together when its currency is hopelessly debased is a practical fact with which we are only too familiar. (146)

As bad as that is, Sayers says that it is only symbolic of a greater truth. What Dante gives us

is the image of a society in the last stages of its mortal sickness and already necrosing. Every value it has is false; it alternates between a deadly lethargy and a raving insanity. All intercourse is corrupted, every affirmation has become perjury, and every identity a lie. No medium of exchange remains to it, and the "general bond of love and nature" is utterly dissolved. (147)

Below this is the Well in which we find the Giants, whose exact placement was what prompted Sayers to reflect on the whole order of Hell.

When the intellect is wholly perverted, what can remain? Blind forces— giant blocks of primitive mass-emotion, the more dangerous because they are not just mindless, like "elephants and whales," but stupid like imbeciles, like crowds, like cunning and half-witted children—a pin-point of human brain in a body of superhuman strength. (147)

This is the realm of Treachery: "Here the final ties which bind man to man are broken: the tie of kindred goes first, and then the tie of country: into these we are born—we did not choose them" (148). After that comes the betrayal of guests and of feudal lords.

Below that is only Satan, and we have reached the bottom of the Hell through which Virgil guided Dante, and Dorothy L. Sayers guided us. If this tour has reminded you all too much of the world in which we live, my point has been made. If it does not, I hope you will look again, because I think it reminds us of what our God can save us from. It thus becomes preparation for the gospel. Then those to whom we preach can follow Dante through Purgatory into Paradise.

26

From Crowded Stable to Empty Tomb to the Sunday Morning Pew

*Preaching Transition through the Cycle
of the Liturgical Year*

O. WESLEY ALLEN JR.

As surely as time progresses out of the past and toward the future, transition in life is inevitable—you know the old line about the only constant being change. We do not make up pithy sayings like that about things that do not concern us. Transition concerns us humans deeply because it is rarely easy. It is unkempt, even chaotic. Whether the change is major or minor, evokes joy or sorrow, whether we have hoped for its potential or dreaded its possibility, change involves the unknown, the unexpected, the uncontrollable.

No wonder people turn to their church community to help them in times of transition. The help we are able to give follows the onset of the transition. Preachers rarely get to direct the transitions in the lives of our parishioners. There are times we work for and preach toward change, but more often we deal with changes pastorally and prophetically as they occur. We do not plan them in advance, write them on the church calendar, or type them into our PDA. We *respond* to them. We try to help our congregants manage their messiness. We attempt to influence change's outcome *after* it is under way. When we use worship as part of this response to significant transitions, we turn to pastoral rites, such as baby dedications, baptism, confirmation, baccalaureates, weddings, healing services, funerals, and the like—occasional services meant to address very specific pastoral, emotional, spiritual, and physical needs.

But for the purpose of this essay, I want to change the after to a before. I am not looking to argue that we can or should try to control transitions before they occur in our congregants' lives. I simply want to ask how preaching and worship week in and week out helps or can help our congregations *prepare* for a life in which transition is fairly constant. In the linear progression of our

236

lives, transitions mark radical changes between what was, on the one hand, and what is or what will be, on the other. Worship, however, is built on repetition. Sunday to Sunday we may have different themes, different hymns, different sermons, but our basic pattern of worship remains fairly stable. To varying degrees in different Christian denominations, this repeating pattern extends to an annual cycle of a liturgical year. So the question, refined slightly, is how might preachers and worship planners/leaders be attentive to the regular patterns and annual cycle of worship to *prepare* our congregations for transition? How can regular, repetitive ritual practices prepare our congregants to deal with significant change in their lives whenever and however it comes?

To move toward an answer, let's begin with the nature of ritual itself. While those who study ritual have had long and heated debates about nuances of its nature, for our purposes *ritual* can be defined as *the patterned enactment of a community's myths.*[1]

First, what is meant by "a community's myths"? When ritual and liturgical scholars speak of myth, they do not mean to evoke the colloquial sense of the word as false stories. Instead, we are using "myth" as a technical term referring to the foundational narratives, histories, symbols, and beliefs of a community. Mythic foundations can include both literal and nonliteral elements, the historical and fictional. They are multilayered, complex beyond any simple naming, and demand interpretation.

As such, myths are identity forming. The history, narratives, creeds, and symbolism claimed of a community determine who the community is and how its members live in the world. Of course, the identity formation—this shaping of our core beliefs, attitudes, and behavior—is not simply a matter of intellectual reflection on the myths. Thorough identity formation involves the *patterned enactment of the myth*. What does it mean for a community to *enact* its myths in ritual, in worship?

What is not meant by this language is that communities *re*-enact their myth. Ritual is not putting on Christmas pageants or passion plays that recount the ancient story. Enactment is not theatrical rehearsal. It is, however, dramatic in the sense that ritual *dramatizes* a community's mythic understanding of God, self, and world. The community does not simply gather to repeat the ancient content of the myths. Instead it gathers to perform the contemporary interpretation of the traditional myths. The community actualizes the narrated understanding of the meaning and purpose of existence. It doesn't just report the myth (past tense); it is enlivened by it (present tense).

---

1. For a good survey of the development of ritual theory, see Catherine Bell, *Ritual: Perspective and Dimensions* (New York: Oxford University Press, 1997).

To unpack this idea of ritual as the patterned enactment of a community's myths further, it might be helpful to recall J. L. Austin's influential little book titled *How to Do Things with Words*.[2] In it, Austin proffers what has become known as "speech act theory," which has profitably been applied to the study of ritual and liturgy. Austin notes that we usually think of language as functioning referentially—speech refers to something external to the speech itself. The word *tree* refers to an object in the world. The word *anger* refers to and describes a particular emotion over against other emotions. The word *run* refers to a certain kind of action that is a distinct type of behavior.

Austin notes, however, that some expressions do not point to something beyond themselves. If I say, "I promise," I am not referring to some external promise. Speaking the words *is* the action of promising. When I officiate at a wedding and say, "I now pronounce you husband and wife," I'm not referring to something I have already done or will do later. I am not narrating something I am doing outside of the expression. The pronouncement itself ritually joins the couple in wedlock.

It is in this sense that we can say ritual *enacts* a community's myths. The purpose of Christian worship, for instance, is not referential. We may "tell the old, old story," but we do not gather simply to rehearse what used to be. Preachers refuse to leave the biblical text in the ancient world—we "apply" its content to the world today. We do not sing songs like a choral performance; we sing our prayers for today using words from our forebears. In our particular Christian tradition, we might say what ritual does is *anamnesis*, the Greek word for remembrance.[3] Without getting into the historic debates about what does or does not happen at the Lord's Table, we can say ritual does not simply remember the myth (past tense), it re-*members* the myth—puts its meaning and significance together in the community (present tense).

So how does/can the patterned, Christian enactment/re-membrance of the church's myths prepare our congregations for transition? One could offer a range of answers to this question, rephrased in this manner. The way I propose to approach it is to look for the way in which transition itself is a key element of our myths and to see how the church has enacted this ultimate sense of transition in the liturgical cycle.

In the ancient Near East, many cultures viewed time as being cyclical. Classic symbols of this understanding of existence are the wheel and the *uroboros*, a serpent swallowing its own tail. Based on their experience of the rotation of the seasons (spring, summer, fall, winter) and the parallel agricultural stages

---

2. J. L. Austin, *How to Do Things with Words*, 2nd ed., ed. J. O. Urmson and Marina Sbisà (Cambridge, MA: Harvard University Press, 1975).

3. On Christian worship as both *anamnesis* and *prolepsis*, see Laurence Hull Stookey, *Calendar: Christ's Time for the Church* (Nashville: Abingdon Press, 1996), 28–33.

on which survival depended (planting, growth, harvest, death), these cultures interpreted divine participation with human reality in the same pattern. Gods were incarnated, were present with humanity, died, and were resurrected annually. The central locus for revelation in this mind-set, then, is nature.

The ancient Hebrew worldview was quite different. The Israelites viewed time as linear. An arrow is a better symbol of this view than a circular serpent. Time is past, present, and future. It begins with God calling light into being and moves teleologically toward the end God desires for the world. In this tradition, the central locus for divine revelation is history. The Hebrew Bible portrays God as acting creatively, providentially, and redemptively throughout the advance of time. This is why so much scholarship has been able to read the Bible through the lens of salvation history, even if it has too often been a heavy-handed approach with the texts.

But even in this linear understanding of time and God's activity in history, the First Testament clearly demonstrates an ancient value placed on the cyclical *experience* of time. Even as the creation story of Genesis 1 portrays God as setting the linear progression of time into play with the creation of light, days are marked off as the cycle of night and day. Moreover, the cycle of the week is presented as part of creation itself, anchored in the weekly liturgical practice of Sabbath. Then, of course, add to that the fact that as the history of Israel progresses, a range of annual celebrations develop, marking both regular agricultural events (such as the Succoth celebration of harvest) and onetime historical events (such as Passover, commemorating the exodus).

So whereas in many cultures time was viewed as cyclical, Hebrew culture viewed time as linear. The Hebrew people, however, used cyclical *patterns* to *enact* the *mythic* understanding/experience of God working through and accompanying us during all the changes that occur in linear time. God moves the world along in a linear fashion—from past to future—but the Hebrew people enact the meaning of God's movement through history cyclically— day to day, Sabbath to Sabbath, festival to festival.[4]

The early church is heir to this paradoxical worldview that was very much a part of first-century Judaism.[5] The New Testament presents God as intimately involved in the course of history. Indeed, in accordance with God's providential plan, Christ appeared once and for all, in accordance with God's providential plan, at the right time—at the eschatological moment, the *kairos*

---

4. For a brief review of the relation of the evolution of the Hebraic religious calendar to other ancient understandings of time, see Frank C. Senn, *Christian Liturgy: Catholic and Evangelical* (Minneapolis: Fortress Press, 1997), 19–22.

5. For a general introduction to the evolution of the church's understanding of time, see James F. White, *Introduction to Christian Worship*, 3rd ed. (Nashville: Abingdon Press, 2000), 47–80.

in the center of the *chronos*. For the early church, the Christ event is the central transition in history and thus the central expression of God's self-revelation as God moves the world from Alpha to Omega. For the church, time is linear.

As the church's practices begin to evolve, however, this central historical event is translated into cyclical enactments/experiences of its meaning. The first major liturgical innovation of the church is to move the primary day of worship from the Sabbath to the day of resurrection. This happens early enough that Luke seems to assume the practice of gathering on the Lord's Day by the time he writes the Acts of the Apostles in the late first century (Acts 20:7; compare other possible New Testament references to this practice: 1 Cor. 16:2; Rev. 1:10).

The next major liturgical innovation that influenced the church's experience of time was well established by the mid-second century. It was *Pascha*, the first annual celebration of the church. *Pascha*, the Greek word for Passover, was originally the church's unitive commemoration of the death, resurrection, and exaltation of Christ. Only later did the church break apart this celebration into different days and seasons, such as Lent, Good Friday, Easter, Ascension, and Pentecost.

So the first two significant liturgical innovations of the church related to enacting the end of Christ's life weekly on the day of resurrection and annually on *Pascha*.

The next major liturgical innovation related to the church's experience of time was the celebration of Christ's birth. In different geographical regions, different practices and different dates were assigned for celebrating Christ's nativity. In the East, the church celebrated Epiphany on January 6. It was a unitive celebration of God's revelation in Christ that included the birth, the epiphany to the magi, baptism, the first miracle at Cana, and the transfiguration. In the West, the church celebrated Christmas on December 25. As the practice of East and West came together, Christmas became the primary day for celebrating the birth, and subsequent days celebrated the other revelatory moments in Christ's life.

The picture we get then is that within the first few centuries of the church's development Christians enacted our central myth on an annual cycle anchored around the ultimate transitions of human existence—the beginning and end of life. In the centuries that follow, the liturgical calendar continued to develop, but all of the seasons are connected to one of these two. Advent leads into Christmastide, and Epiphany flows out from it. The nativity of Christ anchors the first half of the church year. Lent prepares us for Eastertide, which culminates on the day of Pentecost. This half of the year is anchored by the death and resurrection of Christ, ritually enacted during the Triduum—Maundy Thursday, Good Friday, and Easter Sunday.

Instead of using a circular pattern, the church created and has, to various degrees in different traditions, maintained an elliptical experience of the Christ event in Christian ritual. As an ellipse, the annual cycle has two foci instead of one center. The high ritual points of the church year, every year, are at one end Christ's being brought into the world and at the other Christ's departing from it. Every year we enact the movement from birth to death and resurrection. In other words, the church year is cyclically patterned on the ultimate linear transitions that define human existence—birth and death. This pattern offers preachers a wonderful opportunity to prepare their congregations for the full range of transitions that come at us in life.

Too often we celebrate Christmas and Easter with a focus only on their historical dimensions. I remember a sermon on Christmas Eve, at least the preacher called it a sermon, in which the main point was trying to reconcile the Gospel of Luke with external historical data to determine the actual year Jesus was born. If memory serves, this pastor argued for the year 6 BCE. There was nothing in the talk about what that birth means in the present.

I remember a sermon on Good Friday, at least that's how the bulletin labeled the speech, in which the preacher, like a coroner on a TV crime show, detailed what happened to Jesus' body on the cross that brought about his death and why she thought he died more quickly than most who were crucified by the Roman Empire. There was nothing in the talk about what that death means to us now.

I also remember an Easter sermon, at least it had a "sermon title," in which the preacher argued for the historicity of the empty tomb over against other people who claimed some other mythological or symbolic interpretation of the resurrection. He said, "If the tomb wasn't literally empty then the resurrection means nothing." That claim is fine and good except the preacher then said nothing about what the resurrection *does* mean in the present tense. These sermons, and the worship services in which they were embedded, were more referential than they were performative. They were reminders without any *anamnesis*. And thus they offered no experience of Christ's transitions in a way that had power to shape our current and future life transitions.

Without diminishing the historical claims of the faith, and without diminishing the claims of the character of the Christ event, the church can claim the stories of Jesus' entry into and departure from human existence as ultimately significant for us today. In traditions that use some form of a prayer of Great Thanksgiving when gathering for Eucharist, the entire congregation usually speaks or sings what is called the Memorial Acclamation. The line is often rendered,

> Christ has died.
> Christ is risen.
> Christ will come again.

At first glance, it sounds like each sentence represents a different temporal perspective. Notice first that we do not say, "Christ *has* risen." The resurrection is affirmed as a present reality. So, it seems that we have past, present, and future: "Christ *has* died. Christ *is* risen. Christ *will come* again."

Notice that first line, however. We do not say, "Christ *died*." We say, "Christ *has* died." Instead of using the past tense, the sentence is spoken in the perfect tense. Whereas the past tense refers to something that has happened and is completed, the perfect tense names something that happened in the past with effects or consequences continuing into the present. Saying, "Christ *has* died," and "Christ *is* risen," is *anamnesis*, ritual *enactment* of our Christian myth.

While the continuing effects of Christ's birth, on the one hand, and death and resurrection, on the other, are manifold, one such effect certainly relates to our experience of such transitions. Every year we rehearse, we enact, we proclaim the movement from birth through death to resurrection in Christ *so that* our congregants might be able to identify and experience that pattern in every stage of their linear lives as Christians. Celebrating and proclaiming year after year in never-ending tandem the way in which God is (not was) manifested in the ultimate transitions of Christ's life prepares our congregations to look for and find God manifested in our own transitions. When the connections between the transitions in Christ's life and ours are made explicit, the liturgical and homiletical repetition serves as rehearsal or practice for our congregations as they face, struggle with, and muddle through the unknown and uncontrollable transitions that constantly are coming our way.

In a sense, the hermeneutical move we preachers must make is to resist always stressing the unique aspects of the story of the Christ event. Sometimes, instead of stressing that Mary was visited by an angel, we simply need to remember and identify with her as a woman having a baby. Sometimes instead of emphasizing Jesus' birth as attended by shepherds and star, angelic hosts and magi, we simply need to proclaim that like us, Jesus was born. Sometimes instead of emphasizing the heavenly voice and the descending dove at his baptism, we simply need to see ourselves as coming out of the waters of baptism just like he did. Sometimes instead of emphasizing what it meant for the Son of God to set his face toward Jerusalem, we simply need to see fellow humans struggling to deal with a fate beyond their control. Some-times instead of speaking in cosmic terms of how Christ died for all, we just need to say he died. And sometimes, instead of announcing, "Christ is risen indeed!" as the central revelatory moment of the Christian story (which it is), we simply need to wonder what it means for us to experience such a radical new birth, for which we can only give credit and praise to God.

This is not to urge that our gospel message become reductionistic or that we must adopt a Christology that does away with the "fully divine" part of "fully human, fully divine." Yet I would argue that for the annual cycle of ritu-ally enacting the Christ event to empower us in our congregants' linear exis-tence, we preachers are free to remind them over and over again that we find our humanness—in constant transition from life to death to life—in Christ.

Contributors

Joanna Adams is a Presbyterian preacher, pastor, and teacher and is known for building bridges of understanding in both the community and in the church.

O. Wesley Allen Jr. is an ordained elder in the United Methodist Church and professor of homiletics and worship at the Lexington Theological Seminary in Lexington, Kentucky.

Ronald Allen is the Nettie Sweeney and Hugh Th. Miller Professor of Preaching and New Testament at the Christian Theological Seminary in Indianapolis, Indiana.

David Buttrick is the Drucilla Moore Buffington Professor Emeritus of Homiletics and Liturgics at the Divinity School at Vanderbilt University in Nashville, Tennessee.

O. C. Edwards is a historian and former professor of homiletics at Seabury-Western Theological Seminary, where he also served as president and dean. He is an ordained priest in the Episcopal Church.

Craig Gilliam is the director of the Center for Pastoral Excellence for the Louisiana Annual Conference of the United Methodist Church. He is adjunct faculty at the Perkins School of Theology at Southern Methodist University and consults with churches and other organizations across the country.

Sidney Greidanus is Emeritus Professor of Preaching at the Calvin Theological Seminary in Grand Rapids, Michigan.

John Holbert is an ordained elder in the United Methodist Church and the Lois Craddock Perkins Professor of Homiletics at the Perkins School of Theology at Southern Methodist University.

Gary Kindley is the executive director of Counseling, Consulting & Inspiration Associates, LLC in Dallas, Texas.

Thomas Long is the Bandy Professor of Preaching at the Candler School of Theology at Emory University in Atlanta, Georgia.

Mary Martin is the pastor of Poetry United Methodist Church in Poetry, Texas.

John McClure is the Charles G. Finney Professor of Homiletics at the Vanderbilt Divinity School in Nashville, Tennessee.

Carver McGriff served as senior pastor of St. Luke's United Methodist Church in Indianapolis for twenty-six years (1967–1993), building the congregation from 900 members to over 4,000 members at the time of his retirement.

Alyce McKenzie is an ordained elder in the United Methodist Church and professor of homiletics at the Perkins School of Theology at Southern Methodist University.

Jonathan Mellette is the senior pastor of Florence United Methodist Church in Florence, Texas.

Kent Millard served as a pastor or district superintendent in South Dakota for twenty-three years prior to his appointment as senior pastor of St. Luke's United Methodist Church in Indianapolis, Indiana, in 1993. He continues to serve in that capacity.

The late **Ella P. Mitchell** was professor of homiletics at the Interdenominational Theological Center, Atlanta, Georgia, and mentor for students at the United Theological Seminary, Dayton, Ohio. In 2004, Henry and Ella Mitchell celebrated their sixtieth wedding anniversary. Ella passed from this life on 20 November 2008, and her funeral was held at the historic Ebenezer Baptist Church in Atlanta, Georgia.

Henry Mitchell is the former dean of the School of Theology of Virginia Union University in Richmond, Virginia.

David Mosser is the senior pastor at First United Methodist Church in Arlington, Texas. He is an adjunct professor of homiletics at the Perkins School of Theology at Southern Methodist University.

Mary Alice Mulligan is interim minister at Eastgate Christian Church (Disciples of Christ) and affiliate professor of homiletics and ethics at Christian Theological Seminary, both in Indianapolis.

Carol Norén is an ordained elder in the United Methodist Church and has been the Wesley W. Nelson Professor of Homiletics at North Park Theological Seminary since 1993.

Sharyn Pinney is a psychologist practicing in the Dallas, Texas, area. She serves as a consultant to the Supervised Ministry Program at the Perkins School of Theology at Southern Methodist University.

Robert Stephen Reid is the head of the Communication Department and director of the Master of Communication degree program in organizational communication at the University of Dubuque, Dubuque, Iowa.

David Schlafer is an Episcopal priest who has taught philosophy, theology, and homiletics at a number of seminaries in different denominational traditions. He currently focuses his professional energy as a conference leader and preaching consultant across the United States and in England.

Fredrick Schmidt serves as the director of Spiritual Formation and Anglican Studies, and professor of Christian spirituality at the Perkins School of Theology at Southern Methodist University. He is an ordained priest in the Episcopal Church.

Robert Schnase serves as Bishop in Residence of the Missouri Area of the United Methodist Church.

Frank Thomas is the senior pastor at the Mississippi Boulevard Christian Church in Memphis, Tennessee. He is an adjunct professor of preaching at the McCormick Theological Seminary in Chicago, Illinois.

Thomas H. Troeger is the J. Edward and Ruth Cox Lantz Professor of Christian Communication at Yale Divinity School. A preacher, homiletical theologian, poet, and flutist, he has focused his scholarship and creative work on the place of the imagination in preaching and worship.

Joseph Webb has worked and taught in all aspects of journalism and media. Since joining the faculty in 2007, he has been a professor in the Department of Communication Studies at Gardner Webb University in Boiling Springs, North Carolina.

The late **Rodney Wilmoth** was senior pastor at Hennepin Avenue United Methodist Church in Minneapolis, Minnesota, from 1994 to 2004. He formerly served as senior minister at St. Paul UMC in Omaha, Nebraska. Wilmoth was a noted preacher in the Protestant Hour radio series. Wilmoth died on 11 February 2009 at age seventy-one in Tucson, Arizona.

Starsky Wilson is pastor and teacher of Saint John's United Church of Christ in St. Louis, Missouri.

June Alliman Yoder is Professor Emerita of Communication and Preaching at the Associated Mennonite Biblical Seminary in Elkhart, Indiana.

CPSIA information can be obtained
at www.ICGtesting.com
Printed in the USA
BVHW080232270123
657041BV00014B/169